Femi Euba is a Ph.D., MFA, MA., playwright, theater director, actor, novelist, and scholar. Currently Professor of Theatre and English at Louisiana State University, he studied acting at the Rose Bruford College of Speech and Drama in England, Playwriting and African American Studies at Yale, and Literature-in-English at the University of Ife, now Obafemi Awolowo University. His works include *Archetypes, Imprecators, and Victims of Fate*; *Poetics of the Creative Process*; *Camwood at Crossroads*, a novel; the BBC Radio plays; and full-length plays such as *The Eye of Gabriel* and *Dionysus of the Holocaust*.

For WS and all the creative artists that have influenced my work.

Femi Euba

EXPERIENCING WS

The Making of an Artist Scholar

AUSTIN MACAULEY PUBLISHERS™
LONDON • CAMBRIDGE • NEW YORK • SHARJAH

Ordering Information
Quantity sales: Special discounts are available on quantity purchases by corporations, associations, and others. For details, contact the publisher at the address below.

Publisher's Cataloguing-in-Publication data
Euba, Femi
Experiencing WS

ISBN 9781643789828 (Paperback)
ISBN 9781643789835 (Hardback)
ISBN 9781645365822 (ePub e-book)

Library of Congress Control Number: 2020909717

www.austinmacauley.com/us

First Published (2021)
Austin Macauley Publishers LLC
40 Wall Street, 33rd Floor, Suite 3302
New York, NY 10005
USA

mail-usa@austinmacauley.com
+1 (646) 5125767

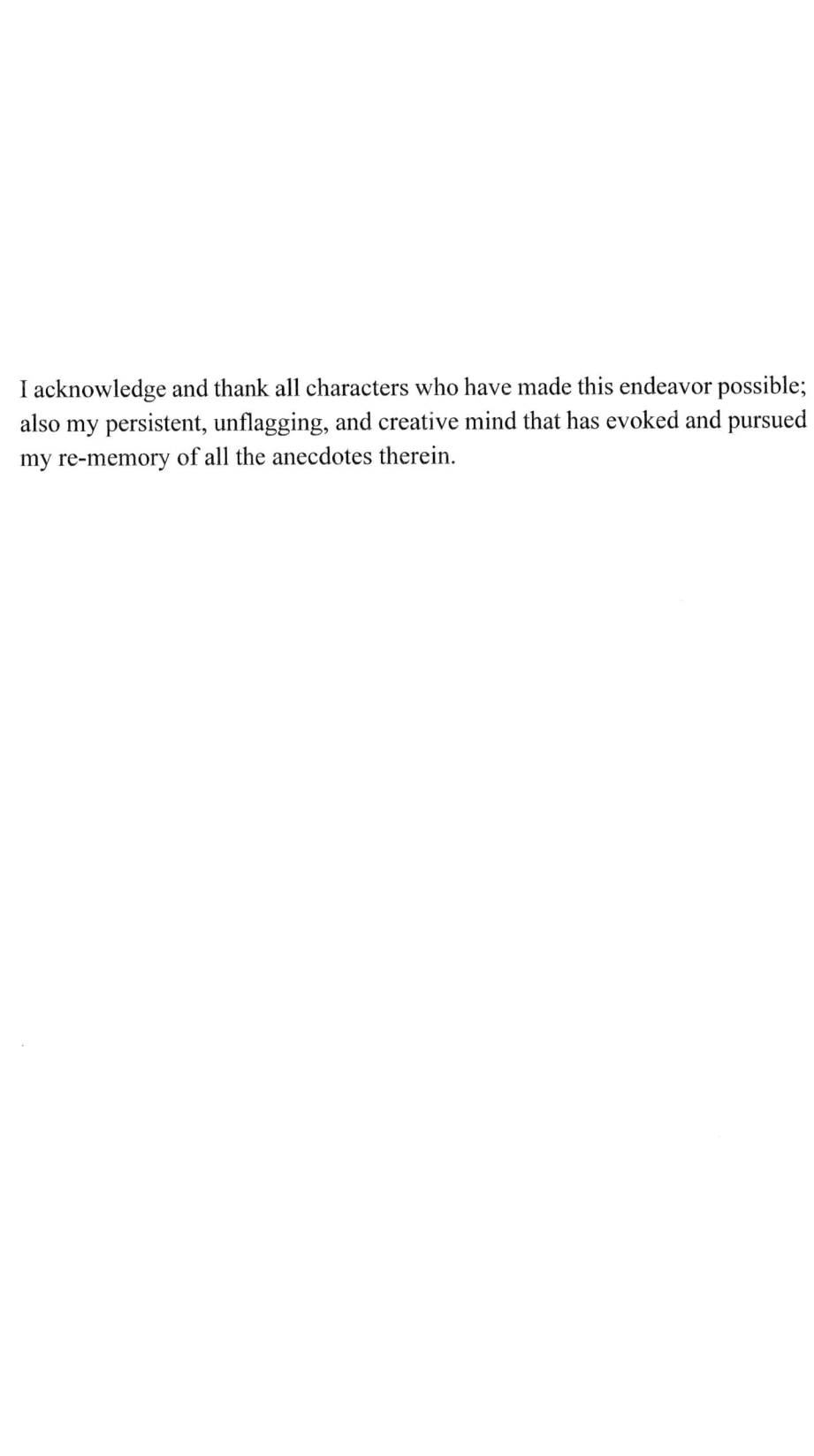

I acknowledge and thank all characters who have made this endeavor possible; also my persistent, unflagging, and creative mind that has evoked and pursued my re-memory of all the anecdotes therein.

Prologue

The Ritual Process of Artistic Experience—An Overview

I, alias BBGD, had entertained no ambitions to writing a memoir. Such an endeavor, to my mind, should be left alone to people of great importance, such as my former mentor, brother, and friend, Wole Soyinka. This is especially so when such people are much older and are only looking back at their accomplishments and the summation of all that had contributed to their success. But perhaps that's old thinking, since memoir writing seems to have expanded its horizons to include people who have something to say about life and how they've survived an event or a predicament. Nevertheless, I still stand by my own understanding.

Regarding that, yes, I could boast to a certain degree of some artistic success—come to think on it, in acting as well as playwriting and directing—experiences of a career that could describe some form of development or structure. But these achievements, to my mind, were nothing that could conjure up an interest to a considerable number of audience-readers, or could whet the appetite of a following of fans, such that Wole Soyinka commands. A Yoruba proverb comes to mind, strange as it might seem to apply here: "If you have to eat a frog, you might as well eat one with eggs (of gold)"—the parenthesis is by implication. In other words, in the context of a memoir, if one decides to embark on such a project, one should make sure it is potentially functional, fruitful, and therefore worth the effort. The question is, whether my career efforts and achievements merited such a preoccupation. On the other hand, perhaps like Anton Chekhov was, or as WS has often expressed, I am sometimes given to self-deprecation.

What triggered the present endeavor to legitimize a memoir in its own right, an obvious change of mind, began about ten or so years ago. It was at the inauguration of what came to be known as Soyinka Festival—an idea fashioned at the time by the imaginative foresight of a young Nigerian, then a graduate student at the University of Southwestern Florida, in Orlando[*]. There,

---

[*] The student, at the time, went by the name, Jamin, or later, Ja Ori.

9

I presented a paper entitled "Experiencing Soyinka: Reflections on 2002 and the 1960s." In the paper, presented in a roundtable to a few other scholars who attended, I reminisced on the last production of the Soyinka play in which I participated, *Oyedipo at Kolhuni* (an adaptation of Sophocles' *Oedipus at Colonus*), and the experiences that initiated and launched my acting and theater career in the 1960s, under the tutelage of Wole Soyinka. What significantly aroused the reflection was the distinctive parallels I felt could be drawn between both periods, even though separated by about four decades. One period initiated an acting career while the other re-engaged that profession after some years of seeming inactivity, thereby calling attention to its rather dubious development and what transpired in between that hiatus.

As it happened, at close regard, the perceived dormant state was rather specious and therefore superficial; alongside the acting had developed other artistic/creative forms, namely playwriting and directing. These, in fact, would seem to have taken over the acting experience, submerging its possible development into an acknowledged, though fond and nostalgic, oblivion. However, the takeover called attention to the possible reasons that much later confronted me—reasons why I had allowed the seemingly artistic coup to happen in the first place. This situation will be engaged in Chapter One—or Scenes One, as preferred for the memoir—and more fully in Scenes Nine.

Indeed, it was a response to the presentation at Orlando that facilitated my interest in writing a memoir. What was expressed in the paper drew the attention and fascination of my small audience, especially that of a younger professor, the late Dr. Esiaba Irobi. It was Esiaba that made me conscious of the fact of the presentation as embarking on a prize project. He saw the paper as an initial skirmish for a larger project that could describe a special relationship between a mentee and his mentor, and meant to capture the interest of a larger audience. As Esiaba visualized it, the project fashioned by such an idea could elicit dimensions of the mentor that nobody else could talk about but the mentee—perspectives that spanned some forty years of relationship.

Thus, after much contemplation, the project grew from paper presentation to book form. In addition, it has expanded in scope, from acting to every aspect that describes or privileges my person as a theater practitioner. For, looking at and assessing each aspect, whether as actor, director, playwright, or in fact as scholar, Wole Soyinka happened to have had an influence, in varying degrees of course, in every one of them. And, as the book began to gain form, especially with a focus on the making of a theater practitioner, it became convincing to me that the memoir could stand in its own right to engage the interest of the curious reader.

Although my acting career seemed to be short-lived, concentrated in two or three time periods, the total experience spread over many years encompassing three continents. Apart from the acting, it included not only productions that involved Wole Soyinka either as playwright or director, or as both, but also the many productions I directed, some of which were of Soyinka's plays. Furthermore, while these experiences dated back to the launching of my acting career through the preliminary encounter with Mr. Soyinka, between 1958 and 1962, they presupposed my training at one of the best conservatories in England at the time—the Rose Bruford College of Speech and Drama—and, thereafter, my professional thrust into the career. In fact, that opportune thrust, which spanned less than a decade (from 1962 to 1970), included some noteworthy productions—two Soyinka's, one of Shakespeare (*Macbeth* with Alec Guinness as Macbeth). It also involved an encounter with prominent theater personages, such as Bill Gaskill, Lindsay Anderson, Simone Signoret, and of course Sir Alec himself—all of whom were conversant with the increasing popularity of Wole Soyinka during those early years. The experiences also germinated other artistic interests, mainly playwriting and, later, directing. Furthermore, they remarkably increased my fascination for the other WS of Strafford-upon-Avon, where I paid frequent visits to immerse my creative energies and culturally nuanced thoughts in productions of the Bard's plays.

The second period of acting flourished six years later, between 1976 and 1986, that is, after graduating from the Yale School of Drama as a playwright, and working for two or three years as a visiting artist at a college-preparatory school for women, the Ethel Walker School. As fate would ritually have it in 1976, both mentor and mentee arrived in the same year at the young University of Ife (the now Obafemi Awolowo University), where they became academic colleagues. The mentee was hired as a professional artist/lecturer in the Dramatic Arts department—that is, after some 14 years spent abroad in England and the US. Mr. Soyinka, on the other hand, after some six years in political exile, took appointment at first to consolidate the Department of Comparative Literature, but after a year or two became the Chair of Dramatic Arts. It was the period that fully developed my relationship with the distinguished playwright and, quite logically, my acting proficiency. Also, more formally, it situated other artistic interests (directing, playwriting), and my scholarship. More significantly, it was those years that allowed me to begin to inter-relate all theater interests with one another, thereby manifesting their integration in the books and plays to be later written.

Kongi oooh, Kongi eh,
Oga tiwa, Wole Soyinka,
Kongi oooh, Kongi eh! [†]

Thus, the ritual appellation-chant, like an oriki,[‡] celebrated the poet-playwright-director, among professional actors and students alike at Ife. Long christened as Kongi, after the title and central character of his *Kongi's Harvest*, Soyinka had come to accept the nickname as logical and fitting. All that (the play, its production and the christening) happened during my absence from Nigeria and stay abroad, in London to be exact. I was, however, aware of the production and its subsequent development into film through the media that flashed across my ears and eyes. Also through intermittent encounters with the personage in England, mainly at the Transcription Centre, in London Mayfair. Anyway, the appellation and chant were unfamiliar to me until I was back home, especially the various versions of their development that made them so fitting. More about that in due course. Suffice to say for now that the name had stuck, and it will recur in this memoir among other monikers chosen to identify my former mentor, such as Prof., Br'er Wole, and WS. Their employment in the volume is often by instinctive choice, depending on sound, mood, occasion, and period of engagement.

Br'er Wole, short for Brother Wole, probably deserves further explication within its Nigerian (Yoruba) application. Not to be confused with the "Br'er" often found in New World folktales, such as "Br'er Rabbit," the term is indicative of the respect usually given to seniority among the Yoruba, or Africans for that matter. Initially formulated for an older brother, it often extends loosely to any older male individual of the peer-group of the real brother, or in general to any male person worthy of the respect of the tender. It was the term applied frequently during my rookie years as Mr. Soyinka's research assistant and a foundation member of his first theater company, the 1960 Masks.

Consistent with appellations, the memoir has opted for the third person in the name of BBGD, by virtue of its usage by the poet-playwright to variously accost his mentee. Even though the acronym/nickname predated its relationship with the mentor, the voice privileges WS and the relationship, observing both at an artistic remove, so to speak. Where, on occasion, this designation is difficult, BBGD responds to alternative names—such as Henry,

---

[†] Oga – used variously to signify respect and authority. Here it is tantamount to "Chairman." Thus "*Oga tiwa*" means, "Our very own Chair.
[‡] A Yoruba praise-chant used to inflate the ego.

a penname used when he was in high school, and for his first ventures into fiction, writing short-stories for the radio. On very rare occasions, he has responded to Femi, his given name by birth. As a matter of fact, "Henry" came by way of colonial upbringing and, for some incredible reasons, through a fascination for the Plantagenets in Shakespeare's plays. The penname had persisted among his high-school peers and through his years at the Rose Bruford College.

"Bem-Bem-GuDu," blasted the Sergeant Major.

"Ye-sah!" responded the junior barrel-rotund officer, who instantly jumped out of the small platoon file, gave a vibrant salute, and awaited the orders of the SM. The infantry was marching uphill back to the barracks, somewhat tiredly, perhaps after a morning drill or some other operation. For the World War II was on and was felt in Lagos, as in many British colonies, through occasional sirens. Here, on the island and capital city, the high wailing drone kept the community guarded and alert, and sometimes sent them to shelters to await further orders.

That officer's image was the only figure that fascinated the schoolgirl eyes of BBGD's favorite auntie, the image of the Hausa officer, young and fat, with a stomach that could consume a "ton," according to the late Auntie Iyabo. Instantly, the image cross-faded to her nephew, a two-year-old rounded kid, known to enjoy enormous meals, whenever, wherever, whatever and with whomever. Thus, the appellation had christened the kid and got circulated among all the members of his family and relatives. Unfortunately, there was nothing he could do to prevent it from close friends of the family, such as the Johnsons. As stated, the name preceded its relationship with WS, who only got wind of it almost two decades later.

To be clear, there should be no presumption that the young recipient had ever liked the nickname. In fact, he had often shown his dislike with a terrible frown as he grew older, except that there was nothing he could do about it. Even though he declared it out of bounds among his peers, sometimes they dared him and faced the consequences of his scathing retort. But, because of his apparent dislike, few had chosen to just hum or thump its tonal value, like the tom-toms of the talking drums. This was the gesture-version that WS had sometimes adopted, that is, when he got wind of the naming several years later, through the playwright's closest friend, the late Femi Johnson (OBJ), an older son of the Johnsons. By that time, his previous dislike for the appellation had somewhat dissolved or mellowed into a rather numb but explorative amusement. For, as he discovered, he could sometimes put it to very effective use.

The accosting name, like a praise-name, had stuck; BBGD could do absolutely nothing about it. Under its usage by WS, he had come to enjoy its full creative potential, with the undercurrent amusement that even he, Kongi, probably didn't know the exact story behind it. In fact, there often arose a customary incitement by the poet-playwright, a threat to let the cat out of the bag, an inciting threat to reveal the true story behind his hummed accolade to the curious, uninitiated ears of their colleagues at the University of Ife. That seeming intimidation often amused BBGD no end, supported by a soft smile that called the playwright's bluff, daring him to unclassify the classified, so to speak, if he could.

Thus, the choice of the third person omniscient becomes evident. It is to enable the author to observe and hold BBGD (the mentee-turned-actor-playwright-director-scholar) and his activities with WS (his distinguished mentor) at some contemplative, artistic, critical, and often humorous distance. It also allows the author some latitude at invention and creativity, especially when events seem to blur or strain (only to be expected), and in an utterly desperate need for reconnection. Rather than leave a writer in first person hanging and helpless with guilt, such moments encourage the third person the initiative to respond creatively to factoids of imagination, indeed with impunity.

As for the development of the narrative in scenes as opposed to chapters, there is no specific justification, except that it stands to reason, given the somewhat dramatic graph the memoir suggests. Initiated by reflections on the events of 2002 and 1960s, the memoir subsequently ventures in moments, from BBGD's rookie beginnings, through his artist's training and conflicts arising, to his professional maturity. It then comes back to resolve questions raised of his artistry, as fashioned by the events of 2002, which he thereafter legitimizes. Ultimately, these moments describe the rites of passage of an exemplary theater practitioner, inspired and conditioned by a mentor-mentee relationship. Like in any drama, and from the point of view of BBGD, it describes a ritual process that expresses a need of becoming, which, through sacrifice inherent in conflicts and determination, results in favorable outcome beyond his expectations.[§]

[§] Ritual process has been of interest, variously, in the author's works. See *Archetypes, Imprecators and Victims of Fate: Origins and Developments of Satire in Black Drama*, Greenwood Press (CT, Westport, 1989); *The Gulf* (play), *Longman* (Lagos Nigeria: 1991); *The Eye of Gabriel* (play) Alexander Street Press (Alexander, VA, 2002), and *Camwood at Crossroads* (novel), Xlibris Philadelphia, PA: 2007.

Scenes One

The Call and the Calling: The Lure of a Dynamic

"H'm, BBGD!" accosted the familiar rich and hearty tenor voice at the other end. It was unmistakably WS's. And who dared hail him with that appellation other than Kongi? "What are your plans next summer?" the caller continued to ask, after the receiver's initial burst of laughter that acknowledged both voice and acronym.

"Nothing much, why?" BBGD responded.

"It's the project we briefly talked about last year in Canada. Possibility of going to Greece with my adaptation of *Oedipus at Colonus.*"

"Oh yeah? It's happening, is it?"

"Yes. But let me e-mail you fully about it—dates and all. Just want to know if you're still interested"

"But of course. Gee, thanks!"

BBGD received the expected e-mail a week or two later, locating the date of the production in early July, 2002. Rehearsals would be in Las Vegas for a month, that is, the whole month of June. WS was at the time the first Elias Ghanem Chair in Creative Writing at the University of Nevada, coordinating a new program as the Director of Literary Arts in the International Institute of Modern Letters. But BBGD noted something else in the e-mail. The playwright wanted him to mail him an audition piece as soon as possible, since it would not be possible for the Louisiana State University professor to be at the general auditions of the play, *Oyedipo at Kolhuni*, the following week in Las Vegas.

He didn't quite understand why he should audition at all. Yes, he hadn't acted in years, but surely Kongi should be familiar with his capabilities. Unless, of course, he wanted him for the lead role, which was unlikely and he certainly didn't want that anyway. That role would probably go to one of the people he was auditioning in Las Vegas, consisting of, apparently, members of the University of Nevada Conservatory. The question was: Is the adaptation for an African cast or a mixture of African and Caucasian? It would seem the latter. He remembered being told in Canada by the playwright of his intentions to bring some members of his old company from Nigeria and the U.K. If so, what might this mean? That he wanted these former actors in the principal roles? Perhaps, but more than likely he was probably thinking of these actors in terms of dancing and the play's evocation of the Yoruba gods, which, obviously, would require the Yoruba members to authenticate. Still, that didn't answer the question why WS wanted an audition piece from him. However, he recalled the way the director had auditioned in the past—everybody sat and read in the round, whether or not someone was earmarked for a role. Now that he was himself a director, BBGD thought it might just be a question of hearing and balancing voices in order to be able to cast as coherently as possible. That, certainly, would be the case if he were attending the audition; but he was not.

His initial reaction was to ignore that part of the message. He dared Kongi not to cast him because of it. Should he take his chances and face any consequence, even though the adventure that Greece imaged was gnawingly irresistible?

After mulling things over for a day or two, he decided to go ahead and record two speeches on a CD, one from Sophocles' *Oedipus at Colonus* and the other, his favorite speech in *King Lear*, the one by the old ogre in the terrible storm scene that ends, "I am a man more sinned against than sinning." He struggled over the recording in several takes, and almost abandoned the idea—he had never appreciated listening to his own recorded voice. At last he heaved a sigh of slight satisfaction at the last take, then decided to give his former mentor a call, to find out where to send the CD.

"Too late," affirmed the almost dismissive voice at the other end. "Don't worry about it." Knowing the playwright well enough, that didn't signify the end of the matter; rather, as far as he could determine, it was more the fact that the playwright-director had changed his original plans, whatever they were.

"You mean you've cast it?" BBGD wanted clarification.

"Yes, somewhat. I have a part for you though."

"Okay, but as to that. I hope it's nothing big. I'm not looking for anything big." BBGD decided to make himself clear on the matter. "Something small, but worthwhile, you know?" His thinking, in fact, would be in keeping with his perpetual, but modest reluctance to act, let alone engage a leading role. Since his professional London days, he did not often feel compelled to do any more acting, especially when he got back to Nigeria. He had the opportunity to get on stage when he was at Yale, but he did not pursue it, since he wanted to focus on playwriting—although the real reason at the time might be his feeling of a kind of insecurity on the American stage. The uncomfortable position, he felt, was not unusual for any actor to find himself in.

After Yale, his directing interests began to take shape and be put to test, first at the Ethel Walker School, a college-preparatory school for girls.

16

Actually, during that span of two years, two stage opportunities had come his way, both at the Hartford Stage; he accepted one engagement but had to turn the other down because of sudden urges to go back to Nigeria. More to his liking was a directing project that came his way, really out of the blue, which in fact involved a few professional actors from New York. Some luck!

Then, back in Nigeria, at the University of Ife, his instincts to decline roles became rather tenuous. He found himself always having to reconsider his position for one reason or the other, especially when it concerned a Soyinka play.

"Yes, nothing big," assured the playwright-director with a kind of croaky, mischievous laugh. "It's the character of Chieftain—I think you'll like it."

Come to think on it, the endeavor of acting had almost always faced him with certain terror, at least at the initial stages. He had heard many actors express similar feelings. In his case, he was convinced it had something to do with what ultimately and instinctively veered him away from taking acting head on as a profession. Whatever that was, he was to later find out.

Looking back at this histrionic part of his career, he concluded it was a significant part of his whole artistic development. For, he was convinced, it formally triggered off into existence his other artistic abilities. Yet, now, far from the histrionic "madding crowd" so to speak, he often teased his mind about what would have happened if he had taken on the challenge, especially when he placed himself in relation to the acting career of some of his conservatory peers at the Rose Bruford College. For only a few had succeeded to catch the limelight.

He felt gratified that whatever he did accomplish described an artistic graph of its own, in the light of the principal roles he had played, most of which were by WS. This, along with his accomplishments in his other artistic pursuits, did not allow him to entertain any regrets, especially on occasions when nostalgia for the art suddenly overcame him—often when he visited London and saw shows at the Aldwych or the National. He had wondered whether his nascent but promising talents before he left the London stage would have come to much, whether they would have gravitated eventually towards being in one of the major theater companies, such as the Royal Shakespeare Company or the National Theater. This possibility, after all, constituted his fleeting aspirations during those days after Bruford. He often recalled the comments and advice of his agent at the time, Mae Bleazard, during the somewhat long waiting periods between engagements. She would console him that such a talent as his sometimes took a long time to make a breakthrough, since typecasting was often the name of the game in show business, even for the stage.

She had, therefore, encouraged him to be patient, an advice that seemed, ultimately, not to have stuck to his eardrums, so to speak. But then again, thinking about it, perhaps he would have eventually drawn the attention of the British Royalty, and got celebrated with an august award, such as an MBE or an OBE, just like his Jamaica-born friend, Yvonne Brewster, or his countryman, Peter Badejo. Or even a knighthood! Sir Henry... He chuckled at the outlandish thought. But who knows, as WS would have said, who knows!

One thing he did know was that accomplishment wasn't fated to be. Or, put another way, his *Esu* or fate essence, at the crossroads of decision-choices, did not signify in that direction. But then, does the godhead ever point in any specific direction? For at those crossroads of his presence, he often leaves the choice to individuality, which has to immerse itself into the spirituality of selfhood, in order to make the right choice. The nascent actor's process of that fate, as it turned out to be, followed a different path, a different road. And, as it turned out to be, he was not ungrateful for the choices he made, especially thinking of his relationship with WS, one of the best he could ever seek in the field of theater—with a Nobel Laureate to boot!

Be that as it may, there was something he often felt was his handicap in acting, something quite apart from the challenge posed by the correct enunciation of the Queen's English—a fact that Rose Bruford College would not allow him to forget, but rather intensely infused in his self-conscious sensitivity. Even that obstacle, he felt, could have been surmounted. After all, it wasn't uncommon for developing or established actors to employ some speech coach, and he did just that in London for some time. No, the handicap he implied was not the fact of a speech disability, if indeed it could be called that. There was something else, something that subconsciously made him not to prioritize acting as a profession, something that would take him some forty years, since his first forays into acting, to consciously diagnose.

Yet, there was such a time that it seemed acting, indefatigably, was his ultimate calling. There was a calling, to be sure, which blossomed in its own way for a while, but turned out not to be the ultimate.

*****

He had been having a siesta snooze in his favorite armchair at 2 Carter Street, his family residence on the mainland of Lagos, waking up intermittently to distant trickles of the news from the Rediffusion (Radio Diffusion Service). Suddenly, the mention of Wole Soyinka jolted his earlobes, which he lifted and cocked towards the transmission box on the living room wall by the cuckoo clock, above the piano. He was delighted he caught the entire segment, loud and clear. The writer, who had been in England for a few years, had returned home to Nigeria, with a grant from the Rockefeller Foundation to do research on West African indigenous drama. The drama personage, with a master's graduate of Leeds University, was also in the process of forming a theater company.

BBGD immediately made the connection with the story he heard only a few days before. He had chanced upon Sola Rhodes, one of his friends in high school, who had in fact bragged about his relocation to the University of Ibadan, and about working for the well-known home-comer. A crust of envy had settled on and creased his forehead, which must have delighted Rhodes. Recalling that emotion, as skeins of snooze quickly vanished from his eyes, he became immediately determined to do some investigation for possible action. A research in West African indigenous drama echoed in his mind, and images of the adventure that echo manifested, glittered before his eyes. The possibility of his participation in that adventure became simply irresistible.

He thought of his brother, who had recently also come back from London and was stationed in Ibadan, as the regional Head of Music of the Nigerian Broadcasting Service. He was convinced that the two *tokunbo*[**] knew each other well. This was enough to make him proceed with his objective, which instantly illuminated two hurdles of action.

At first, they looked like difficult hurdles, for in front of them were obvious cautioning obstacles. He had become somewhat settled to a job as an office clerk, usually the first opportunity of employment that presented itself to high school graduates. Not that he was expected to stay in such a job for life; an unambitious few did. But it was deemed a worthy and productive period of decision-making about what to do exactly with one's life after high school. That period could last at least two years, enough time for the high school leaver to feel proud as a responsible salary earner. The time could, of course, be shortened or be non-existent for individuals from wealthy families who could afford to send their children to study abroad. Some, in fact, were sent earlier enough to English high schools, sometimes as high-brow as Eton. For BBGD, that possibility was simply unthinkable and it had nothing to do with the hurdles that confronted him.

After graduation, he had been drafted to the Public Works Department (PWD) for his first employment, an office job he hated right from the beginning, especially thinking about what some of his peers got landed with, no doubt through their influential parents—a strategy that his father obstinately

---

[**] Literally, one who comes back from over the seas. It could be used as nickname or proper name.

opposed. For starters, the physical appearance of the office was a far cry from those of his friends—indeed, what could one expect of a PWD office, other than metal desks and chairs in an open dingy-looking enclosure amid wooden crates, pylon parts, and pipes. Unfortunately, his chemistry and physics grades were not that impressive to win him jobs in the medical laboratory, like his friends, Ayo Craig and Toyin Martins. After a few weeks at the PWD, he got his mother to persuade his uncle to get him another job, even if clerical, at the Ministry of Health Headquarters, where ACO Dawodu was the Chief Accountant.

That change was effected hardly six months before he heard the announcement on the Rediffusion. To then go back to tell his parents and uncle that he now wanted to follow a pipedream, with no monetary prospects, seemed a non-starter, a senseless proposition that would hardly fly.

Actually, the hurdle was not as impossible to leap across as he had thought. His father reveled in the arts, especially music. He must have been curious, immediately after BBGD's graduation, what profession in life might capture the interest of his seemingly not-so-clever second-born. When he posed the question, BBGD had made known to him that while he had no wish to pursue music and follow in the non-exciting footsteps of his brother, drama was a possibility. He felt he possessed some instincts for that subject far more compellingly than for music. Known fact. From about the age of 8, he had tried his fingers on the keyboard and found the endeavor hopeless, at least as far as his father's tutoring went, and his meager capacity to read notes.

However, the gravitation to drama didn't come as first choice. Initially, he was vacillating between being a journalist and a lawyer, both of which instantly received objections from the ultimate decider, his father and his astrological readings—that is, for whatever reasons the stars foretold his father. But in terms of drama, there seemed to be an accommodation. When the constellations were consulted, they aligned BBGD's astrological path more with the profession—and this indeed was fortunate to the hurdle at hand.

As such, when he approached his father with regard to working with Wole Soyinka—that is, after his brother had arranged a meeting with the researcher himself—he felt fairly comfortable with his expectations. Chappie, as his father's friends called him, was quite familiar with the personage of the writer and his family background. He had no objections to leaving his son in the hands of such a person. What concerned him, or rather what seemed to raise a caution for him regarding the hurdle, was BBGD's missed opportunity to earn a good salary to save for unexpected developments. That was also the concern of his mother, whose opinion, in terms of strategy, he had to first seek in order to assess his chances.

"Let's see what your father says," she had responded. Far be it from her to stand against her son's wishes. This meant BBGD would have to find a favorable time to introduce the delicate matter, preferably when his father was enjoying a good afternoon meal.

"Have you considered that?" Chappie calmly threw the ball in the court of his sometimes rebellious second-born, sucking the marrow juices out of a piece of a cow's succulent legbone. "The inability to earn good money and save for a rainy day, have you considered that?"

"Well, I have. But, it's an opportunity to work with a theater person. This will enable me to pursue drama," he emphasized just to prod his father to a fact already sanctioned by astrology. At first, the type of theater he had in mind was more academic than artistic. He must have seen himself in the future pontificating on drama and theater among his prospective students.

"We'd like to talk to Mr. Soyinka," his father concluded after a long digestive pause—of the spoonful of rice and spinach stew he had heaved in his mouth, masticated to satisfaction and swallowed with ease.

"And you're going to have to talk to your uncle about this," his mother added, coming into the dining room from the kitchen where she had heard it all.

BBGD well knew he could not avoid his uncle, since he had gone out of his way to get him the job he had liked—a clerk at the General Hospital branch of the Ministry of Health, where he was only a stone's throw from his laboratory friends. But getting some approval of his parents, first, should make confronting ACOD somewhat easy. And, just as he thought, the crucial point again was the question of stability.

"Why do you keep hopping from one job to another? You're barely a year at the hospital job. And now you want to work on something else, a job with no secure future?" His uncle's concern and admonishment, which he understood well, was not without cause. A rolling stone obviously gathers no moss. Even that early in life, it was an adage that was often flung at kids, exemplified with true stories that occurred inside various families.

"What does your father think? And Sisi?" BBGD believed ACOD added his sister's nickname only for curiosity, for he was certain that, as siblings, their apprehensive thoughts were similar.

"They both seem to be supportive, sir."

"Well, if they're supportive, there's nothing more for me to say. Just don't come back to me again looking for a job. I wish you the best of luck," he added as he resumed scrutinizing the accounting ledger. ACOD was well aware of Chappie's artistic propensities and perhaps, at least in that respect, a father was a better judge than an uncle, an accountant, to direct his son's career path to maximum profitability. But where's the profit in acting?—BBGD almost heard him questioning in between his accounting thoughts.

Mr. Soyinka was given an honorable hearing, treated to homemade cookies—Sisi's much sought after, delicious shortcakes. He emphasized the fact of limited funds of the research and therefore an infrequent income for BBGD. However, he confirmed resourceful opportunities capable of serving his assistant's theater interests, and promised to take good care of their, apparently, talented son. Issues of lodging did not seem to present any problems. He would of course stay at home when in Lagos. As for Ibadan, apart from the possibility of staying with his brother, BBGD could also stay with Uncle Pekun, a well-established accountant with his own firm. He, in fact, owned the house Akin, his musical brother, was renting, next door to his uncle's mansion. Other than these arrangements, he thought no further; he was quite certain Br'er Wole would see to whatever developed on the road within research periods, that is, in terms of lodging and eating.

*****

"Nice and smooth." Kongi's voice exalted in the uncomplicated richness of the character he seemed to have devised for BBGD. He said the script was on the way. "Let me know what you think after you've read it," he added.

BBGD was delighted to be working with his former mentor once again. He had left that possible door open when he left Nigeria more formally in 1986. But it had been a difficult possibility since. Two years earlier, in 1984, at the University of Ife, he had participated in the feature movie Kongi had written and directed, *Blues for a Prodigal*. Though not on the same lavish scale or commercial dimension with Hollywood or Pinewood, the production had taught BBGD a lot about filming. Earlier in London, in the '60s, he had experienced some TV or film productions but only in minor parts or as walk-ons. Once there was a possibility of being landed with a major role, but it didn't materialize. More about that later. As such, *Blues* was his first serious work and major role in film. After that production, his mentor had retired from the university. Two years later, BBGD had resigned from his position and come back to live more permanently in the U.S. He felt more determined about his resignation by the fact of Kongi's retirement, as well as the fact that Nigeria was becoming more worrisome to live in as an academic. But he realized that moving overseas might make subsequent collaborations with his mentor somewhat difficult. Film participation might be his best bet, since a stage production would involve lots of systematic rehearsals, for which he might not be able to take a long period off from his new US academic responsibilities.

Case in point was the 1986 production of *Death and the King's Horseman* at the Lincoln Centre. That was his first year at the College of William and Mary. By the time he knew anything about the production, let alone having time to make probable plans, the cast was already made. He only knew about it when he got a sudden call from Kongi, asking him if it was possible for him to go to New York and assist in a two-day workshop with the cast, that is, prior to the director's late arrival. Lucky he was able to fulfil the obligation at short notice—Virginia was not very far from New York. The objective was to familiarize the actors with the Yoruba cultural nuances and the tonality of words in the play; these, to be expected, were foreign even to the African American, let alone American actors.

However, more to the point, such a production, happening in the US, would have been a good possibility for collaboration. If he were still in Nigeria, there would have been no question about that. But not being there, out-of-sight-out-of-mind adage seemed to have succeeded as the order of the day; he was not remembered until it was critical for the director's schedule. On him BBGD had squarely put the blame. The unfortunate instance made him recall similar ones. There was the production of *The Road* in 1965 when he was just getting out of the Rose Bruford; again in 1973 with *Madmen and Specialists* when he was at the Yale School of Drama. Possibilities of acting engagement and exposure all rendered futile through Kongi's sometimes bewildering thoughtlessness.

In spite of the difficulties that living overseas presented, he had continued to open his mind to any other possibility of collaboration with WS. Nothing however had materialized until *Oyedipo at Kolhuni*, the adaptation of *Oedipus at Colonus*. Then he had become a full professor of worth at Louisiana State University. And, as luck would have it, the production happened during the summer months of vacation.

*****

Both *Blues* and *Oyedipo* could serve as two career-end milestones in BBGD's professional experience, the former ending the University of Ife years, and the latter putting an end to his spasmodic nostalgia for acting. Not that this latter end was anticipated, but it became evident through certain facts. After so many years of emotional seesaw regarding his acting on stage, he felt the production of *Oyedipo* served two purposes. First, the fact that he still had the capable resources in him; second, he was able to confirm for himself what he had often concluded to satisfy his mind when he felt the sudden nostalgia. It was the fact that, although he considered himself a very good and creative actor, there were obvious limits to his artistic priorities. It was a conclusion that often foregrounded and justified his other commitments more convincingly—directing, playwriting, teaching, and scholarship. To be sure, these comforting zones were often short-lived and hardly strong enough to put a permanent seal on his rather strained love affair with acting, but, by the end of *Oyedipo*, it was a done deal. What remained nostalgic was not the thing itself but the fact of its beginnings, placed against the experience of that final production.

*****

Four decades seemed to have passed by within a twinkling of an eye...

He had come upon a picture of the production of *A Dance*, in his box of oddities. He remembered it was one of the two pictures that made the theater critic page of the *Daily Times*—as the Dirge-Man he was holding a whip and looking defiantly at Agboreko, the oracle priest. The other picture that made the page featured the playwright as Forest Father, giving instructions to Aroni, one of the forest creatures.

"Of all the pictures taken, yours had to be the one chosen!" exclaimed Br'er Yemi Lijadu, who played one of the leading roles, wagging a finger at BBGD as if he had committed some crime. But then the radio drama producer instantly went on to cover up his obvious flush of envy with "Good, good!" Too late. BBGD's eye just in time caught the spoiler for Mr. Lijadu's intended admonishment. His mentor and playwright/director was just then coming in their direction.

There was something about the man that always made BBGD nervous whenever he was near him. He didn't feel always welcomed in his presence, and were it not for Br'er Wole, he felt he would simply be nobody in Lijadu's eyes. True, the Head Producer of Drama had assigned him small parts on and off in the radio drama he produced; but those roles, he felt, were always grudgingly given, by the very fact of his association with the playwright/researcher. Thankfully, the producer had no authority over the casting of *A Dance*; for left to him, the rookie actor would probably not have played one of the Triplets, let alone the Dirge-Man. But then, he probably would not have met him if he hadn't met WS, who kindled his interests in acting and made those roles available to him. There would have been no "1960 Masks" to accommodate his first acting experience. As such, probably Lijadu, best friend of the playwright though not a favorable person to him, was an inevitable encounter. A decree of the good and evil complementarity of fate made manifest, so to speak?

He brushed the negative thoughts aside. There was no sense contemplating what might not have happened, for what had happened was what needed to have happened. He was at the right place at the right time, and all that came with that given moment in time should be accepted as parts of the whole design.

A Dance of the Forests, as far as he could remember the production and his state of mind, was loaded with imagery and cultural nuances expressed with Soyinka's command of English, all of which made the play somewhat difficult for BBGD to understand at the time. Try as he may, he could not for the life of him remember much about his performance, except that, reflecting now on the three parts he played, the oddity of his costumes, as the Dirge-Man picture showed, somehow reminded him of the oddity of the Chieftain's in *Oyedipo* (a pith helmet and khaki "safari" jacket over Maori sarong). That oddity as a matter of fact reflected those of all the three parts played in *A Dance*. As the Slave Dealer, he was in khaki jacket and shorts, and a pith helmet—he remembered the way his character had deviously greased the palm of the Historian (played by the late Ralph Opara) with a bag of money, so the Historian could falsify history. As one of the Triplets, he wore a grass skirt, had a masked face and configurations painted on his bare chest—he remembered the way he and the other two Triplets circled the Half Child in the last scene. But, above all, he had enjoyed being the Dirge-Man, in a gray gown, almost ankle-length, littered with fetish.

The determined entrance of the rather frustrated, omen-sensitive-botanist Chieftain, with his butterfly trap-net, also, somehow, recalled the energetic bursting-in of the ritual-euphoric Dirge-Man. Impelled by the drummers, the acolyte, with a whip in his hand scattered the crowd round him as he launched his recitative: "Move on, eyah! Move apart…"

By some association of thought processes, he had also recalled the event that sanctioned that performance as proof of his "calling," against another in *Oyedipo* that gave credence to the quality of his final performance of the "call."

It happened during the hiatus between the Lagos performance of *A Dance* at the J.K. Randle Hall and the one anticipated for the Arts Theater at the University of Ibadan. At WS's Ibadan residence, the newspaper reporter had arrived and was ushered by BBGD into the sitting room, an open area that overlooked a small balcony revealed through the French window by the partitioned long curtains of locally handwoven fabric. The room was barely furnished. There were two sturdy locally made oak arm-chairs, a sofa, side-tables, and artifacts of carved Yoruba masks. The cushions and small pillows had matching covers of tie-dyed fabric.

In deference to his mentor, as culture demanded of juniors to seniors, BBGD had moved, after WS had welcomed the reporter, from this area to one of the rooms in the inner chamber. That was where he usually slept whenever he stayed overnight at the house. This was always decided by time. For although Uncle Pekun's house, his formal sleeper, was about a mile or two away, the roads at night were not well-lit and could be dangerous.

He had been told vaguely of the interview, a chance for the playwright/director to speak in defense of the Lagos production, which had mixed reviews. The themes and intentions of the production had, obviously, been misunderstood. They were dismissed in not very complimentary terms by the *Daily Times* critic, a supposed friend of the playwright. As such, WS wanted to set the record straight.

When the interview started, BBGD, feeling very curious and anxious, had eventually submitted to temptation and moved locations. He had tiptoed from the guest bedroom to the corridor that led to the living room hidden by a wall. This enabled him to keep his ears close to the opening into the room curtained with strings of cylindrical bamboo beads. He had kept clear of these noisemakers so as to prevent any accidental rustle that might call attention to his eavesdropping.

As far as he could remember, the reporter and the playwright had talked about theater in general, about the play, its themes, its relevance to Nigerian Independence, the multiplicity of actors in the production. These went back and forth, back and forth... Then came the question that lifted the ears of the rookie actor to sound bites of his interest and intense curiosity:

"Acting would seem to demand something of an extrovert of the actor, don't you agree?" probed the reporter.

"How do you mean?"

"I mean, I've always thought of actors as extroverts by nature. Isn't it so?"

"Absolutely not. That's a misconception," the experience of the playwright pointed out with confidence.

"Very well then, is there such a thing as an introverted actor? I mean, can introverts make good actors?" The reporter seemed to wish to come to terms with his ignorance, perhaps based on misinformation or preconceived ideas.

"Certainly," came WS's unequivocal response.

"Really?" The reporter's ignorance was alarmed.

"As a matter of fact, I have one in my company right now."

"Really?" The reporter's helpless repetition revealed his utter curiosity, which obviously beggared the follow-up question: "Who's this?"

It was a leading nudge that the playwright, for some reasons, did not wish to take up or respond to. The reporter, on the other hand, also for some reasons, allowed his curiosity to lapse seeking no further pursuit. In vain BBGD strained his ears; he was beside himself. He almost forced himself out of his secret hiding to prod the reporter to quest his curiosity further.

Rather, the reporter seemed satisfied with the hanging response. Could he have assumed that the playwright assumed he knew—which would seem outrageous? Or was his silence compelled by a fear of knowing the complete truth—a contradiction to the biases of his preconception? The rookie would have preferred a confirmation of some sort, spelt out directly for the benefit of his selfish curiosity. However, ultimately, he felt somewhat consoled by the fact that the puzzle was in reality not hard to resolve. For who else could have been the referent other than the silent eavesdropper behind the wall? His thoughts ran up and down the cast list and found no one else fitting that role other than himself, who, after all, had been referred to as "the silent one."

Another thought that boosted his ego was that the playwright, probably feeling the nearby presence of his assistant, deliberately decided to keep him guessing. Or, perhaps, he didn't want the knowledge to go too far into his rookie head, hereby making it swell with dangerous premature praise?

The production of *Oyedipo* was to be a kind of regathering of the "tribe," that is, the actors that constituted Soyinka's theater companies in the 1960s—the 1960 Masks and the Orisun Theater. Thus, the occasion was to celebrate memories of the good old days. BBGD recalled the first mention of this intention at the Soyinka colloquium in Toronto. He was very excited by it, even though he knew he would probably be the only member of the original "nucleus of the Nigerian National Theater," the 1960 Masks. Most of the other members had followed very different paths from Theater; he really didn't know any that metamorphosed into the new Orisun. By the time of that transition, he was already in England in an effort to pursue studies in drama.

However, as it eventually turned out to be, for many reasons, the main being logistics and economics, the reunion had never happened as anticipated. Apart from BBGD, certainly the oldest member not counting WS, there were only Tunji Oyelana (of the former Orisun Theater), Folabo Ajayi Soyinka, Kongi's sister, and Anthony Ofoegbu, the youngest member and a professional actor in London. The last name, let alone his face, was unfamiliar to BBGD; the London actor's relationship with Soyinka began long after he had left Nigeria.

There was also Peter Badejo, the distinguished dance choreographer from London. His relationship with the playwright also happened after BBGD's exit. But he knew the name and did meet the dancer a couple of times in England, during his visits there from the US. Whatever Peter's previous relationship with Kongi was, the playwright had always wanted to work more formally with him as a choreographer. The rest of the *Oyedipo* company consisted of members of the Nevada Conservatory Theater of the University of Nevada in Las Vegas. Intensive rehearsals of the play went for a period of four weeks under slightly stressful but tolerable conditions, before taking the production to Greece.

Casting back to his humble but determined beginnings, BBGD reflected on the mixed pool of actors that also constituted the 1960 Masks. There was the Lagos crew, from various walks of life, some of them university colleagues of the playwright when he was a student at the University of Ibadan a few years back. Out of this lot, the only member that had probably received some acting training or experience was Olga Adeniyi Jones. Wife of Dr. Adeniyi Jones, she was nee Rhodes, of the well-known Lagos-Brazilian family (cousin of Shola Rhodes, BBGD's high-school friend). She had recently returned from England with her medical doctor husband and was easily persuaded by WS to join the company.

Apart from her, BBGD presumed no one else had any experience beyond probably high-school or college acting. Some might have had adequate knowledge of drama, to be sure—such as Yemi Lijadu, Ralph Opara, Francesca Pereira, Patrick Ozieh, and Funmilayo Asekun—but none in acting per se. However, being the playwright's peers and older, he gave them their due respect. Furthermore, since he also had some Brazilian background, he felt some kinship with the Rhodes and the Pereiras, although not as elite-demonstrative as they made up to be.

The other half of the company, the Ibadan group, consisted of members of the University Players at the University of Ibadan. In terms of logistics, the mixed pool meant the company had to rehearse in two locations, alternately—Lagos and Ibadan. However, because of the student academic responsibilities of some of the Ibadan group, and because its members had limited access to transportation, it was not often possible to get the group to rehearse in Lagos. More often, each group was rehearsed separately; and when it was necessary for the whole company to rehearse together, the Lagos group went up to Ibadan by carpool.

As assistant to Soyinka, BBGD had enjoyed the adventure that the rehearsals accorded him. Whether in Lagos or Ibadan, or together in Ibadan, he had been present at all occasions, doing one thing or the other for his boss, so to speak, that is, something other than driving. Regretfully, he couldn't drive. As to that, he recalled the rather humiliating encounter with Sola Rhodes, when he first learnt from him about Soyinka's intentions:

"You, Wole Soyinka's assistant?" He doubted the credibility of Sola, since his friend was sometimes given to exaggeration and name-dropping; but he was obviously full of envy.

"Yah," Sola tinged his blunt response with pride, which touched his apparent rival all the more to the quick with anxiety.

"B-But I want to be his assistant too," BBGD snapped, as if Sola had robbed him of his rightful place.

"Well, can you drive? I'm his driving assistant," Sola rubbed it in.

No, he could not drive, that he could not deny. It was a fact as stark and blatant as two plus two equals four. Two plus two equals four, he pondered the thought, as if he needed a reminder of the obvious simple addition.

In spite of his obstacle, he had become Soyinka's assistant, although with the secret hope that he would take up driving lessons in the near future. Then he would become a more complete assistant.

Four decades have elapsed between that calling of the 1960 Masks and the call to participate in *Oyedipo*, he mused with wonder as he closed the album that initiated his thoughts, putting it aside for the moment.

At first glance, the calling and the call seemed unlikely comparatives. Or, at best, they were two moments that indicate naiveté and maturity. But, on second thoughts, both derive from similar, somewhat idyllic fascination with a dynamic and his art. He felt extremely indebted to WS, for providing that initial impetus of encouragement to what, up till that point, was an uncertain interest in theater, let alone acting. If, as he thought during his high school days, acting had to do with just memorize lines, his remote interests in, indeed hatred for it, would have been justified. What came to mind as a defense of that hatred were the high school classes that required certain level of memorization, like dates in History or translations from Latin into English and vice versa.

History dates! He could not ever remember them. Try as hard as he could to put them in his head, they just didn't sink into the storage of memory. Rather, they scuttled the surface, like sand sprinkled on a smooth metal head-piece. He had to devise other means of remembering them, such as association of events and letters. Latin took a similar forgetful session, especially when he was studying for the West African School Certificate, the graduating exams of high school. Many of his classmates preferred to cram the available translations of the Horace, Ovid, or Virgil set for the exam. As far as he was concerned, that endeavor was lunacy. He later admitted that laziness and his aversion to memorization had to do with it. Actually, his attitude really paid off. It forced his critical understanding of the Latin sentences, phrases, and idioms; that ultimately got him a high grade.

Participating in *A Dance of the Forests*, he came to realize that acting had to do with more than memorization of lines. It had to do with the repeated enactment and development of scenes during rehearsals. It was those times that made the lines more and more familiar and therefore provided gradual understanding of the character. Not that he was conscious of this transformation during that production. For the way he got his lines in and was able to switch characters, from Slave-Dealer to Dirge-Man to Third Triplet, was something of a miracle for him. It was afterwards, when he began to think about his experience, that he understood the importance of the process, that seemingly tedious repetition of lines and going over scenes again and again during rehearsals. That process paid off; like magic. The lines and character changes, all of a sudden, became second nature during the actual performance.

The perpetual but progressive repetition, surely, was the hard work that made possible the seemingly effortless product. Something relating to character and the action of the play seemed to be discovered anew during and after each repetition. This understanding, in addition to the comments of his mentor regarding introspective actors, made him to be more convinced of his prospects in theater and acting. Then, the urge to satisfy this passion as quickly as possible became evident, especially as other theatrical opportunities around him began to play comparative temptations against his mentor's vision of theater.

The upsurge of interests in cultural development, initiated by Nigeria's Independence, had brought about mushrooms of popular theater companies and activities. They were all modeled after the already existent Yoruba travelling theaters companies such as Herbert Ogunde's. What had fascinated him was the ability of these companies to draw audiences, and therefore their propensity to make money, at least as far as it appeared to him. That inclination, obviously, was not the initial objective of his mentor. As such, BBGD's lack of understanding of these things lured him towards some of these groups, although their often-demonstrative expertise in singing and dancing did not have much appeal to the rookie. He felt these were antics a bit more than what he could stomach.

"You should come and join us, help us develop the company," a director of one such companies had enticed him.

"Well, I am in Wole Soyinka's company," BBGD defended.

"You're interested in that kind of theater?" the director rebuffed, almost with sarcasm. "Intellectual and academic. Who needs that? How do you attract audiences that way? You want audiences for your production, you should try and attract the people, anybody you can get, to come and see your show. That's how you make money. An actor of your caliber should be in our company."

He had resisted the enticement of what transpired between him and that director. He came to dub him by the name "Mr. Moi-moi eleelo…" [††] from a song he heard during a production by his company. He had liked, especially, the way the song had integrated the *moi-moi* seller's ad-call into the main action. He had struggled to resist the lure until, defenseless, he couldn't bear any longer the gnawing pain the resistance inflicted in his head. And stomach, if he may add, since *moi-moi* was one of his favorite meals. He had to seek relief from his ailment at all costs by consulting his mentor.

"Well…" Br'er Wole had simply shrugged. "Don't let me stop you," he continued with his customary, matter-of-fact stare, shot straight at his assistant's knuckle forehead. "If you feel that's what you want at this beginning, don't let me stop you." Then, thinking better of it, he must have felt it was his brotherly duty to help his assistant's understanding by further providing informative explanations: "Listen. I know those companies glitter with excitement, but some of them will not last, I can assure you. My company and theirs appeal to different audiences. Personally, I don't think their process is the right thing for you."

BBGD had taken in the advice, and churned it carefully in his head; it was the gentle persuasion he needed. He did not talk about the matter any further, nor did he have inclinations to consider any contrary argument, which he believed was really no match against his mentor's rationale. And then, it came down to the barefaced question: Which company of actors would he rather mingle with? Those of the 1960 Masks, whose class and intellect he had much more in common with, or those of Mr. Moi-moi eleelo, whose education probably didn't go beyond high school?

The call to perform in *Oyedipo* (at the dusk of his acting career, so to speak) was not beset by novice conflicts with other theatrical lures, such as those that confronted him at the calling. Both moments and circumstances, however, were obviously compelled and fated by the irresistible dynamism of a mentor, who had faith in him as an actor. That dynamism had fostered certain intimidation in him, which had persisted from that dawn of experience into its dusk. The trepidation had gained gravity; rather than becoming subdued, it got compounded by the experiences he garnered over the years between these moments. While he had yet to analyze for himself the exact nature of his affliction, he discovered quite early that the sensation was far from dissuading or pulling him away from the dynamic, as one might expect. Rather, it drew him more towards this personage, in fact making him almost always do his bidding.

This lure, as he dug deeper in to its characteristics, really had nothing to do with mundane or surface attractions, such as adventure or monetary concerns.

Or, as was customary with some other people he knew, it had nothing to do with the human tendency to rub shoulders with fame, the ultimate of which, in this case, was his mentor's Nobel Laureateship. Rather, the lure, it would seem, was predicated by the very dynamism, and the more he perceived or felt this zing, the more he was convinced what it had to do with. It was imbedded in the playwright's corpus, in the works that had gradually affected his sensibilities, probably more intensely as an actor over the period of four decades. Initiated by the poetry and lyricism of the Dirge-Man in *A Dance*, the energy had run through subsequent plays, the ones he actually performed in and those he saw or read. By the time of *Oyedipo*, it had become more crystallized, like diamond, even amidst the tussle and bustle of conflicts that buffeted that production.

More about *Oyedipo* in later scenes. But, in terms of his discovery of comparative moments in the play's production and that of *A Dance*, an emotional wave of new perception, all of a sudden, filled him with certain warmth. It was regarding a complimentary comment of equal faith in his acting made by his mentor.

Rehearsals of the play, as usual, had been somewhat daunting and harrowing—by the very presence of the playwright as director. His trepidation had come to the fore, perhaps compounded by all familiar and similar experiences he had had over the years of collaboration. The rehearsals in Las Vegas came and went, so was the only performance of the play at Delphi. During these, he had, as usual, experimented with voice and character, which, again, had got him in trouble—because of the way these explorations seemed to have threatened the vision of the playwright. Throughout the rehearsals, and the one performance on the makeshift stage at the foot of a hill in Delphi, he had had no way of knowing how WS had overall taken his interpretation of the Chieftain. He had not dared to ask him directly, at first, because of a confrontation they had during the rehearsal.

He had not been present at the postmortem discussion of the production the day following. For, as the company was leaving Greece the day after, it was the only morning he was able to go and communicate with the gods at the sanctuary of Apollo. He had to go early before the heat of the day made it impossible. He had apologized after the fact, but heard of the baffling proceedings straight from the horse's mouth. Taking advantage of this, he instinctively confronted the criticism-immune playwright:

"Well, how did you feel about the production on the whole? You haven't even told me whether or not you liked my performance."

His friend-brother-mentor-colleague gave him one of his direct uncomplicated stares, then responded: "I wore the jacket you gave me, didn't I? If I didn't like your performance, I wouldn't have worn it."

BBGD had worn the referenced jacket, made from handwoven fabric, to one of the receptions prior to the performance. WS had liked it on him, and the mentee had gone on to tender it as gift the day following. He took the comment and held it in the silence of the smile that curled his cheeks. Just like the reporter's inquiry with regard to introverted actors, there was no need to pursue the playwright-director's response, because he understood it as genuine. How could he not, after four decades of intermittent experience of it.

Scenes Two

Looking Through the Lens of a Prospective Mentor

More than anything else, BBGD was fascinated by any opportunity to go on a tour. In all his eighteen years, his parents had never allowed him to go out of Lagos of his own volition—well, except to Ibadan, some 80 miles away, which could be called a suburb of Lagos, so to speak. That time, he had gone to visit his father's friend in the GRA (Government Reservation Area) created by the old British colonial government in an attempt to distance their presumed superior officials from the natives. Each important Nigerian city had a GRA. But gradually, just before and after the British left, it became occupied by the Nigerian elite in governmental administrative positions. Such was the case with his father's friend, Jack Smith, who had recently come back home after a long stretch in England. Going to Ibadan, then a sprawling city, was the only travel he had made outside Nigeria on his own. Virtually that is, for it was only made possible when another friend of his father decided to go and he was allowed to tag along. His parents had no car to boast of.

Come to think on it, he faintly remembered travelling with his mother, when he was very young, to visit his granduncle, a government official of the British colonial. He vaguely recalled some preparation for the visit; he was about four years of age at the time. He remembered being stood on an armchair in the dining room and got dressed up in travel clothes by his mother very early in the morning, so they could catch the train to Oshogbo at Iddo Station located just after the main bridge connecting the island of Lagos to its mainland. That was his only memory of it, except that his mother and aunties had often teased him about what happened on the train on one of those journeys. Apparently, he had helped himself to some fried plantains bought at one of the train stops by the passenger sitting next to him. This uncontrollable food-compelled behavior, which only added credence to his appellation, "Bem-bem-gudu," had put his mother in a very embarrassing, apologetic position. Apparently, the passenger had not minded at all.

"Yes, I could do with another assistant." Mr. Soyinka's response had been a joyful hymnal to his ears. "But we'll be doing a lot of travelling; I don't want to take you away from your office job."

That certainly was no deterrent. It was like asking him to choose between a plate of "jollof" rice and fried plantains, admittedly his favorite teenage dish, and an opportunity to satisfy his hunger with epicurean delights. The adventure that touring involved was just too much to resist, despite what he had come to enjoy in his civil service job—paying the intern probationary nurses at the end of the month, the responsibility for which he had been dubbed "Chief Accountant of the Prob-Nurses." What he had enjoyed most was the small power he seemed to have wielded with that job, which secured him respect and various flirtations from the young nurses, and also provided his friends at the medical laboratory access to the women. Nevertheless, the educative prospects of the adventure seemed limitless.

Chappie's approval of his son's otherwise precarious objective was not difficult to fathom, and therefore not limited to astrological enlightenment. For his father's various artistic inclinations were all too apparent. First was his extraordinary creativity that fashioned many of his children's toys and those of his neighbors. For instance, BBGD's wooden train, tricycle and pedal car, handed down no doubt from his brother, but updated, were items he had designed and built with his friend, Peter the blacksmith. But then, he had also demonstrated his abilities with amateur acting by, no less, his involvement with the Lagos Operatic Society, a colonial organization under the auspices of the British Council. A few Africans, like Chappie, who had a classical musical background, were graciously admitted into the organization, while others, who were not as musical, begged to be included in the elite society. It was here that Chappie, with proud enthusiasm, had the opportunity to play minor roles in the works of Gilbert and Sullivan such as *Trial by Jury*, *The Mikado*, and *HMS Pinafore*. He was by no means a token of colonial graciousness, for he was adept at piano and taught all his children to play running the keys of that instrument. BBGD, as it happened, was not as connected to playing as his older brother, Akintunde, who made a career of it, or his junior sister, Tinuade, who at least accompanied the morning hymnal at her senior high school. But above all, Chappie in his younger days, apparently, was a real dandy with his three other friends, Jack, Joe and Jock. They constituted a group called the Lagos Concert Party, much in the frame of the Black Minstrelsy, although without the customary exaggerated facial features. BBGD had always been fascinated by pictures he saw of the tuxedoed group, all with piano, banjo, saxophone, drums etc.

BBGD, as Mr. Soyinka's assistant, received some stipend whenever possible. Nothing significant, however, to write home about. Thankfully he could boast of some savings, which constituted almost all his monthly salary from his former civil service job. He had lived with his parents where he was not expected to pay any rent or feed himself. Hence, apart from a few clothes he sometimes bought to keep up with his teenage peers, he had no imposing expenses. With Mr. Soyinka, he also did not have to pay any rent. He sometimes found a space to sleep in his apartment, at first in town and then, when it was available, in his bungalow at the University of Ibadan as a Rockefeller Foundation researcher. However, that living arrangement was possible only when it was convenient for his mentor, that is, when there was no likelihood of a female visitor coming for the night. Most of the time, when he was in Ibadan and not in Lagos taking a breather, he stayed with Uncle Pekun, the well-known accountant, especially, among the Indian and Pakistani haberdashery community. That was where he enjoyed watching his first television shows, since his parents in Lagos possessed no TV.

When on campus at the University of Ibadan, he, through Mr. Soyinka's arrangement, ate in one of the university halls among the undergraduates, an option he always took advantage of with delight. Realistically, at his age, that was the place he should be—at the university. The ideal process expected of high school leavers was to study for the HSC (Higher School Certificate) for a year or two at a high school or some other pre-university institution that offered the program. With that accomplishment, the individual had the chance of securing a competitive bottleneck placement at the only university available at the time—the University College of Ibadan. As the ill-luck of Lord Misfortune would have it, or was it his Esu's accountability, BBGD could not immediately do the HSC, let alone get admitted to the university. He must first try and improve on his low grade in English, which downgraded him to a Grade Two rather than the most cherished Grade One in the West African School Certificate. A mere Pass in English, his favorite subject? He could not believe it, nor were his English teachers who saw him as a writer, based on the short stories he wrote and which were often read over the radio, enjoyed by all listeners. Everybody was puzzled. He was convinced, although he could not prove it, that it was a case of grade mix-up or misallocation. Unless it was a case of his natural experimentation with the English language that got in the way with the examiners!

Being on the university campus, mingling with the undergrads at lunches or dinners seemed to give him some kind of false belonging. Often, he was able to discuss and talk with them as if he was one of them. He also had one or two as friends, and often went to their rooms to have a chat. There, he found himself accepted as the research assistant to the man they all had admiration for. As a kind of consolation at moments of truth regarding his insecure belonging, he felt it was only a question of time when he would either be at that university or, like Wole Soyinka, go abroad to study drama at some English university, which he considered a far better objective. Perhaps his mentor could help in this, he had wondered.

However, he was a little envious of Sola Rhodes, who had a way of mingling with some of the white lecturers, for reasons that was not clear to him until later, when his friend's assistantship with Mr. Soyinka suddenly ended, thus making BBGD the only assistant to Br'er Wole. Sola had all along claimed to be some kind of probationary college student, a fact the naïve apprentice did not bother to verify even though he could not figure out how that could be. He was later to find out that it had to do with Sola's so-called white professor friends, but for the moment, BBGD seemed quite satisfied with his friend as a possible college student; hence his envy. But then, with what he later knew, he felt that, with a little prodding, he should have fathomed the nature of the professors' relationship very easily at that initial stage. He only had to make connections with the goings-on when they were in high school. For two plus two equals four.

One strange morning, out of the cerebral and celestial blue, the principal, Adeyemi Degbite, B.A., M.A., Ed. D, went out of his style to deliver a scathing sermon in the school-chapel, something to do with older guys who should be more responsible than taking advantage of younger ones by having illicit relationship with them. He was ready to dismiss instantly anybody reported to him as guilty of such an outrageous, inhuman, and heinous crime. For such an act of sinfulness, he elaborated, was unpardonable by God.

BBGD, at first, naively missed the implications of the principal. Students who were more streetwise at once knew about the activity and the referent. They therefore, instantly, made it their duty to propagate, through the grapevine, their knowledge in coital, sodomized whispers, which eventually got flicked into his ears and, at once, beggared obvious questions. For, if the principal knew what he said he knew, why didn't he expel instantly, as he threatened, the unnamed person and culprit of his spiritual venom? For the referent, going by those cutting words of Oga, the principal, surely deserved immediate expulsion. If this person, whose name went unnamed, received only a warning, why was the punishment just a warning? Why was he given the privilege of staying further in school? Those were the burning questions that everybody in the know was asking.

The low whispers that started from the chapel, trickled out somewhat loud outside it and then went berserk. For there, among the gossips, it only took a slightly graphic prodding before the images were understood with unmistakable clarity, without any pretentious prevarication. The culprit in person was no other than *langalanga* Rhodes! [‡‡] How, indeed, could the parent-sheltered pupil that he, BBGD, was could be so naive and unsuspecting about a person he called a friend?

Actually, his relationship with Sola, if at all it could be called real friendship, was somewhat flawed, even before the revelation. Other than being an imposing-looking classmate, they were friends because they were both descendants of the so-called krio-elite, a Lagos Creole circle, who, so-named, often earned the derisive acknowledgment of those who considered themselves the real McCoy, that is, the unadulterated indigenes. To be sure, the krio-descendancy of BBGD's family, unlike that of some others, was not necessarily measured in terms of money but rather in status. But then, neither was that of Rhodes' family for that matter, if only they could honestly, as opposed to their pretentiousness, own up to it. However, this was not the issue of the flawed relationship.

At Lagos Baptist High, BBGD's cloud of envy was premeditated by an assumed competition existing between him and his friend, with regard to their relationship with Principal Degbite's wife. Rhodes, for some reasons, always vaunted himself as the obvious favorite. He was always seen in the principal's apartment, or in the office of Madame, as she was called, helping the family with this and that, especially with the children he sometimes babysat. For BBGD, it was an assumed relationship he aspired to better if not prove wrong, which resulted in the "love" poem he forged out of his head in praise of the favored beauty and object of his contemplation—Madame. The sonnet seemed to have succeeded at the initial stage of its author's vying for patronage, but, alas, only for an insignificant period of time. For it certainly was not enough to displace Rhodes from the grounds he had already firmly secured in the principal's quarters, as opposed to BBGD's seeming priority access to only Madame's office.

As such, the more he thought about it, knowing what he now knew, he felt Rhodes relationship with the Degbites was simply inexplicable, let alone unhealthy. Or, could the Degbites, initially, be as naïve as he was? But then, as baffling as it was confounding, that relationship had continued after the principal's sermon, a fact that he deemed so unconscionable, especially so if it was a gesture of some cover-up.

At any rate, he felt that if anybody deserved the friendship of the husband and wife, it should certainly be him, for he knew them both long before the

---

[‡‡] A Yoruba onomatopoeic for a tall and lanky person

molester ever came into the picture frame. They used to be neighbors in the Olowogbowo area of Lagos, living not very far away and round the corner from BBGD's family. At the time, both were fledgling teachers in the same Baptist high-school they graduated from, that is, long before they both got a Baptist missionary scholarship to go and study at Lincoln University in the US. In fact, he used to pass by their two-roomed living quarters, one in a long line of apartments behind the Methodist church, built by their ethnic relative, one of the affluent timber contractors of Lagos. On the way to the local dumpster about half a mile away, he would see one or the other looking out of the window and would tender his greetings. And when the time came for BBGD to proceed from elementary to high school, and he was unable to make the grade for the much-coveted CMS Grammar School, it was the husband that had come to the aid of his family, making it possible for him to get into Baptist High instead.

Not ungrateful for the favor, BBGD had often felt inadequate overall, that is, when he considered the facts. For, because of the high school's American-based system of education, he had lost two years of formal high school education, that is, as compared to his brother and some of his peers at the CMS Grammar school, who had graduated at the ideal age of 16 as opposed to 18. Thus, while his indebtedness to the Degbites was a given, for which he was thankful, he felt it should be consequent to his being their favorite, as opposed to their option of Rhodes. As far as he was concerned, his rival should have been dismissed, given his hideous coital activities that became full blown to BBGD's sheltered naivety in due course.

Two plus two equals four…

Whispered voices came from behind the plywood partitioned room as BBGD sat in a kind of anteroom area. He had sat there for over thirty minutes, waiting for his friend to emerge from the locked door of the room. He had nothing urgent to talk about, really, and he probably would have left if the whispers did not arrest his curiosity. Sola's voice, for sure, he could decipher, but the other voices (at least two others) were impossible to fathom. What could possibly be going on in there, he had wondered, the inscrutable tête-à-tête mixed with giggles? He had intended to call only for a few minutes, drawn no doubt by the extraordinary taste of Mama Rhodes' famous "puff-puff" doughnuts. To get faster to the house from Baptist-High, he had taken the back route. He had walked along the narrow one-way busy bus route that came toward him and went back as far as to the Ikoyi Cemeteries, past the Race-Course, where the British colonials and the Lagos Krio elite gambled on horse-racing weekends. Coming from Oil Mill Street side of the school, away from Broad Street, he had cornered into, and walked down Igbosere Street on to

Campus Square and into the narrow stretch towards the Tinubu Square bus terminal. Just a few yards from the bend into the square, he had halted in front of the faded yellow stucco house, arrested by the all-seeing penetrating eyes of Mama Rhodes, whose sumptuous frame on the gutter-slab had occupied almost the entire threshold.

"Good afternoon, mah," he had greeted her calmly.

"Ah, my dear. Your friend is at home," she indicated, and BBGD had squeezed by her into the passageway that led to back of the house.

"Sola, are you there?" He had knocked on the door of the partitioned room.

"Who's that?" the response was jumpy and querulous.

"Me."

"Ah, Euba." Recognizing the voice, he felt more secure. "Wait for me. I'm coming." And the whispers and giggles had adamantly continued.

When he finally showed his face, noticeably flushed, he said with a smile: "I'm tutoring these two kids in Algebra. Why don't you come and join us?"

Apart from his waiting for more than half hour, BBGD's sixth sense counseled reluctance. At any rate, he had to get back home, and no insistence at joining the group could change that. Not even an appearance of puff-puff at that stage would have altered anything—and there was always the freedom to choose to take the delicious pastry home. However, no puff-puff came along, and the idea of Algebra was somewhat perplexing. For, Mathematics was hardly Rhodes' forte, so why he should be tutoring some juniors in his weakest subject was hard to conceive. He tried hard to determine the possibility, but to no avail. He probably would have dismissed the thought without further ado, if Oga Degbite's signifying sermon of sodomite iniquities had not intruded by some association. The revelation snapped his eye nerves into twitches as he turned to step out of the anteroom, insisting that he had overstayed his time and on his need to hurry back home.

As it turned out, Rhodes never did any touring with Mr. Soyinka. Justly so, BBGD reflected in hindsight, flash-alarmed by wicked images of his friend's busy schedule of activities on the university college campus. For Rhodes' vaunted claims, of university studies, were only believable if indeed he was a student, even though the exact nature of his studies were a suspect. But those claims turned out to be false. BBGD's efforts to gain something tangible from Br'er Wole regarding the sudden resignation of the driving assistant's duties, were met with the customary throaty rumble of the voice, which produced nothing meaningful to interpret. He could only surmise that the researcher knew something he wanted to protect the rookie's seemingly innocent ears from hearing, but as to what that something could be was difficult to comprehend. All that became obvious was that, after the production of *A*

Dance, encounters with his supposed co-assistant became very infrequent, reduced to a mere sighting with this professor and that, or a quick hailing across campus to, apparently, a lecture or on some errand. And so it was that BBGD came to be the only acknowledged research assistant of WS, although, alas, lacking in any driving experience.

Years later, to resolve the simple equation formulated by his friend's enigmatic sightings on campus, years later and out of the blue, the assumptive deductive factor confronted him on the streets of Earl's Court, one of his favorite habitats in London during his professional acting days.

"Hello there!" accosted the rather thin voice behind him. When he turned to look, he recalled the face that had familiarly struck him a few seconds before as it passed by. Therefore, looking at the figure more thoroughly the second time, something began to connect, although at first with difficulty.

"Remember me? Ibadan University campus…"

"Yes…yes of course," he finally made the connection though not quite fully. Perhaps he was one of the lecturers involved in some play production? That much he thought he knew. Rapid incidents raced through his mind to determine the true identity of the figure in front of him.

"English department. *That Scoundrel Suberu*," the accosting white man further juggled his memory. Yes, yes, he knew it had to do with theater. Now that he mentioned it, he recollected the English man (or perhaps Scottish) somewhat in relation to that production, into which WS had thrust him by some arrangement with its director, Geoffery Axworthy. The pale and rather lanky accoster was hardly that director with whom BBGD had crossed paths many times years after that production. The intruder went on to introduce himself more formerly, although deafened by the passing traffic and crisscrossing thoughts that beleaguered his mind, BBGD had failed to register the exposition of the stiff-upper-lipped.

"Yes, yes," he pretended to get it. Not that the man cared much, for he had continued to puff on into the wind regardless, as if he were chatting with one of his former students in the cast of *Suberu*, a Nigerian adaptation of Moliere's *That Scoundrel Scapin*.

"Are you now living in London? Or what are you doing here?" The longwinded finally diverted to ask.

"Actually I'm here on vacation. I'm living in the US at the moment. Just came on a visit at a friend's."

"Marvelous, marvelous. I live not far from here. In South Kensington. Look, what are you doing this evening? Perhaps you can come to my house for dinner? Then we can catch up with old times."

"Ah…certainly." BBGD's first thought was to make up an excuse, but somehow, he reconsidered. What the heck, a free dinner was not such a bad idea.

"Great." His small moustache exalted with a spread of smiles. "Shall we say, 7pm?" Then he gave his address and direction to it.

BBGD may have missed the sound bites that could have summoned full recollection, but another opportunity came full blown at dinner, and how could he not have guessed!

"Where's Sola Rhodes these days? Back in Nigeria? I saw him quite a few times here when he was studying law."

That was it, right there, and with all its antecedents—and probably what Br'er Wole's unintelligible mumbling had tried to protect him from. The man was one of the lecturers Rhodes had mingled with, a relationship that probably led to his disappearance after *A Dance*. BBGD now had an inkling of why he had been invited to dinner, a plate which really had nothing much to offer— the usual thin English roast beef, a few spuds and Brussels sprouts. The bottle of wine served was a favorite of the period, although he would like to feel he had graduated from Beaujolais, thanks to WS for an eye-opener to other brands. It became evident to him that his glass was in constant refill in spite of his cautionary gesture of decline, but he knew his limits and therefore kept his senses acute and alert to any slight change in equilibrium.

He had been completely overwhelmed since he entered the house, struck by the numerous priceless Yoruba carvings that filled the walls, especially the famous Ibeji sets. There must have been hundreds of them in pairs on shelves framing almost every wall of the man's semi-detached. This initial amazement was immediately buffeted with horror by thoughts of the lootings administered, with impunity, to his country's treasures by white colonials, as they began vacating the country in droves just before Independence. Seeing the writing on the wall that their time was limited in the formerly dependent colony, these colonials had disappeared, vengefully, claiming what they thought was their right to claim.

"Where did you get all these?" he had queried with a wry smile.

"My collections. Aren't they just wonderful?"

Collections my arse! BBGD had muffled. The anger he had tried to control unabashedly transmitted strands of disgust onto his contorted face. He could imagine how much the little sparrow-face had paid for them, if at all, and how much these collector's pieces would fetch should the looter decided to sell them.

"All these made my stay in your country worth the effort," he had punctuated with conclusive effrontery.

Then, to add insult upon injury, when BBGD decided the evening must end and it was time to leave, the insensitive calculating "spindle" had dropped the bombshell: "Going? I thought you were spending the night here."

"Here?" An involuntary chuckle broke through his larynx, making him to consider looking at his watch. He quietly blamed himself for not paying much attention to time until now, which, along with the wining, was consistent with the preplanned ambitions of his host. He also noticed for the first time that the lights had dimmed to a relaxed glow around the table.

"Yes. I have an extra bed."

"N-No, thank you. I really have to go."

"How're you going to do that? You can't get any tube or bus at this time."

"Well, I'll take a taxi." By this time BBGD was adamant, the full implications of pointed razor-nose's suggestions staring him in his lightly tipsy face.

"Tch-tch-tch. Very expensive this time of the night."

"I don't care." With that, BBGD got up, thanked the man for his dinner and walked out. A light sweat had developed and formed on his forehead, but he was quite convinced it wasn't because of the wine. For the bombshell had recalled much of the conversation of the evening, nothing significant but roundabout talk about university days, his cottage on campus and the students that came by to his dinner parties, including Rhodes. He was quite convinced that his guest had been among them, which BBGD could not for the life of him recollect. And was this where everything was leading—to reconnect with his frivolous colonial past, and have a night fling with one of his campus sidekicks?

Fortunately, a taxi had come his way as he got out of Tim Thompson's semi-detached. As he rode back to Earl's Court, musing over the evening's experience, he was convinced more than ever that the man had nothing significant to do with the production of *Suberu*. He was probably present at some point during the process, since he was a lecturer in the English department. But, certainly by the time of the production tour, he was no longer relevant or the situation was no longer ideal to his needs. Neither the man nor Rhodes was part of that production, into which he was drafted rather late, specifically for its anticipated tour. Also, he felt he probably could have made the connection much earlier than he did, especially if he had been able to make some sense of Br'er Wole's rumblings, or had been informed more properly about Rhodes' vaunted excuse and exit from the 1960 Masks and his assistantship. Ultimately, however, he understood the position his mentor took was what his parents would have expected of him—shield their son from terrible experiences lurking in the dark, awaiting the naivety of innocence. It would not be the only time BBGD felt thusly protected.

*****

He heard the sound of the truck on the driveway gravel pulling up in front Uncle Pekun's two-story mansion. It was unmistakable, and he only looked through the shutters to confirm the Rockefeller Foundation Land Rover on loan to WS for his research.

"Praise be," BBGD muttered. He hadn't heard from his mentor for about five days—since he last deposited him at the house, to allow him some breather he did not need. No, it was more a breather for Br'er Wole than for him. For as far as he was concerned, he could never tire being around a dramatist he wished to emulate at all costs.

He had come to understand his mentor's social breathers, so to speak, not in so many words. Once, upon a lazy afternoon, when he really had nothing to do except to wait for his boss' next orders for an errand, the playwright-researcher had come out of his bedroom and, taking one blunt look straight in his assistant's eyes, had mumbled something of a prologue to an affirmation, something to the effect that what he had to say was certainly not a result of what was often referred to as an artist temperament, which he didn't believe he had, even if it existed. But, the simple upshot of his main point was that he preferred sometimes to be alone. Earlier that morning, coming out of the shower, BBGD had, out of curiosity, applied a few puffs of his mentor's cologne on his neck, which of course tickled the olfactory senses of the playwright as soon as BBGD entered the living room. Quite naturally, it was easy to relate that action and the guilt of being found out to the present breather-mumble, and it did cross his mind; but he dismissed it instantly as petty. For, he had, within a short space of time in their relationship, come to respect his mentor's privacy, although he always wished he could be a part of it, which involved his colleagues and women friends. BBGD had little or no experience in that area and hoped he could learn a thing or two from his surrogate brother, especially so since he had played a kind of go-between with regard to the several missives he had delivered for him at the Queens' Hall— the women's dormitory on campus.

Confirming the Land Rover, he hurried outside with a streak of smile, suspecting there was something in the offing, something that would get him back to his mentor's bungalow, well situated at the back of a cul-de-sac overlooking a wooded, squirrel-infested area. He had been allocated the

Rockefeller bungalow, one of four on campus, when it became available after the *Dance of the Forest* production.

"I want you to take a small part in *That Scoundrel Suberu*. They're going on tour and they need somebody to take an extra role," Br'er Wole instructed.

"Really?" That was all he could say, although with some enthusiasm. Such rather short response was not unusual. Whether it was a speechlessness compelled by awe, or the fact that he was simply limited and had nothing much to say, BBGD had always had some difficulty at indulging himself in verbal expression. This inadequacy often led to a lot of awkward silent moments between him and his mentor, who always seemed to have a way with words, and had unusual expressions come to him very easily—which, of course, was not surprising. The playwright always had a spirit of activism about him, which his assistant admired and wished he could also acquire. Perhaps such an achievement was all in good time, although he did not think he had within him any making of it or a characteristic compulsion for it.

"Well, will you do it?" the researcher seemed to need some affirmation.

"Yes. Yes." But what else could he say. He had nudged his mentor many times, about when the company would have another show, or when they would do another production of *A Dance*. He had felt a certain yearning for the stage after it closed with only a few runs. They had talked about the output of the many Yoruba theater companies in Lagos vying for recognition, and he had understood his mentor's position. In fact, he had come to realize that simple adage, "Not all that glitters is gold," and that patience often had its delayed but rewarding results.

"Okay. Geoffery Axworthy wants to see you tonight at rehearsals. 7 o' clock." And, probably as an afterthought that the researcher knew would delight the rookie: "Or you can come with me now."

"Yes please." That was not a hard decision. He loved to be in the company of his mentor, however speechless it might end up.

In spite of his nudges and expectations, BBGD was somewhat petrified about the audition and being in *Suberu*. He had seen a performance of the play in the Arts Theater; all the actors were university students, mostly in the English department, which sponsored the project for its drama emphasis. And although he had acquired two or three as friends, for example Dapo Adelugba, who played the lead, he felt they were all so good and he could hardly compete with them. He did not know the original play although knew of Moliere through high school encounters, such as *The Miser*. He had found *Suberu*, when he saw it, very hilarious, especially the way they had adapted and manipulated some of the English translation of the dialogue into the local pidgin English. He did not believe he was capable of responding, like the other actors, to the wit and humor of the dialogue enough to actually make people laugh. *A Dance* was certainly not a comedy, although there were some funny moments, such as when he, the Slave Dealer, bribed the shiftless Historian with a bag of trinkets. In fact, he was not conscious of the humor in the exchange until the audience laughed. In contrast, *Suberu* was consciously satirical and therefore comical; its comic lines had nothing in common with those in *A Dance*. He slightly regretted not participating in plays in high school, which exposed him to Moliere, Shakespeare, Sheridan, and Oscar Wilde, etc. His only theatrical effort was in a mock trial project, which he enjoyed directing. He simply did not have the calling at the time.

However, what seemed to override all his tremors of acting was the opportunity to go on an extensive tour. That was a first for him in his highly sheltered life. And, although he would still require some approval from his parents regarding the touring, he felt the formal rules of his late teenage existence could be broken, and certainly indulged, through the intervention of his mentor, whose trust, after all, they had approved.

Mr. Axworthy thrust him the script of the play, and showed him the scene he wanted him to look at. There was nothing much to it, the role of a hysterical servant, who seemed to thrive in announcing bad news. Years later, when he became more familiar with the Moliere play, he realized that the character was an adaptation of Maid, a servant. In fact, the original actor for the show on campus was a woman, but she could not, for some reasons, make the tour, which worked well for BBGD to take up the role instead as a male servant, who in the Nigerian context spoke pidgin English. Axworthy explained the situation and instructed the relevant actors to act out the moment immediately before the servant's entrance.

"Come in, alarmed, wide-eyed with horror and exaggerated gesticulation," Axworthy advised.

"Okay," responded the rather frail nervous voice.

The character made two entrances in the play. Two or three trial runs for each scene ensued, along with Axworthy's demonstration, and it was over. BBGD was in. He even received applause, much to his surprise, from the university actors, who immediately welcomed him in as a comrade, a gesture that seemed to vanish his previous fears. They must have liked his wild gestures and horror-widened eyes—which was what he was told to do, surely. Later, he would know the correct word for such acting was "ham." Supposedly, it was suitable for farces such as that. Again, much later on, when he knew more about Moliere, and understood the Comedia dell'Arte convention that such acting was based on, he would slightly disagree with the way he was simply told to "ham" the part by the colonial know-how.

There was hardly any time between the full rehearsal of the play and the tour; just enough for him to dash to Lagos to tell his parents and back. As expected, their approval was not difficult and hardly needed the expected intervention of his mentor. The playwright drove him to Lagos where he was going anyway for a day or two, then returned him for the tour, which was to covered some cities in the western part of the country, then across the Niger Delta and River Niger and on to the Eastern region—all within two weeks.

There were probably many reasons why the researcher wanted his assistant to go on tour with the company. One at least was factual to him. Perhaps, in order to justify the importance of BBGD's inclusion in the company to Axworthy, he wanted the assistant during the tour to keep an open eye on any interesting situation or event that might come his way, cultural events that had the ingredients of drama, which could be in the nature of dances, ritual performances or festivals. It was to be his formal introduction to the processes of research. However, not given anything to document with other than perhaps a notebook, nothing like a camera or a tape recorder, BBGD did not take that charge too seriously. And so that idea seemed to have gone out of the Volkswagen Minibus window as they traveled from one location to another.

WS put him in the hands of two of the actors, for them to look after him, although there were no formal instructions or a list of what they should or should not do with him. And there's the rub. BBGD used their duty as guide not only to learn more about university life, but also gather a few things about what it took to be a man, something he was only able to watch his mentor do, as opposed to asking him directly. At any rate, try as he may to emulate him at every social turn, he found himself discouraged as much as possible from that part of the playwright's life. The only explanation that he could come up with for the obvious reluctance was a supposition that seemed to make sense—his mentor's promise to his parents to take care of their son. As strict disciplinarians, his parents must have summoned up an unusually strong sense of responsibility in the researcher.

It was in Asaba, the last city in the Western region before the River Niger, overlooking Onitsha in the East across the river, it was there that these manhood matters mounted and rose to a curious and crucial climax. He had heard, in the male-actors circle, that Asaba women were easy lays, which made him excited and anxious.

Before this and before embarking on a long drive towards the East, they had had quite a few performances in the Western region, in places such as Ondo, Benin, and Warri where he had met his maternal grandmother in person for the first time. Between and during these performances, he had got acquainted with the only two women in the cast. They knew he was WS's assistant and seemed to be interested in knowing his mentor better through him. Therefore, they were always around him. As such, he felt quite comfortable and warm with the smell of their various perfumes, body lotion and talcum powder.

They got to the town of Asaba in the evening and, as planned, had no intentions of crossing the bridge to Onitsha until the following morning. So they stayed the night at a cheap hotel, where plans materialized to hunt for Asaba women in a village brothel as soon as they finished dinner.

"Have you been to one before," inquired one of his actor-guides, a confident smile furrowing his dimples.

"N-No," BBGD shamefully admitted. "Have you?"

"Oh yeah. Many times!" Freddie's braggadocio puffiness, though somewhat belittling, gave the apparent novice the assurance that he was in good hands.

"Are you sure you want to try it?"

The cautionary addendum almost instantly deflated him, but he quickly mustered: "Y-Yah." It was a defense that did not find support in his conscience. For what does one do? He queried himself as he struggled hard to cover up any sign of virgin doubt. With no problems of pregnancy to worry his mind, he convinced himself it was only natural to get serviced with experiences of this all-important objective of teenagers by an experienced servicer. Many times his mentor had driven to some night clubs in Ibadan where such things could happen but without him. Although tempted many times, he had not dared to go on his own, what with the parental pressure of admonitions that always found their way into his thoughts to prick his mind. Such promptings had prevented any rendezvous with women either in Lagos or Ibadan.

Not that he found himself wanting regarding a girlfriend. As a matter of fact, he had one, openly, for the first time after graduating from high school. CK, so called, was a nurse he knew from the clerical job he left at the General Hospital. But shameful as it may sound, his skirmishes with her had only been limited to deep kisses, which she taught him. Moreover, it wasn't the case of not being curious enough to want to push things further. He very much wanted to, especially the way he and his friends circulated certain facts among them about nurses. The belief in the main, that they were notorious with sex. But, the crux of the matter was, as long as he was under the roof of his parents, and the all-seeing eyes of uncles or aunties, he could not override the thumps of guilt hammering in his heart. As such, the frequent times that his testosterone ran riot were merely wasted into his underpants at crucial moments of kisses. Or when exaggerated images of sexuality were entertained or evoked among his friends, such as the images in Kama Sutra, or of frolicking doctors and nurses in hospitals. As to the latter notion, the "Doctor" serial novels of Richard Gordon were ready proofs. However, more to the point of celibacy was the serious possibility of pregnancy before marriage, a fact of the drumbeats of parental pressures that had cluttered his young Christian mind. And the question of where to perform was always a problem. He was not as free as some of his more able friends, who lived in Lagos but far away from their parents in other towns or cities.

Yet, another crucial factor was the question of disease, which became operative when the subject turned to prostitutes. His heart as usual sank a little at the prospects of a trial experience that now confronted him. The possibility of a protective, which his guides suggested, surmounted his fears a little. But he had no experience with these things, and to ask about their usage could be somewhat unmanly and therefore embarrassing.

"Here, let me give you one." Freddie's offer seemed to seal the deal, although BBGD was still very nervous about its application.

They had gone into the compound in a village not far from their hotel. There, a few women were sitting at large on benches under an almond tree, waiting for possible customers. Following the lead of the others, BBGD had with curiosity approached the woman of his liking. He did not know why he made the selection, except that she looked young and healthy, with a quiet smile teasing out of her mascaraed eyelashes and talcum-powdered face. A reddish blouse and a knee-length indigo wrap-around, from locally woven cloth, displayed her cocoa-butter-lotioned arms and legs, which she parted with taunting abandon as she sat on the bench. Reading his intentions, the young woman had got up and led him into one of the unpainted cinderblock huts lining the circular compound.

"How much?" BBGD had flipped at her, with a rather awkward naivety. The room, as far as he could make out from the dim lighting, was bare, except for a foam mattress on the raffia-matted rug, and an aluminum basin on a small table with a pail of water beside it. On the wall hung an expandable wooden clothes-rack with a few odds and ends.

"Five shillings." She had tendered her hand, scrutinizing the naivety of her client with quiet amusement. He understood the gesture to mean, pay before any activity, which was a little odd to him. But, with no experience, he had complied, dipping into his pocket to fish out one of the two five-shilling notes he had hidden there.

The hostess had put the money in a container on the table. She then proceeded to remove her blouse, revealing cups of what looked like a clean but well-worn bra, which concealed what he imagined as young breasts, that is, judging by the pointed cups. He looked forward to feeling these as soon as he could. In his neighborhood in Lagos, at the central community water-pump, he and his friends had sometimes indulged themselves at night with that foolishness. Pretending they had come to draw water, they had suddenly aimed at the nipples of the already sighted breasts under flimsy blouses, then took to their heels before their faces got clawed.

Contrary to expectation, and much to his disappointment, the woman had not removed her bra to reveal what he thought was his right to see and fondle. Why, he had wondered, but not been courageous enough to ask. Now that he was able to probe the bra more closely, he found that the low lighting had been a little deceptive. The cream pigmentation on the bra was not so much from overused faded color. Rather, it was from stains of accumulated and dried up sweat and lacquer, which various washings had failed to remove. All this had flashed across his eyes within a twinkling of an eye, as he was beleaguered with thoughts about how to proceed.

He watched the woman simply hitch up her wrapper to her waist and then proceeded to the mattress.

"Come now," she beckoned him as she lay face up and legs astride.

He felt something was not right about this. Some of the X-rated movies he had watched flashed across his mind. He saw nothing like this for comparisons. The experience he got through those movies and through stories told, even if exaggerated, had usually emphasized certain nakedness. Something was not right about this; as such, he too was under no obligation to remove his pants. He clumsily brought out the durex, under the watchful curious eyes of the young professional. As he unzipped his pants and bent down to a close prostrate proximity of his objective, his eyes spotted something on a lip of the revealed vagina, which held his curiosity. Zooming in intently on to the spot, his sharp eyes determined the object to be some scab. That immediately sent his thoughts back to the list of signals he had gathered from friends. Craw-craw, perhaps![§§]

"What's this?" he asked.

"What?"

"That." He pointed nervously at the spot.

"Dat be not'ing. Come now." Without any concern, she gave him a reassuring smile. "Come. Let me help you," reaching towards his penis.

"No! No." His mind had frozen up with an instant misgiving, causing immediate shrinkage of his organ, which no action or prepping up could now help. He recoiled like a wounded, nervous animal.

"Wetin now? You no wan do again?"

[§§] Used for a number itchy genital rash, including lice.

"No." He stood up and proceeded to zip up and buckle-belt his pants. His face felt flushed with quiet anger and disappointment. "Can I have my money back?" His voice was brusque and matter-of-fact, but he was not optimistic about the response.

The young woman simply smiled and shook her head with negative calm. "If you no wan do, dat no be ma fau't," she added.

A rather suffocating breath of humiliation overcame him, not because of the money he failed to get back, nor because he failed to proceed with his objective, for which he felt no regrets. And yes, the five shillings, he considered, could buy a lot of snacks and edibles, but he countered the thought with an easy rationale—what that same money might have cost him if he had gone through with the act. No, the real humiliation arose from the consideration of how to play the situation off with his guides, who, presumably, were enjoying themselves with the choices they made—although how exactly they did that was anybody guess. For, it occurred to him, next morning as they reconnected and were boarding the minibus to proceed with their journey East, it suddenly occurred to him that truth may never be found out. For what he overheard and then was told was all too vague and fuzzy:

"How did you make out?" one asked the other.

"Fantastic. How was yours?"

"Great." Then, spotting BBGD, they both approached him. "How was it last night, man?"

"Not bad." His naïve innocence at first got the better of him.

"What do you mean?"

The challenge was unexpected, so he immediately changed his tune:

"I mean, good. Good."

"How much did you pay her?"

He wished they wouldn't pursue the matter any further. "Five shillings."

"Five shillings? That was cheap, man. I paid ten for mine. But I spent about one hour. How much time did you spend?"

"About the same." Luckily for him at that moment, before they could continue their rather busybody prodding, one of the two women in the cast came by.

"You're going to sit with me on the bus this morning, aren't you?" she insisted, and he found himself being pulled away without any resistance. He felt the rescue as godsend, and as he got on the bus, the possibility of certain consolation entertained his mind.

From the beginning of the tour, he had been more at home with the two women than with his so-called guides. This fact and its reasons had not been obvious to him until later, that is, after the two had shared him alternately as

51

seat mates in the minibus. It was not difficult to see that there was some competition between the two. It was certainly not because both were very interested in him vis-à-vis intimacy. Of course, he would have liked that, especially at an age when he wished some woman would take the chance of experimenting with him, preferably in the woman's own room. Such an opportunity had not been possible with CK, his nurse-friend, for many reasons. All said, he had enjoyed the fondness the women seemed to have showered on him, sharing with him candies, cookies and such snacks. Stella, the woman that came to his aid, had even allowed her head, once or twice, to lean on his shoulder to rest her eyes. That delighted him, and even produced certain sensations in him, although to no avail. It all had to do with his feeling of inadequacy. Perhaps the situation might have been different if he were their university peer.

Much of their conversation, however, always ended up with something about his mentor. They seemed to have much respect for him as an excellent writer. More significantly, he had also captured their interests as a young, possibly wild, bachelor. Or was he? For there were stories abound.

"I hear he is married to an English woman."

"Not to my knowledge." BBGD indeed had no idea.

"That's what I heard. And that she had a baby for him."

BBGD wished he knew all these details. "Perhaps he's not married. Otherwise, why didn't he bring her back home?"

"Well, perhaps they were just friends," she wondered.

"Perhaps," BBGD concurred, then went on to supply a supposition. "Perhaps when she got pregnant, he escaped from her, because he didn't want to marry her." He had heard such stories from his parents.

"Yes. That's the trouble these men sometimes got themselves into." That conclusion had come across as somewhat regretful.

BBGD had wondered where on earth these rumors had emanated from. Much as he had kept his ears on the alert among his mentor's friends, he had heard nothing definitive about his marital or single status. All he knew was that he had come back home via Paris. Both women expected him to keep his eyes vigilant, nose to the ground and ears more alert.

He knew of a few men who had actually brought home white wives. Rumors had it they had to marry them so the wives could work and help them financially while they studied. In so doing, babies came into the picture along the way, and then they could do nothing but bring their white wives home. Perhaps the decision had something to do with responsibilities expected of a Nigerian father to his child. However, as it soon became obvious when they came home that their choices were far from satisfactory. He was to find out years later that some of these women, regarding beauty and intelligence, paled in comparison with many others he had mingled with in London, let alone among the crème de la crème. Perhaps his mentor fell into such a trap, although he could not imagine him choosing an "Ugly Teh-Teh,"*** as some of them were ridiculed in Lagos. Eventually, the humiliation that resulted made the men become victims of daughters-of-the-soil, who sought to relieve them of their white wives by any means necessary. Many, as expected, succumbed, an action that sent the white wives back home in shame and disgust.

"Serves her right," BBGD's father had concluded, regarding one white woman that came into the family of one of his friends. "Everybody was so relieved that Kintunde came to his senses and gave ear to Tola," he added with assertive triumph.

BBGD made himself available to both Stella and Lara, and whether Br'er Wole knew of their intentions before the tour was anybody's guess. What became clear was that they were willing to take their chances and stake their claims, whether the famous, up and coming playwright was married or not. But, another reason for his inclusion in the touring cast soon began to entertain the naïve but imaginatively ambitious traveler. Was he supposed to find out for his mentor, during the tour, what these two women were up to? Was he expected to divulge the information to the pleasure of his boss' ears on his return? If that was the case, how could the novice have been so naïve, especially as he had gradually become more experienced in his go-between duties?!

On such missive-exchange opportunities, he had sometimes found himself demanding from the women responses to the delivered notes from his mentor, even when there was no need for any. Such was the case with two very competitive women, who willingly and gladly responded to his requests, along with a packet of cookies or lozenges to boot, or even a coin. However, while he did not know exactly what happened as a consequence of the transmissions, the two women all of a sudden disappeared from the Rockefeller bungalow—unless, of course, each rendezvoused at the time he wasn't present at the house. That was quite possible although very doubtful. Admittedly, on many occasions he had found himself booted out, so to speak, for one reason or the other—all in the name of the solitude an artist deserved unto himself from time to time—he often knew who was still in and who was definitely out. Yes, he was quite convinced the women in question probably disappeared on account of their feline-vicious competitiveness, which negotiated their displacement by

---

*** From an African boxer nicknamed as such.

a new aspirant to the playwright's boudoir. Two plus two, surely, should equal four.

His reflection in fact replicated the very fates of Lara and Stella, his two actress-friends in the cast of *Suberu*. Sure enough, through some feminine art or device they did appear at the Rockefeller bungalow at some point after the tour—coming at separate times of course. Their appearance and stay, however, was all too short, and remembrance of their presence almost faded into oblivion, except for the fact of what developed during their short tenure. First, after the initial engagement, the competition shortlisted Lara, who seemed to have been delighted for being so favored. But then, all of a sudden appeared another interest—the cool, calm and more calculating Laide, who forced a reconsideration in her favor. Lara remained in view for a little time, vying for a recognition of her as more suited to the researcher's creative, literary, and scholarly proclivities. But, after some time, judging by the frequency of missives and who came more often to the bungalow, it soon became obvious which cookie got crumbled. In fact, the quiet beauty was so good that she became the one favored to marry the playwright (that is, his first formal marriage) and bearer of four of his children. That affair and much of its long life happened after BBGD had left the scene to go and study in England. It, however, proved to him beyond all reasonable doubt, that the young intellectual and playwright probably didn't marry the English woman. Or, if he did, she was evidently becoming displaced by one of the daughters-of-the-soil. Displaced like the rest of them, BBGD acknowledged with a whiff of delight.

"Serves her right?" he echoed the vindicating words of his father. But his thoughts were inconclusive about that justification; as such, his attitude was rather short-lived. However, that notion, along with the experiences he had with the daughters-of-the-soil combatants of the white lady, made him construct, through his curious lenses, another point of view of his mentor. An image of a dynamic, whose potency and Ogun-sanctioned [†††] sexual proclivity made him an irresistible stud among women.

It was a fitting attribute he wished he could emulate, albeit so far denied him because of various conflicts—chiefly, parental indoctrination, but also Christian pontifications against pregnancy, disease, and premature marital responsibilities. All these obstacles, he felt, he could have surmounted,

---

[†††] Ogun, god of iron and metallurgy, who has severally inspired Soyinka's creativity and scholarship as principle of creativity and patron of the arts.

perhaps, if Br'er Wole would only put him in the right direction. But, looking at it another way, it was possible that putting him among university students on a production tour was probably an indirect, intended thrust by the mentor to put his mentee in the right direction of experiencing the world. Case in point, the people that were supposed to be his guide introduced him to a brothel—he had read somewhere that such an introduction was lavishly practiced in some countries as a legitimate cultural norm. In his case, that idea had practically led to nowhere and his parental imperatives had obviously prevailed.

Thinking about his experience, he couldn't help teasing his sense of humor with a Yoruba proverb: "*Akara d'enu akayin; akara d'okuta.*" (When the delicious *akara*[‡‡‡] comes into the mouth of the toothless, the crisp-fried delicacy becomes a hard rock!) The situation, he felt, might have been different if the educative factor was more direct, taught or handed to him, as it were, by the genius trickster that he considered his mentor to be. But, as he gradually came to realize and conclude it, the creative artist's disposition seemed averse to taking on such responsibilities.

*****

It was his second visit to Enugu. His first was with the University Players in the production of *Suberu*. This time he was travelling directly with his mentor. The first visit probably initiated the second—at least, he would like to think that. He did not find any cultural event to record during the *Suberu* tour. This was partly because of his research limitations, but then there was hardly any time to spend on such endeavor. Hopping from one city to another with the theater group did not provide any opportunity for any investigation. At any rate, he was quite preoccupied with mingling with the university students, exploring new friends, and enjoying the theater experience with them. However, really more through rumors that brushed into his ears than direct inquiry, he brought back rumors of exciting possibilities for research. It was only to be expected that indigenous rituals, such as in festival celebrations, were just waiting in the villages to be explored. Thus, this second time round, they had all the apparatuses for research—tape recorder, camera, as well as notebook.

They had put up for the night at the residence of the late Christopher Okigbo, poet and librarian at the University of Nsukka. It was the first time Mr. Okigbo and his mentor met since their student days at the University

---

[‡‡‡] A delicious snack made from battered beans and fried, with condiments, in small balls.

College of Ibadan. As such, they had so much to recollect, about life, pranks and, of course, women. BBGD had an earful of episodes revealing the aptitude of both men as comrades in female-hunt.

"We'll go into the village tonight, not far from here. I've arranged for some dances for you to witness. Afterwards, we'll bring some back here. Okay?"

"Great," Br'er Wole acknowledged, abruptly, casting a cursory eye on his assistant.

BBGD saw the glint in the eye and mistook it for inclusion. They were enjoying a delicious dinner of pounded yam with stew combination of okra and bitter leaf, Igbo style, prepared by the poet's steward/cook. His novice eyes lit up at the prospects of being formally christened with sexuality in the hands of those who knew. The welcoming and seemingly supportive face of Okigbo, which affirmed his reading, transmitted that much. He should probably have exercised some caution, since he had gained no body language of encouragement from his mentor to verify his conclusion. Rather, he was convinced all would be well, with Okigbo's support.

He should also probably have guessed by the division of rooms. Okigbo would remain in his room, while the guest room went to his mentor. And BBGD? He was to take the sofa turned cot in the living room. Actually, this arrangement could also be interpreted in a different way, as three separate spaces of desired actions. Why his space should be open was, of course, anybody's guess; but that could be argued by virtue of his being the junior member of the pack. He decided not to deliberate too much on this situation, preferring instead to be optimistic. On an earlier occasion of the research tour, another friend had offered a guest room and both researcher and assistant had slept on a big bed; both had lain on it at opposite positions. It was an awkward situation for them both, but they had endured it.

After dinner and a little rest, the two comrades got up and acknowledged it was time. BBGD felt he read Okigbo's inclusive eyes correctly. He therefore jumped up from the sofa with great hope, and followed them outside to the host car.

"I think you should stay here," the researcher mumbled the discouraging words to the assistant, which at obstructive once halted and dashed all his hopes to the ground.

"Is he not coming with us?" Okigbo was rather carefree about the matter.

"No."

"Then perhaps we bring him somebody?"

"No!" the researcher was emphatic, then went on to mumble something else, perhaps to the effect of being accountable to his parents.

BBGD's silent anger was immediate, with puffed up face and tearful eyes, red like crests of hot coals. He turned away briskly to hide the embarrassment from his assailant, head bowed, and went back into the house to sulk.

Damn! Why couldn't he be given the opportunity? Why couldn't he also enjoy what they would enjoy, what should certainly make him a man?! If the host comrade didn't mind, why should his guest? They'd come back with two young women, all to themselves, and he would have nobody. Nobody! He imagined what it would be like to have sex with a young village woman with young firm breasts. It could be quite an experience of a lifetime! These women must be easy catch in this part of the country also. For a moment, he wondered whether his non-inclusion was a punishment for what happened on the way to Enugu that morning?

They were on the well-tarred new Onitsha-Enugu freeway. He and his boss, for most of the time, had been in their customary mode of silence, with nothing to say to each other. The researcher had suddenly had a brain wave. The road had been relatively quiet, enough to wish to engage in some experimental activity, if only to break the monotony of being on the wheel and provide the much-needed relief, if only temporary.

"Here, take the wheel. It's high time you learnt this." The researcher had pulled up and made BBGD take the driver's seat, then directed his ignition and pulling out on to the road. "Keep your eyes focused on the road. Keep still, don't turn the wheel, it's a straight road…" He tried to calm his assistant's nerves, helping him along with the pedal and the brake. As his first lesson, he felt all that the learner needed to do was just to be able to focus and control the wheel. After some minutes of instruction, which included one or two scary moments of manipulating nervous wheel turns that deflected the car to the right and then to the left (and this probably raised a few curses from drivers coming in the opposite direction) his instructor gave up. "To be continued," he indicated after he made the truck to pull up again on the dirt shoulder.

As far as BBGD was concerned, it was a welcome exciting moment, thinking his performance was all it took to drive a vehicle. However, his ego quickly sobered up as an earlier situation in front of the Broadcasting House in Lagos flashed across his mind—his rather embarrassing struggle, one rainy day, when he was being directed, by yelling voices across the rain, to put the same Land Rover in ignition, put it in gear, move up and get it to Br'er Wole and his friends under the canopy at the front entrance of the building. That incident, which almost resulted in a crash, gave him the jitters whenever he remembered it.

He brushed that aside. For the real incident that prodded his present thoughts happened some minutes after his short driving lesson. He had settled back to his seat, and the former silence between him and his mentor had been restored—which made the whole situation, upon reflection, rather stupid and baffling. For whatever got over him all of a sudden was mystifying. It was as if some intoxication incited by the excitement of the driving lesson had got his senses out of whack. No doubt, fate had to do with it. Was his fate under the direction of that fateful/fatal god, Esu Elegbara, whom the Christians would rather dub the Devil, albeit in error? On second thoughts, the incident was more like devil-driven than the trickster-capabilities of Esu. For if it were under that god's influence, to what avail, he had wondered? What lesson or awareness was he supposed to reflect upon? He had not been able to come to any satisfactory understanding on those terms.

The tape recorder (a Grundig for that matter, new in the market at the time) was for some reasons kept to his left, wedged against the door by his foot. It was his charge to guard and bring it along with him whenever they needed it for recording. He knew how to manipulate it; this he had practiced several times over to become second nature. But what happened? At that lightheaded moment, at a cruising speed of about 70 miles per hour, he felt the need to open and close the door on his side, as if to satisfy himself that it was properly secured. Hindsight could shed no sensitive light on justification for this action. But there it was, at that split tragic second of open and close, the deed was done—the machine had slipped through the crack.

He knew the stupid mistake was made and the immediate consequence. Both he and his boss heard the crash on the asphalt and the truck had swerved a little from the involuntary nervous application of brakes. He was speechless for the first few seconds, numb and dumbfounded with horror.

"What happened?" The researcher's reaction was urgent.

It took the assistant another few seconds before his mouth could break the silence: "The recorder."

"What happened to the recorder?" The researcher pulled the Rover over to a complete stop and simultaneously cast a swift glance behind him as truth stared him in the face: the Grundig was lying some distance away on the dirt side of road.

"Shit! Why did you open the door?"

"I-I d-didn't think the door was well locked."

"That was stupid. Why did you keep the recorder there in the first place?"

BBGD could not give a plausible answer. He could only keep his head bowed in shame.

It was obvious that his mentor was mad, even though he tried to conceal it, as he manipulated a reverse of the vehicle to the broken machine. It was an incident for which the rookie could never forgive himself, and which was to remain intact in his head.

Was that the cause of his non-inclusion to the sexual plan? Some minutes after they left in Okigbo's car, he decided to explore a possible rendezvous on his own, even though he recognized that idea was dumb and fruitless. He headed in the direction the car went, straight down the road, which he assumed would end up in the village. By some luck he was right.

There in the village square was dancing and excitement. He looked around to spot where his adversaries had placed themselves, sitting on a bench beside a local chief, who, obviously, organized the dance for Okigbo—at a cost probably, or some contribution to the chief's coffers. A crowd had formed to watch the spectacle, which was fortunate for BBGD—he used the spectators as much as possible as shield, relegating himself to the shadows like an agent in mufti. He enjoyed the dance for a while, women in skimpy red bands firmly rounding off their firm breast with a tie at the back; short red split skirts to match, revealing black drawers and young thighs; pounding feet to the jig of anklets; jerking waists in quick flirtatious succession to the sound of drums, cowbells and penny whistle…

Among the crowd were also young village women, perhaps friends and colleagues of the dancers. He looked around for possible contact. For a moment he was hopeful, but then resolved the night was a lost cause. Without a guide, like Okigbo, how could he even start to talk with anybody? Who did he know in these parts? How could he find out who was what? Even if, as he thought, the catch was probably easy, what did he know about the village, or the language, or the available right woman to select? For a second the incident at Asaba during his tour with *Suberu* flashed across his mind. Without a guide like the expert Okigbo to introduce him as a voyager from the big city, he knew all was naught.

The tease of the dance against the hopelessness of his situation was just too much to contain. He knew he must get back home before the lucky rakes came back. With reluctance, he shook off his misery and dragged his feet away from the spectacle to head back to the house. On occasion, he cast a gaze back, not at the scene, but to check whether Okigbo's Morris Minor was coming behind.

He had gone to bed on the sofa-makeup before they came back, but not quite asleep. He had struggled to keep himself awake until they arrived. When he heard the car pull up in the garage, he became alert but pretended he was fast asleep. They walked stealthily past him in whispers, one voice in Igbo language, which he could not understand but it seemed to be giving the women some instructions regarding the procedure. He managed to catch the figures of the invaders in silhouette before they disappeared into separate bedrooms. He felt he recognized the two dancers, even though they were no more in their dancing costume. Perhaps they had showered and powdered; perhaps they still retained the village odor, which might give the guys extra taunting and libido. Then silence. No more was heard from within the concrete walls and oak wood door. All was left to his young imagination, which went somewhat awry and wild, and which finally gave up to sleep.

He actually thought he would see the women at breakfast, which, on second thoughts, was a naïve expectation. What happened through the night escaped him, so was the disappearance of the women. He was almost certain they left before the first crow of the dawn. He had also hoped some comments about their performances would flail across his ears, either at breakfast or sometime before he and his boss set out back on the road. But then again, on second thoughts, that expectation was simply naive. The rakes joked about everything else but that—unless they spoke in peer-codes unfamiliar to him. And perhaps it was wise and considerate of them not to discuss the matter in his presence, sparing him certain torture. One thought wished they had spilled the beans, but another felt to do so would have been cruel and unforgiving. It couldn't be simply they were trying to preserve his innocence. What innocence?

Scenes Three

An Introvert at Large

Introvertedness was a condition that had beset BBGD from childhood, at least when he began to express himself lucidly enough to know what he had said as opposed to what he had not, or left unsaid. His parents had observed, from early childhood, that he liked to study or scrutinize an object for quite some time and then launched an attack, whether to tear the object apart or put it in his mouth or play with it—whatever his instincts directed. A case in point was the incident on the train, on the way to his granduncle in Oshogbo, some 150 miles away from Lagos. Apparently, he had studied the passenger opposite him as he hailed a *dodo* (fried plantain) seller, at one of the station-stops, to the train window, bought the fresh, leaf-wrapped, palm-oil-fried snack or lunch, and set it on the stationary train-table dividing the to and fro seats. He had watched the man unwrap and apply a warm delicious piece of the plantain cuts through his teeth into his mouth. Then, suddenly, BBGD leapt forward and attacked the wrapper, an action that his mother pulled him away from, just in time before obvious catastrophe. Of course, that inability to attack with success resulted in a burst of screams—which he knew how to do so well, a seeming contradiction to his introvertedness. But that seemed to be the only way available to him to get his way, which, sometimes, was not successful, in which case he would continue to cry until he became tired or cried himself to sleep. In the case of the *dodo* passenger, the man too willingly let his mother allow him to partake of the snack, an opportunity he capitalized on until the last cut. The embarrassment of his mother for the inability to keep her child under control of home etiquette was only too apparent, validated by her abundant apologies.

The attitude, as stated, was sometimes in his favor; at other times it led to detrimental consequences. Two situations had always perplexed him whenever he reflected on them. One was trying to comprehend a problem in Arithmetic, a bane of his childhood.

"What is 2 plus 2?" demanded his teacher-auntie living with his family. She was helping him attend to his homework.

BBGD stared into the ceiling, as if it was a magical space that transmitted invisible answers.

"You won't find the answer up there. What is 2 plus 2?"

"Errrrr."

"Look at me, look at me. 2 plus 2?" Her tone had become sterner, which, however, had begun to worry BBGD. For its seeming harshness only made matters worse, disrupting his contemplation and therefore blocking off any thought-avenue to possible answer. And yet, the matter had better be resolved before his performance came to the ears of his father.

"Come on, this is so simple, BB. What's wrong with your empty head?"

Since something may truly be wrong with his head, and empty at that, as it seemed obvious to Auntie Iyabo, he could do nothing but to resort to a quiet crying.

"BB... BB...stop crying." Determined to help her favorite nephew get through his difficulty, she persisted with a more softened tone, "Look at me, look at me. Two...plus two..." She applied her fingers to explain the numbers.

"F-F-Four," he answered with caution.

"Alleluyah!" Auntie Iyabo exclaimed with joy, which transformed BBGD's tight face into a certain relief and broke a smile.

That was a simple example. How he got through the more difficult problems of multiplication (actually, all pupils struggled through that, from kindergarten to middle high, learning the tables by rote from 1 times 2 to 12 times 12), not to talk about problems of algebra, history dates, trigonometry etc., or even of spelling! How he succeeded surmounting those challenges of his childhood and teenage-hood was something that had always dazzled his mind with sheer amazement. And perhaps his success was partly due to the inventiveness of his favorite aunties, who had often come to his aid by using all the visual power they could summon to induce the correct answer.

He was not so lucky with playing the piano, that art of signs and abstracts, under the direction of his not so sympathetic father, who did not seem to have time to appreciate the possible positive results of his introvertedness.

"Wrong!" Chappie's voice boomed from the dining room to the sitting room, where BBGD was attempting to interpret the notes and play them correctly on the keyboard. As usual the interruption disrupted his thoughts, so that the hieroglyphics became fuzzy or blurred before his eyes. This made his nerves tighten as he tried to repeat the musical phrase, which, again, ended with a discord.

"Wrong!" the stern voice interrupted again. Surely the delicious mouthwatering dish that sweetened his father's esophagus could induce more tenderness. Or perhaps that was the very cause of the reaction, that is, the intoxication that may have resulted from the succulent delicacy, the *mokoto*, the stewed cow leg whose furrowed juices were being sucked to the marrow. For, the third time that voice of doom came again, it was always followed by angry footsteps getting up from the dinner table and charging to the piano with a ruler or cane, to apply a few smarting smacks on the offending fingers on the piano.

That was the ultimate deterrent or detriment to the growth of BBGD in terms of learning how to play the piano, perchance to become a musician. He often got the right note after he had successfully in his head matched the abstract with the animal it represented—for C is for cat; D is for dog; E is for elephant, G is for giraffe, and so on and so forth. Unfortunately, the contemplation was often too long a process for the musical ears of his father, whose responsibilities and anxieties were for his second son to access and master the smooth rhythm of the notes as quickly as possible. That objective and demand, to be sure, had precedent—his older brother, by comparison, was a genius at reading those incorrigible signs and symbols.

How he got through these oppressive states of childhood would always be a puzzle to him. But one thing he was certain about was this, a comparison of his abilities with his brother's in terms of music was a bad idea. Reflecting on those years later, and in spite of his ruler-ached fingers, he would ultimately rather not put the blame on his father. For that was the way all colonial-trained parents had learnt from their Victorian indoctrinated colonial masters. What was obvious in the end was that the experience had pointed to an important consideration in BBGD's mode of creativity, a fact that had gradually dawned on him. For, the apparent product of 4 resulting from 2 plus 2, he thought, was the indisputable conclusion of any traditional, mathematical mindset. But, the possibility that 2 plus 2 could be 5, for instance, could only come from a creative intellect backed up by compelling considerations and creative possibilities that factored in. The 1 that made up the 5 may simply be a matter of possible invention of a virtuoso!

Another ironic contradiction to his silence-compelled contemplation, yet an attribute to his fertile creative instincts, was that sometimes, at moments he decided to open his mouth to speak, he was given to certain exaggeration. It was a condition that his brother, Akin, and Br'er Wole ultimately knew and indulged. More about these contradictions later.

*****

"Both of us drove in silence most of the time, but I guess we got by," Br'er Wole would respond, rather humorously, to his friends, especially after a long trip.

He was not always sure what exactly his mentor felt about his silence, whether it was annoying, or gratifying. From his point of view, far be it from him to interrupt the researcher's thoughts, as some other assistants might have done, certainly Rhodes, whose outright loquaciousness was always devoid of any serious inquiry and therefore amounting to nothing. On the other hand, the researcher, surely, might have wished for some light conversation every now and then to break the silence, more so during long and sometimes difficult driving. However, what he was sure about was that his mentor never simply talked without substance, even to pass the time. As such, he did not suffer those pure drivellers gladly, the "Totofiokos"[§§§,] as he often referred to them. Knowing full well that his handicap smacked of certain inadequacy, BBGD discovered that the chronic characteristic sometimes placed him at a disadvantage and other times at an advantage. Thoughts of either consequence raced through his mind.

Almost always at Ibadan, especially on campus, there descended at about 6pm this sudden cool evening breeze from nowhere, that is, after a rather scotching and humid afternoon. On this particular day, it descended as usual as night shadows were slowly creeping in between the woods on to landscapes, driveways and threshold of faculty bungalows; on to student dorms through the wide branches of the frangipane trees that stood in front of some of them. BBGD had just finished dinner (his favorite mashed black-eyed peas and fried plantains) at one of the male dorms and had wandered outside in his own time to wait for his mentor. By the time the Land Rover picked him up, it was getting too dark to distinguish clearly the features of an approaching figure in the curve of the parking lot, let alone that of the person occupying the front passenger seat of the truck. But somebody there was to be sure, as far as his penetrating eyes could bore through the closed windows. And that meant he would have to manage sitting at the back, on one of the narrow blanket-cushioned ledges that bridged and humped over each of the back wheels. Before getting inside, he went around to the closed window of the driver's side, simply to make his presence felt, and, of course, to confirm his conclusion— that the figure was a woman's. Who else would take his usual seat from him— unless, as it had happened on occasion, he yielded the seat in deference to his

---

[§§§,] Totofioko: a character in one of the junior-high readers, often given to unnecessary drivel.

mentor's peers, like Mr. Yemi Lijadu? Or, perhaps, again on occasion, it was one of the students contesting for the playboy's attention.

So, it was a woman; but who? He had not seen this one before. Certainly, it wasn't Laide, the student he had come to know as the researcher's real girlfriend, nor any of the others. But who? As far as he could decipher in that brief moment of time, she seemed to be wearing a print dress associated with Ghanaians. Apart from the dress, what confirmed this for him, more than anything else, was the headgear tied the way he had seen it on Ghanaian women, edges of the scarf tied around the head and flipped up at the back, like the tail feathers of a saucy sparrow.

He keened his ears, finetuned to his receptive resources. The tarpaulin cover that divided the front from the back of the army-type truck, with its centered fuzzy plastic viewing aperture, was usually an easy transmitter of messages from front to back. But all he could hear of the low-toned dialogue between the woman and the researcher came across as in whispers, muffled by the inevitable drone of the moving truck. The woman must have appeared in the bungalow after he left for dinner. The plan was for his boss to pick him up and drive him to his uncle's at Molete, about ten miles from campus, where he was to stay until his services were needed again, whenever that would be. Usually not more than two or three days—unless the researcher wanted to travel alone somewhere for a few days, like to his parents in Abeokuta. So, what could have happened between the time he left for dinner and the present, he wondered?

The mischievous silent one kept his ears glued to the tarpaulin, but no luck. All he could go by, which helped to connect the dots was that minute or two hiatus of dialogue that slipped through the humming of the idling engine before the truck pulled away from the hostel. His eardrums strained to fade up the volume of the sound bites so he could analyze more efficiently:

"Well, what do you want to do about it?" the male voice blunted.

"I want to keep it," the female voice insisted.

"If that's what you want. But I think you should consider that option well…" At which time the engine revved, perhaps in anger, and the rest of the dialogue got lost as the truck pulled away.

But two plus two should equal four…

Is the woman pregnant and wants to keep it? Is she going to have to marry her? What about Laide, his favorite girlfriend? But he already has a wife in England, according to the intercepted transmissions between the playwright and his friends. How about that? So, this Ghanaian woman, where did they meet anyway? Couldn't have been in Ibadan, or he, the assistant, would have seen her. Are they driving back to Lagos when they drop him off? He was as anxious as a gossip.

As it happened, that was the one and only time he saw the woman, and since nothing else came to his ears about it, he gathered the matter was resolved. In fact, he forgot about the whole thing after a long while.

Several years had passed. He had been abroad to England, then to the US and after had come back to Nigeria. They had been years crowded with events and experiences, educative, political and professional, years that had made everybody, including him, grow up. It was after all those years that encounters connected him back to that evening's tête-à-tête. By then, all secrets and suspense of past situational circumstances had dissolved into the fluidity of general facts. Kongi, as expected, had married the quiet but persistent Laide, and four children had come out of that wedlock; but then through circumstances, husband and wife had sought and gained divorce. Yet, all the products of that past, including the ones outside marriage, had grown and remained alive and well, all in the absence of BBGD.

A young woman, then a student at one of the universities, was introduced to him as Kongi's second child but not by marriage, a qualification he understood because he had come to know the four children of the legal marriage. So, if the young beautiful woman standing before him was the second child, then the first must be no other than the London child he was told about but hadn't met.

By some devious waves of transmission, flashes of the past suddenly rekindled and became connected with the present. Confirming the young woman's appearance and demeanor as Ghanaian, he could now, if only by speculation, construct the image of her mother, the mystery woman in the Land Rover several years before. In fact, now that he got it, all other dots came in view and also got connected. The young woman was the so-called Independence child, so known among the playwright's inner-circle of friends—referencing her conception on Nigeria's Independence Day.

He had been tempted to ask WS, now his colleague at the University of Ife, regarding that past and what he BBGD knew, just for the fun of it. But, deciding against it, he had concluded there was no need to do so. At any rate, he did not think the rake would have remembered his connection with the incident. His silence, he thought, could be one advantage up his sleeves, about something no one else knew or witnessed, except him, something only waiting to be voiced or footnoted with amusement when an opportune moment called for it.

*****

66

"All you do is stare. You don't say anything. And you don't smile either," Yemi Lijadu, Br'er Wole's best friend at the time, expressed rather as a joke with a puffed smile on his face. They were in the office of the drama producer. "How do you two get along anyway?" he added.

"Oh, you mean with the silent one. We manage." Br'er Wole, casting a look at BBGD, smiled affirmation.

"But have you noticed how he always gets attention?" Lijadu went to his main point.

"What do you mean?"

"Just look?" He tendered the page in the *Daily Times* to the playwright. "Of all the pictures that were taken of the show, his had to be the one chosen for publication, along with yours."

BBGD simply smiled, taking it as a compliment rather than an expression of implied envy. What else could he say? At any rate, he could not quite understand it as envy. Reason being both Lijadu and his friend were well on their professional paths of success—Lijadu, as Head of Drama; WS, as a veritable dramatist, at least as far as BBGD was concerned. Fact was, he probably wouldn't have come in contact with Lijadu, or radio drama for that matter, but for his mentor. He wouldn't have got involved with the famous radio serial, *Safe Journey*, in which he had sometimes been allowed to play very small parts, a privilege by virtue of his mentor. In comparison to either of them, he was nobody. So, why the seemingly envious remark, one might ask?

The picture in the *Daily Times* that the radio producer was referring to was from the production of *A Dance of the Forest*, BBGD's first real efforts at acting on the stage. There he was in his rather tattered costume-gown as the Dirge-Man with a whip in hand, looking at Agboreko, the soothsayer, and querulous Old Man, who seemed to be demanding some oracular answers from the priest. The other picture in the paper showed his mentor as Forest Father, with one of the forest creatures, also looking for answers. BBGD knew both scenes very well, although he did not at the time see the importance of both pictures as a statement of a relationship in progress, that is, of the mentor and his mentee. And how he came to claim his part as Dirge-Man only affirmed the statement.

Before any auditions or rehearsals of the commissioned play, Wole Soyinka had formed the 1960 Masks, at first consisting of some of the playwright's friends, such as Yemi Lijadu, Olga Adeniyi Jones, Funmi Asekun, and Ralph Okara; later others were drawn from the University of Ibadan Players. On Sundays, the Lagos group, including BBGD, met and were drilled with improvisations conducted by the playwright. As a first experience, the improvisations in the beginning proved an obvious handicap to the assistant, at least the ones that involved dialogue. Since he was a man of a few words, he was very self-conscious when he compared himself to the others, who seemed far more adequate at expressing themselves in improvised words. On hindsight, he really should not have been, since none of them had the experience the playwright must have had. What, in some cases, appeared to be confidence could be argued in terms of seniority. Participants, such as Lijadu, were the playwright's peers, who preferred to be known as seniors and therefore tended to look down on anybody below their age group. BBGD, the youngest of the group, felt he was treated as if he were the only rookie to theater and the stage, when in fact most of them were also that, so to speak, in terms of not having had a formal professional training. As for Lijadu, it seemed he always browbeat his possible inadequacies in improvisations with a kind of self-inflicted stammering, in emulation, no doubt, of the colonial stiff-upper lip.

BBGD did not quite understand the importance of the improvisations anyway, although as he felt more comfortable acting in front of his seniors, he gradually got better at it. But he still would prefer to say as little as possible. Years later, as he knew more about the nature of the exercises, what seemed original exercises to the rookie turned out to be nothing of the sort; the playwright probably imparted what he himself learnt through workshops, at places he had been, such as the Royal Court Theater in London. BBGD would also end up there at some point.

In the exercises that demanded no speech, he felt more at home and therefore faired very well. It might even have struck the workshop director that he had an aptitude for mime, a characteristic that became confirmed for him when he was in England, studying acting at the Rose Bruford College of Speech and Drama. In short, the preliminary exercises had obviously helped his mentor see his acting capabilities, which encouraged the playwright to draft him into the 1960 Masks. Not that either had any other choice really. The playwright was looking for young actors to feed his company, supposed to be the nucleus of the Nigerian National Theater company, as he put it in an interview on the radio. The rookie on the other hand, because he showed interests in theater (through being the researcher's assistant), was an automatic draw. The exercises and formal introduction to the stage only went on to hone his acting abilities.

"Find that wallet, BB," observing the rookie, the playwright imposed on his imagination.

"W-Where?" BBGD naively queried.

"I don't know. It's up to you to look for it and find it."

That was all that he needed. It became obvious to him that the wallet was imaginary and it was up to him to find it wherever. He instantly recalled the living room at his uncle's house; thus, he searched under the rug, in between the leather sofa cushions, and in the cabinet with glass shutters that revealed the decanter and various drinking glasses; below it, where another set of shutters hid the liquor. No luck. He looked around and "Ah," he remembered, he had placed it on the TV stand! Goodness gracious, how could he be so forgetful?!

"Good, good," his mentor had acknowledged his seemingly realistic efforts.

*****

Move on eyah! Move apart
I felt the wind breathe—no more
Keep away now. Leave the dead
Some room to dance…

He had listened to the playwright render the whole of the Dirge-Man's recitative during the first rehearsal read-thru. The words and rendition were music to his ears. They had gathered round, sitting in a circle in one of the recording studios of the Nigerian Broadcasting Service in Lagos—the prospective actors for the first formal full-length play by Wole Soyinka. The play was commissioned by the New Republic journal to celebrate Nigeria's Independence from British colonial rule. The research assistant had heard from his boss, in a radio interview, that the company, to be called the 1960 Masks, was to be the nucleus of the Nigerian National Theater. Up until then they had not done any major research tour, which he was looking forward to. He somewhat felt the impending production and its national objectives could be some calling to a career. Even though he had shied away from acting in high school, he felt a calling at this time might be more appropriate. With no inclinations whatsoever toward music, who could better steer this ambition in the right direction other than this stalwart, just recently come back from the land of the theater.

The round gathering at the radio studio and the way the audition was performed suited the liking and introverted temperament of BBGD, although, to be expected, he was very nervous. The first read-thru was random, each dialogue taken in succession by each person in the round—a method he would come to associate with WS's auditioning. Slightly petrified by this, he always hoped, when it came to his turn, that enormous lines of dialogue didn't fall on him. His hopes for the most part were fulfilled. On one occasion when the speech was long, it was shared by two or three other persons, as directed by WS.

The second read-thru was after lunch. The playwright-director assigned tentative parts to various people before they broke for lunch. He decided to let BBGD read the part of the corrupt Slave Dealer. The novice was pleased with this, not so much because he understood the part as the fact that he was entrusted with a small but substantial part. He was also delighted he would have time during the lunch break to look through the part.

But there was another part that seemed to have fascinated his sensibilities, probably more so than the Slave Dealer. It was that of the Dirge-Man, who appeared in just one scene but rolled through three verses of rather fascinating poetic speech. When they were reading through in the morning, he noticed WS took over to read the verses himself. The way he read them held BBGD spellbound but also stayed very much in his memory. However, when parts were being assigned for the afternoon reading, he noticed the acolyte part was not given to anyone. This got him very curious, and before they started the reading again, he called his mentor up on it.

He sidled nervously to the playwright. "We're going through the whole play again. Right?" he asked.

"Yah. And I want you to read for the Slave Dealer."

"Okay, thanks." He was delighted the suggestion was reiterated to him, but as that wasn't the objective of his inquiry, he lingered to express himself more to the point.

"The Dirge-Man. W-who's reading him?"

"Haven't decided yet who could read it." The rather nonchalant way the playwright mumbled his response almost got BBGD off the track, but he persisted.

"C-can I try it?" His voice, anticipating further negative response, was vulnerable.

"You?" the playwright doubted, looking squarely at his assistant.

"Y-Yes. Let me try it," he insisted as some confidence welled up in him.

WS considered for a few seconds, within which the rookie saw a flash of Lijadu, from the corner of his eye, walking towards them.

"Okay, why not?" the playwright shrugged, and instantly diverted to meet his friend.

Second read-thru began. Nobody knew what had transpired between the silent one and his mentor. As such, everyone's ears were tuned to hearing the playwright once again read the Dirge-Man's recitative. Therefore, the ensuing surprise was genuine and arresting, as they diverted sharp glances towards the unexpected voice of the silent one:

Move on, eyahhh! Move apart…

The beginning was difficult, as he felt almost overwhelmed by the eyes cast on him. But somehow the radiation emitting from those eyes were not at all hostile; rather, they loved him with a certain sensation of warm admiration, which instantly propelled him to gain some confidence. Thus, a kind of intoxication welled up within him, imitating his mentor's rumbling voice and lyrical delivery to the hilt.

> *Daughter, your feet were shod*
> *In the eeled shuttles of Yemoja's loom*
> *But twice your smock went up*
> *And I swear your feet were pounding*
> *Dust at the time…*

He felt somewhat elated, borne aloft by some wind he could not explain. But everything felt good. It was a euphoria he would gradually learn and understand as a danger zone of acting and therefore learn how to control it.

> *…What human husband folds*
> *His arms, and blesses randy ghosts?*
> *Keep away now, leave, leave the dead*
> *Some room to dance.*

At the end of the rendition, he knew he had done justice to the words of the playwright. He stole a ginger look at him from the corner of his eye and caught his faint smile of approval. The gesture was reassuring, but he was not certain he got the part until the end of the reading:

"Well, BB, you might as well take up the part," he mumbled.

"Yes, that was good, lad." Lijadu's echoed praise came as a surprise to him. It was a rare occasion that was most welcome; for nothing specific or definitive ever came out of the producer's often bland non-committal face—as far as BBGD was concerned. He had never felt comfortable or secure in front of the man as opposed to what he always felt with his mentor. The privilege that the Head of Drama sometimes accorded him happened only because his friend, WS, was present. And that also was the case with the small roles he was given in the radio plays. Reflecting on this later, Yemi Lijadu, he thought, was probably one of those people that associated acting with extroverts, so that introverts, like BBGD, in their eyes had no place in that histrionic profession.

His bland and emotionless demeanor spoke volumes, rendering abortive any confidence BBGD might possess. If he could, he would rather avoid him as much as possible. But he couldn't, so he had to learn how to calm his nerves and overcome his challenges.

*****

At first, he blamed his apparent vocal inefficiencies, which had always made him feel rather inadequate, on his academic insecurities and ungrounded intellectual capacities, especially placed against the university students in the company. But then, he gradually convinced himself that having nothing much to say did not mean he had nothing in his head. However, he felt the characteristic tendency was a deficiency that needed attention, since it might be a result of not reading as widely as he should.

He knew he was a lazy reader, in contrast to some in his age group he could call avid readers, their heads always bent to some novel or fiction wherever they were sitting. This was especially so with the pretentious ones that believed they were in superior high schools, taught by colonial teachers. Not to talk about those that got sent to England by well-to-do parents; they came home on vacation to show off their reading habits and superiority, and would not associate with anybody that didn't have similar upbringing.

On the one hand, he sometimes repudiated himself for this seeming languid state, since it might very well be his downfall; on the other hand, he knew he was sometimes given to self-denigration. For he had in fact made some strides to correct some of the problem, especially when he became acquainted with the late Aig Imoukhuede, a *Daily Times* features editor. It was he who introduced him to the short stories and novels of authors such as H.E. Bates and Richard Gordon. That was the time he wrote short stories read on the air of *Radio Nigeria*. He gathered that if he was to become a writer, he needed to read and have some favorite authors. He had also looked forward every Sunday to reading short stories published in the *Nigerian Sunday Times*, usually featured in the magazine section, stories by writers such as his editor friend, whom he always tried to emulate. A few of those stories also came from England, written by Nigerians studying abroad. He specifically remembered one written by Wole Soyinka, entitled *A Maverick in the Land of the Dykes*, which he had enjoyed, although couldn't boast he understood it fully. And, come to think on it, earlier than all these, he had been a kind of Enid Blyton reader, though not as avid as he should have been. And then he had read some of the favorite books at the time, such as *David Copperfield*, *Oliver Twist*, *The Adventures of William Tell*, and *Tom Brown School Days*, which his uncle,

ACOD, had brought back for him from England. However, he couldn't swear he had finished reading any of them. They really didn't relate to him as he had absolutely nothing in common with the characters. By contrast, the stories written by Nigerians drew his attention and curiosity. It was them he tried to emulate, and the short stories he wrote gave him some exposure at school.

"Go get yourself a typewriter," Aig had told his young introverted friend a number of times, sometimes to break the long silence between them while the editor continued to try and focus on his editing. BBGD knew no better than to sit there in admiration of the guy whose story writing had influenced his.

One expresses oneself in writing in silence, doesn't one, he often felt gratified by the credo, which, however, seemed to fit a writer better than an actor. When WS came into the picture, BBGD saw him at first as a writer and intellectual he admired, and wanted to study drama like he did. His researching project appealed to him because of the adventure across Nigeria that it promised. Acting was something he got drafted into along the way. At first, he wasn't comfortable with it. But once he realized that actors were not necessarily extroverts and that he, an introvert, could thrive as an actor, he became more susceptible to seeing it as a profession he could entertain. Thus, when opportunity presented itself in England, he did not hesitate to welcome and snatch it.

*****

"And here's the writer of this funny play sitting at the corner silent, with a serious face," He was challenged by one of the actors at a break in the rehearsal of one of his plays. They were in the recording studio of the BBC African Service at the Bush House in London. "How do you do it, man?" the actor continued.

"What?" BBGD replied.

"Your play is hilarious, man. Aren't you enjoying it?"

"But I am," he responded, creasing out a soft smile on his cheek, slightly embarrassed about being put on the spot. He wished the actor would just leave him alone to listen and enjoy, in unobtrusive silence, the reading of his play. He was enjoying the play's rendering in fact, leaving the knots and bolts of the delivery to Shirley Cordeaux, the producer of the play, whom he had come to trust.

It was probably the fact of being an actor in a conservatory that had led to his understanding of drama writing, but certainly his initial experience with Soyinka and radio acting in Lijadu's radio productions also had a major role in his interest in writing plays for the radio.

It was Pat Maddy, one of his two African peers at the Rose Bruford College who first drew his attention to the call for African actors and writers at the African section of the BBC World Service. It was their first year, but the idea immediately tickled his interest as something he could do. He recalled the short stories he had written for radio in Nigeria. One in particular struck him as a possible idea for drama—*The Yam Debt*. With his experiences in Nigeria, he had an idea what a radio play should look like. And so he had gone into action and knocked out a play within a week and sent it to Shirley Cordeaux, the senior producer of what came to be known as African Theater. The producer had like it and invited him for some revisions, which he did and the play was then scheduled to air for African listeners, or anybody who was on short wave radio band.

Try as he could to write something serious, his plays had always ended up funny. He did not know why but it could be a result of a combination of things. He had performed in the comedy series, *Safe Journey*, back in Nigeria. He had also enjoyed the play of the University Players he went on tour with, although had a small part, an adaptation of Moliere's comedy, *That Scoundrel Scapin*. Also in his first year at Rose Bruford, he had been introduced to the Commedia dell'Arte's characters, many of whom, like Moliere's and some Shakespeare's, he found he could identify with the characters he had seen and experienced back in Nigeria. These were the same or similar characters he enjoyed writing about, which made his radio plays sound hilariously funny. He wrote about them, but sometimes during the process of their creation, he did not even find them that funny. For, as far as he was concerned, he was in a way writing critically about their circumstance, why they happened to be in such circumstance, and how some of them found themselves at a vantage point to turn the tide against their offending "masters."

"But how is it that your villains always tend to win?" asked Shirley Cordeaux, once.

"Well because I see life sometimes that way, I guess." BBGD's response was spontaneous, but he had not quite clearly figure it out in his head.

"Yes. They are very likeable, somewhat."

Shirley's response had delighted him, but again he couldn't quite figure out why it did at the time. He had gone on to be an adept at writing these plays. He had also acted in some of his and some of the other plays, an endeavor and opportunity that had made his other experiences of his training at the Rose Bruford College more endurable.

Acting and writing, it became evident to him, seem to be at opposite poles—one challenging him to be an extrovert and the other celebrating him as an introvert. But, from what he knew and understood, first through his mentor, he was able to relate one with the other and use one in defense of the other. Thus, the credo of his introvertedness had evolved, stabilized and persisted through his acting training. It became the stalwart that he held up to protect himself against those who tried to break his confidence and render him inadequate. Not that he wanted to isolate himself, which would go against all the rules of acting; he just wanted to be himself, one who preferred to be silent and contemplative whenever he felt like it.

"Hey, lonesome, don't be antisocial." One of his peers at the college approached him at some party. He was standing in a corner, a plastic cup of apple cider or some cheap wine in his hand, watching the capering and contorting transformations called dance being performed by his college mates.

"I'm not being antisocial," he responded with deliberate calm, a rather languid half-smile creasing his cheeks.

"Then mingle, mi-lad, dance, enjoy!" his white peer challenged further.

He held his ground and took a sip of his drink, convinced he was enjoying himself immensely where he stood. A person does not have to be demonstrative (as violently as he observed it to boot) before he could enjoy himself. He just wanted to be himself—to dance when he felt like it, to stand and watch the hilarious spectacle, when he felt like it.

At the Rose Bruford Training College, in Sidcup Kent, in order to maintain his artistic equilibrium, he had held the credo against all those who were speech driven, compelled by the notion that actors needed to be extroverts. To be sure, he had limitations. By far the most challenging was the institution's pursuit of the Queen's English as a fundamental and viable medium for the actor's vocal instrument. Granted, he had persevered, albeit against odds, to combat his deficiencies. But then, as he had found out, even that all important agency of speech was only a means to some end, not the defining qualitative end in itself to assess the merits of an actor. Other instruments such as the body and presence prevailed.

Rather than be depressed by the circumstances that swirled around him, he had been able to use the efficient factor, silence, to resist, fend off or overcome the racist fond overtures and pretentions of the faculty and students alike:

"Come on now, my darkies!"

"You wooly head, you!"

"You nig-nog, you!"

"Come on, smile, let me see your lovely white African teeth."

"Your father must be one of the elites. Tell us about your home."

"Tell us about the snakes, the gorillas and chimpanzees!" Actually, BBGD had a short incisive response for that one: "You mean, in the zoo?"

When all seemed to have failed—for everything gravitated towards speech at the Rose Bruford Training College of Speech and Drama—when they tried to present him at the end of his training with a made-up "foreigner" certificate in lieu of the authentic diploma, he had used his only weapon of silence to boycott all graduation ceremonies and refused the insult, until they had reconsidered. His victory, of course, meant compromising with the summer months of extra course work to prove himself. But, after that strategic tolerance, they reconsidered.

Scenes Four

Coming of Age: Conflicts and Challenges

The rumor was confirmed by reliable sources that Joan Littlewood was going to produce and direct *The Road* at her theater in Strafford East. It was welcomed news that tickled BBGD's ears, for he was almost certain it was a production he had to be in. He knew WS had some relationship with Ms. Littlewood through his London days at the Royal Court, which extended to when he was back home in Nigeria. A response to his hurried letter to his mentor confirmed it, also the fact that a few of the old gang from his company, now Orisun Theater, would be coming along to participate. BBGD's interest and availability for the production were very clear, especially since he would have graduated from the Rose Bruford College well before rehearsals that summer. As such, as far as he was concerned WS would do everything to make it possible for him to take part in the production.

Thus, he waited for a call from either WS or Joan herself for him to come to London, from Sidcup in Kent, to audition. That didn't happen. At any rate, unfortunate incidents at Rose Bruford disrupted any possibility to follow up on the matter with his mentor. Or with Joan Littlewood herself, like his South African friend, Alton Kumalo, was able to do through an agent. He had no agent at the time for various reasons.

*****

BBGD had guessed what the meeting with Rose Bruford would be, although did not quite believe the decision would spell out for him the way it did, what with his acting and mime record and his somewhat intellectual bent. All the same, he had prepared himself for the meeting. Rumors had circulated since their first year, among himself and the other two Africans admitted the same year to the conservatory-like college. It was the first time ever there would be such a number of Africans at one time. The college, which specialized in acting and the teaching of speech and drama, had been interested in accepting foreign students, probably to widen their horizons. That was why

BBGD had been interested in coming there in the first place. In fact, before the three (a Nigerian, a South African, and a Sierra Leonean) there had been at least three other Africans, all Nigerians but admitted at different years. One had not finished and had to transfer to another institution; another had finished but was not awarded the bona fide RBTC diploma. Rather he was given the notorious special certificate, designed for certain foreign students, no doubt black.

The third Nigerian, who had graduated at the end of BBGD's first year, and had boasted of being the only black or African ever awarded the legitimate diploma, was Ebun Odutola (later Clark). BBGD in fact had dated her for most of that first year till her graduation. It was through her that the stories of the two former students became known to the newest three Africans—Alton Kumalo, Pat Maddy, and BBGD. She also made them be aware of the possibility of being landed with the infamous certificate. That she was able to escape was quite clear; she was born in England and was able to access the desired Queen's English more readily. She was also liked for her proficiency in Mime by all the small faculty.

Regarding that certificate, the rationale for the three had always been, if the prize-rose could be awarded to one, so was the possibility that it could be awarded to another. Question was, who could it be denied to? So they persisted to working hard to receive it. Unfortunately, Pat Maddy left after the first year—the critical year that decided whether or not a student should continue in the rigorous program. Pat's case, as well as Alton Kumalo's, were tied to the scholarship received from the British Government, which demanded reports of justification for renewal. Pat's development fell short; Alton's merited continuation. BBGD was on a Nigerian scholarship, a compelling foreign money for the college, although his development also merited continuity.

Thus, only the two Africans made it with diligence to the end of the program. And yet, the Rose was good enough for one and not for the other?

"We consider you to be a very good student. Your mime was excellent, and teachers spoke highly of your potential in acting." Rose Bruford's usual, cold emotionless face held BBGD's combative eyes with a certain arrogance that smacked of hypocrisy. Beside her was her aide-de-camp, Greta Stevens, who nodded acquiescence like a stooge to Rose's affirmation. "But your speech let you down, not through a fault of yours of course. Imagine me coming to your country and hoping to speak in your accent, in three years."

"And that's why we have designed a comparable certificate for somebody like you," Greta launched without prevarication. "We felt you should not leave here without anything. So…" she completed her statement by tendering the certificate to him.

"I don't want that." BBGD was as affirmative as his assailants, eyeing viciously the proffered cardboard encased in a folder.

"Look, it's quite recognized. We have awarded it before, in fact to your predecessor, Joel Adedeji. He went back home with it and is doing very well."

"I will not accept it."

"Why?" Greta was curious.

"Because I deserve better."

"Look at your teaching, for example," Rose butted, opening a file on her desk. "You barely passed it. Your supervisor commented you were having communication problems with your students."

BBGD reflected on the supervisor she was referring to. How hypocritical of him, he thought. Yes, he could confess he didn't like the teaching part of the program, but so could some of the other students in his class. In his case, because he was a foreigner, the young pupils to whom he was assigned capitalized on the fact; they indulged in playing various tricks on him as a student and foreigner. He became their bait and couldn't always control their English pranks. Even though the college supplied them with various teaching materials for the particular age-group, it was very hard for him to identify with these materials, which were also foreign to him. As such, engagement of the students' volatile concentration was problematic. Added to that, being at the school only once a week for only one term was hardly ideal for getting to know the students well and following up and improving on previous instruction and experience. But then, the supervisor, when he came to supervise, didn't seem to be very critical of his performance; he seemed to understand and was sympathetic towards BBGD. In fact, he often commented on some strengths he had, a result of his excellence in Mime.

"T-that may very well be. But I will not accept the certificate." BBGD's firmness was final, evoking a pregnant silence for a few seconds and leaving Rose and Greta in a state of awkward helplessness.

Regaining her composure, Greta simply said: "Well, just think about it. Before you make any drastic decision, we want you to think about it."

BBGD rose abruptly and exited the principal's office, knowing full well there was nothing to think about. Yet, he couldn't but reflect on the insult, and the implications of being awarded a certificate as opposed to diploma, which could very well be their final decision even if he maintained his rejection to the end. The gnawing and very degrading fact for him was, how to go back home, which was his intention after graduation, with simply a fake Rose, if indeed it could be called that. His first thought was in relation to his mentor, for this was hardly a way to emulate him. And of course, he would have failed the Nigerian government that awarded him the scholarship in the first place.

His decision to go to the Rose Bruford Training College was in reality by accident. It was certainly not his objective in coming to Britain. Rather, seeing himself in the guise of his mentor, he was going to pursue an academic degree, in his case directly in Theater as opposed to English. He had talked with his mentor about this and the playwright had suggested one of the best institutions for Theater Studies at the time, Bristol University. In fact, WS seemed to have connections there. He felt, with a combination of theory and practice peculiar to that university, he could earn a good degree as well as satisfy his acting potential. To qualify and gain entry, he was first to secure a post-secondary prerequisite, such as the GCE. As such, he was to spend the first two years in London doing just that at the Northwestern Polytechnic where he had enrolled.

Then, in his first year at the Poly, came the opportunity of being awarded a scholarship for drama. He had to consider this in the light of relieving his parents of further enormous expenses accrued from his studies. Also, he did not know whether the scholarship would be available after that year, or when he would be ready for Bristol. He had heard of Rose Bruford before he left Nigeria, and had got the college's brochure through the British Council. With the almost certain opportunity looming before him, he re-engaged his thoughts about Rose Bruford. He applied and easily gained admission.

Therefore, after all his sacrifices, to be denied of the coveted Rose was just unimaginable. For, what vocation could this gain for him at home, he wondered. How could he, with a mere, superficial and unrecognized certificate, face his mentor, then Head of Drama at the University of Ibadan? Not to talk about his parents and brother, through whose influence he was awarded the scholarship, and who toiled and put their resources together to be able to get him to study in England in the first place. He would be a laughing stock and a nobody, that is, compared with some of those actors in *That Scoundrel Suberu*, who not only had a prestigious BA but also could act.

He had justifiably refused the pseudo paper, but he needed to send other messages to Rose and her faculty regarding his objection. His first strategic action was to boycott all the events leading to graduation, including the farewell skits he was to perform with his peers in front of the whole college. Then, since they actually had the audacity to drop the offending certificate in his mail box, he refused to pick it up and made this known to them. It was thereafter that Principal Rose called him again to her office. By then the faculty had met to discuss his situation, at which time he suspected one of the instructors, his favorite speech teacher, James Dodding, had come to his aid.

"Well, we've resolved to let you spend the summer doing active speech work with Mr. Dodding. You will also do a few weeks teaching under the supervision of Mr. Goss when school reopens in August. Based on your performance, we may be able to give you the RBTC Diploma. Is this agreeable to you?"

"Yes. Thank you," he blunted.

"In the meantime, we advise you to take the certificate," Greta added.

"No."

"Don't be silly, take it. It's of no use to us. At best you'll have two certificates."

BBGD considered the honesty of the statement, casting his eyes from Greta to Rose and back again, trying to detect any cloud of deceit hanging beneath their veil of British composure. Seeing none, he rose, thanked them again and walked out, determined to hold them to their word.

Alton had already secured him an acting agent, who quickly got him to audition for the production *The Road* at Stratford East. BBGD probably could have got him an agent also, but he made what, in hindsight, was an unwise decision, with regard to the showcase scene he could have done with Alton and to which agents were invited. In fact, not participating in the event seemed to have ludicrously sealed his fate. When asked by the acting instructor, Leo Baker, to do a scene with his friend for the agents' showcase, he had refused. For one thing, the scene was from a South African play, which obviously would have favored Alton. In addition, he felt he had no need for an agent since he was supposed to be going home anyway after graduation. That decision was an obvious mistake, whose devastating implications he never foresaw. First, because of the ongoing Biafran War, he was advised by his parents not to come home as yet, which meant, staying in London, he would really need an agent. But more devastating was the fact that the acting instructor viciously downgraded his grade in acting from High Credit to a Pass. That might also have led to and supported the administrative decision to award him the fatal certificate.

BBGD considered a direct slap in the face Alton's pride in securing himself, a South African, a role in the production of *The Road*, by a Nigerian playwright. Perhaps a well-deserved one, thinking of the ironic implications of his refusal to do a South African play. Churning that fact in his mind some more, he felt his refusal to do the play really had nothing to do with the possibility of his going home. In reality, it was more because he was a little daunted by the play and the accent the role demanded, although he would probably have surmounted the accent with Alton's help, or played the part with a neutral accent in which he felt comfortable. But the fact that Alton would have an edge over him in front of agents lent itself to a serious consideration. However, there it was, the truth of ironic full circle of a bad decision staring him in the face: Alton got a part in a Nigerian play, a play by BBGD's mentor, to boot. That hurt.

Nevertheless, at the time, he felt at first that all was not lost and he could still be in the production. However, the call he expected from WS never came, and he had no agent to serve him. But then, came the graduation problems at Rose Bruford College, and his confused state of mind drowned all aspirations to strive to make any last-minute effort to participate.

"Sorry about that." WS was somewhat nonchalant with his apology when BBGD confronted him, sometime after the opening of the show. He had caught up with him by phone and had met him at the Transcription Centre, the Mayfair office that was to become the depot of African writers and visual artists. From there, they had gone to an Indian restaurant in Soho. "But why didn't you audition?" he continued, after mumbling some excuses. "You could easily have been in the show. You should have presented yourself and told Joan you had worked with me."

BBGD knew it was partly his fault, and the disadvantage of being silent and hoping things would work the way they would. Well, they worked the way they would and he missed what could have been his first professional production. However, as to the real cause, the Rose Bruford affair, he decided not to mention it. Silence probably paid off in that respect. At any rate, and thankfully, that matter had been resolved before their meeting. He had maintained his refusal to accept the notorious certificate, boycotted every event of graduation. All at the cost of not being part of the farewell show with his peers, performing humorous, satiric gigs and skits before students and faculty. And what farewell was that, he affirmed to himself, when he was to spend the whole summer virtually still in school! His silence of resistance had paid off; they had finally awarded the accredited diploma.

They ate in silence for a little while. BBGD was just getting used to drinking wine, carefully following the expertise of his mentor.

"Anyway," WS broke the silence, "I hope you're now feeling better about that other matter."

What other matter? Did he know about his Rose Bruford problem? Who could have told him? BBGD was beside himself as various thoughts fleeted through his mind.

"What do you mean?" He decided to pursue rather than assume.

"You know…the situation with Ebun."

The mention of that name immediately reinstated a certain heartburn he had tried to control, which now welled up his throat in acid reflux. He swallowed in desperation to prevent being gagged.

She came into his life almost at the beginning of his first year at Bruford, the only black woman and a Nigerian at that. It was a fortunate and welcome relationship. Because of it, he was able to alleviate an otherwise difficult period at a new location, a country-like town in the suburbs of London, devoid of any city life, even though it was only about half-hour away by train from the great metropolis. Actually, the location was in Kent and therefore, in reality, it was outside London.

Women there were, but in 99.9 percent all-white small college, the likelihood of their sidling towards a black man was inconceivable—except for curiosity. This made Ebun, the only African woman on campus, very special, and the fact that she, a third year, chose to move with BBGD, a mere first year. The relationship was an envy of the other two African men—Alton Kumalo and Pat (later to change to Amadu) Maddy. And yet, it was hardly surprising. She was after all a country woman of BBGD, and from the same ethnic group—which she herself must have found fortunate, albeit a bit late in her class-year.

It was possible that the love relationship was on rocky road from the beginning, a fact that one or both of them overlooked. She was in her third year, and had the intentions of going back home afterwards, although that fact was not insurmountable. More than this, her family was materially very wealthy, in contrast to BBGD's, although they could match class with class in terms of education and status. But, as with such wealthy family, Ebun had her high school education in England, a fact that should gnaw at BBGD's chest with envy as it did in his high school days back in Nigeria, when such kids came back on vacation flaunting their Englishness.

All that state of mind should be behind him, since situations would seem to have corrected themselves on egalitarian level. In London, during his one-year stint at the Polytechnic, he had mingled among women of various cultures (English, Indian, West Indian, Nigerian) with enormous success. In fact, quite a few of the women were living in the same hostel as he was, at the Methodist International House in Bayswater, across from Kensington Park. However, regarding the Nigerian women of his encounter, most of them daughters of wealthy families, the uneasiness posed by flaunted wealth had remained. It was always difficult for him to afford what they could—the clothes they wore, the school they went to, the pocket money they claimed, which made life much more comfortable.

The relationship with Ebun would seem have the potential of overriding all that. For her, it seemed to have been a welcome connection she had lacked at Rose Bruford. She might have had some relationship with a white student, but nothing as serious as she would have liked, in terms of quelling her riotous hormones. And she might have gotten carried away by the energy BBGD had put into it. Being the more academic, he enjoyed writing on her behalf, class assigned essays in dramatic literature, which demanded his going back and forth to his familiar library in Bayswater to get the necessary books—on Ibsen, Chekhov, Moliere, etc. He would read the relevant sections of the books, and with incredible dexterity copied the author's words mixed with his own, a crime the lecturers at Bru never detected. Rather, they were filled with wonderment at her intellectual and academic aptitude.

The naked truth soon stared them both in the eye at the end of that year, when Ebun graduated and was expected to go home, although not without some talk of the future. At first, BBGD regretted he was the weaker link, since he had at least two years still to combat with Rose Bruford. But then, an opportune circumstance raised consolations of possibilities in the progression of their relationship. Some two months before her graduation, she asked BBGD to meet her in London at the Waldorf Hotel, where her uncle was staying on a short London visit. She wanted to set the meeting up as a formal introduction of a future fiancé to a member of her family.

BBGD was delighted with that idea, but he was nervous just the same. He wore the only suit he had so far bought in London, apart from his blue Polytechnic blazer, a fine white and black checkered light wool suit. One day as he was passing by a store, in Bayswater, he had seen the suit hanging in the shop window, for a fantastic sale price of 15 pounds. The other suit he had was the light-mohair gray summer suit he brought from home; whose baggy trousers had started to go out of fashion. How he was able to manipulate these two suits in alternate succession for the Sunday services he attended at the Trinity Temple remained a mystery to him. In other words, he often wondered, with a humorous glint, how he had survived the watchful eyes of all those women at the Methodist International House, especially the pretentious Nigerians that had English schooling prior to their present college or university education.

The visit with Ebun's uncle was a little nerve-racking but a bit reassuring. The tall well-cut man knew BBGD's family within the same social class, and although he must have noticed his naivety and crudeness, he didn't take it as a fault that lacked his niece's sophistication, and therefore unworthy of any serious relationship. As far as what later came across to BBGD through Ebun, there was no such contested issue between herself and her uncle. Everything seemed to have augured an approval that signaled some hopes for the future. What became apparent was the responsibility left for him, to make similar overtures to his family. As to that, what was decided between them was that he would go home during the Xmas break to facilitate such an introduction with his family. He would first write to his brother to tell him about the circumstances and then beg him to send him a plane ticket, perhaps using his mother to pressure his acquiescence.

Other than that, Ebun, on her way to Nigeria, was to meet him in Paris, where he would be spending two weeks of summer vacation. Somehow, that didn't happen.

He was in Paris all right, but had to change locations twice, because of his limited expenses. He called to inform Ebun about his progression, waited until his budget was exhausted, and not seeing her made the decision to go back to his digs in Sidcup, thinking she might have changed her mind about Paris. He had hoped he could still catch her in London. No such luck.

According to her, through her first letter from Nigeria, she came looking for him the day after he left—at the location he last stayed, a cheap hotel in Pigalle. He had no reason to doubt her, because she managed to describe the slightly seedy hotel, and the Madame that always greeted him, at the bottom of the stairs morning and evening, in a French he couldn't understand. It was easy to figure it was some sort of proposal—what else could it be in Catholic but Red Pigalle!

After that first letter, to which he replied, still looking forward to seeing her at Xmas, there was an uncomfortable silence. He wrote twice after to break the silence but to no avail, which encouraged suspicions and anxieties to manifest. He knew she had accepted a position at the University of Ibadan, in the department of Theater Arts where WS was the chair. He had in fact written him about his relationship, hoping his mentor would help take good care of his supposed intended. Protection at least from enthusiastic rakes.

When her letter finally came, it was uncharacteristically short. Even before BBGD read its content, he knew what had happened. It felt like one of those premonition-incidents he often dreamed about the day before they materialized. It was all to the effect that she had met somebody else (far above his academic caliber, no doubt), one of the professors in English. Her last statement in the letter was etched in his mind for years to come: "Pray for me." Pray for her?! What craziness was that? Pray for her for dumping him for somebody else. She must be out of her sex-perverted mind—for no doubt, he knew he had lost her under the sheets of some lecturer. The name of the professor was not mentioned, of course. That was made known to him by his brother. John Pepper Clark. The name at once was familiar to him through the plays written by the man, although he might have crossed paths with him once before he left Nigeria. As he thought, it was somebody well above his match at that stage, in education that is. But then, what of it? Was it unthinkable for a woman to wait for a few months? To have consideration and wait only for a few months, for somebody of serious and hopeful intentions? Couldn't she have waited? For the two to talk about possibilities and impossibilities? He felt betrayed, like Hamlet by his mother, who, "with most wicked speed, to post / With such dexterity to incestuous sheets!" He remembered struggling with the lines of that soliloquy a year before in one of his acting classes. Now he could relate more to it and feel the weight and all the implications of the lines.

And now, some two years after the collapse of that affair, in the Soho Indian restaurant, he had to be reminded of that puke-provoking incident! Could not WS have tried to prevent what had happened? For, knowing full well there might be competing agents against him, BBGD did write to him about it, especially when he knew Ebun had been given appointment at the University of Ibadan's School of Drama where WS was the Head. He was supposed to look after her for his former research assistant, like an elder brother to his favorite junior. He wasn't thinking about anybody in particular, and John Pepper Clark's intervention really took him unawares, but he knew the climate he was dealing with. He knew there were hungry "acada" **** wild dogs about that were lurking in the dark, sporting for a young beautiful woman just in town, and from no less the home country of their recent colonial masters. He could imagine the immediate incitement to rush her, not just to welcome her into the community of scholars but with ulterior motives and loined interests. He knew that, and he was slightly afraid of it. But he was almost sure that the young woman would have enough strength to hold her own, at least until she could communicate with the love she left in England, a love that was supposed to be solidified in family circles in a few months. Yet, "within a month…" she allowed herself to be lured into bedeviled sheets, far away from ethnic similarities and commonalties.

"Yah-yah-yah. I've since moved on," he pretended to wave off the incident, trying to avoid his mentor's penetrating gaze. He knew so well that unblinking, blame-voided eyes when the playwright made a blunt, matter-of-fact, no-hiding-in-the-bush point.

"Good," WS agreed, even if he didn't believe BBGD's gesture, and BBGD knew he did not. But what else was there to say about a matter that had best be forgotten, rather than letting it spoil a good dinner of fried Basmati rice, with chicken and lamb hot-spiced curry, chapatti, washed down with good wine. He

---

**** Generic for university academics—often used facetiously.

had gradually got to like wine since he got to London, although all he knew as good wine was Beaujolais or a Chianti. Later on, he was to learn more about others through WS.

"And as for *The Road*," WS continued after a few moments of silent eating, "it really wasn't up to me to cast you. Yes, I knew you were interested, but Joan was the director. We talked about bringing only Dapo Adelugba as Muriana, due to costs. You should have been at the auditions."

"Yah, I should have. But it practically went by without my knowledge. I was also at the time dealing with some critical stuff at Rose Bru. You know, they almost didn't give me my diploma." He knew it had to come out eventually. All considered, it was wise to let his mentor into the picture so he could know the facts as opposed to what somebody like Ebun might have heard and blasted out to her lover and eventually got into WS's ears. He could imagine her flashing out with pride the thought that she was the only Nigerian, if not foreigner, to have been awarded the real diploma, especially since Joel Adedeji before her only received the infamous certificate.

"Oh yes, I heard something about that." Exactly as he figured, BBGD thought. He wasn't surprised the news had already flown to the princess from God's own colonial home country and got manipulated thereafter. "But what happened?" WS queried.

"Oh, I resisted. Rather that, I spent the whole summer doing extra stuff—speech, teaching…"

"But you got it eventually?"

"Yes, of course." BBGD was emphatic, and he knew his mentor was proud of his resistance, whatever it was.

As for the matter of Ebun, BBGD's anger persisted longer than he had thought, especially now that he knew the falsehood she was spreading. His only consolation was that he still hoped to surpass the diploma, some day, with an academic degree that was always in his mind to achieve. He did not know when the opportunity would present itself; he hoped not too long in the future. For now, he wanted to see how far and well he could fare in professional acting.

*****

The poetry reading was organized by Dennis Duerden, the director of the Transcription Centre, in collaboration with the Royal Court Theater. The main attraction of course was WS, who was to do a reading of his long poem *Idanre*. The epic poem was to be read, supported by Nigerian drumming, and actors, who would be reading from select poems by African writers. BBGD knew the other actors through the BBC Radio "African Theater" play productions, in which he had often participated as actor and/or writer.

He was delighted to be among the chosen readers of poems by other African authors, such as Christopher Okigbo, Gabriel Okara, and Alex La Guma. They were to read first before the main event, to whet the appetite of the audience, many of whom were hearing poems by African authors for the first time. Some in the audience were more knowledgeable and informed about Africa and its cultural resources, but others came just for the curiosity of it all. BBGD's involvement must of course be attributed to his relationship with his mentor, which had resulted in his many visits to the Transcription Centre, mingling with African writers and visual artists. Not that he regarded himself as one of Dennis Duerden's friends, or as one of the promising African artists in the caliber of his mentor, James Ngugi, or Christopher Okigbo. Rather, he had decided that going to the Centre as often as he could, even when WS wasn't around, was the only way to make himself felt one way or another.

Thankfully, the Centre was close to many of his haunts, especially the place of his supplementary employment, the Eagle Star Insurance Company, which was within a stone's throw. As such, whenever he was working with the company, in the main calculating annuities, he would constantly make a detour to the Centre, at lunchtime or after work, to mingle with the VIPs, if they were around. Often at such times, there were no Theater or television job in sight to take him away, which sometimes could be months. If there were no artists present, he was quite comfortable to just sit and chat for a while with the white South African secretary, Maxine Lautre, in her office. The advantage of that option was that it placed him in direct eye contact with Dennis in his office, who sometimes would acknowledge his presence, and even endure a little chat with BBGD if in good spirits. And sometimes he got lucky with such an acknowledgment, winning him the favor of a small project that caught the sight of director on his desk. However, he had never entertained any illusions of making any significant impression on this soft spoken, seemingly shy man, whose eyes most of the time seemed to be combating the elements in his psyche in an effort to resolve a problematic, often when he was not on the phone. In fact, the only time he seemed to be at some ease and jolly was when his so-called artist-friends were there, when he would chat with abandon and take them to lunch or dinner.

As it happened, Maxine Lautre, at some point became his landlord for a short while—a subletting landlord that is. He wasn't happy with the arrangement and the pins and needles relationship he had with another subletting landlord in Swiss Cottage—apparently a TV writer. When he intimated Maxine with his woes, she was only too happy to offer him a bedroom in the huge St. John Wood apartment she occupied with her husband, Chris Macgregor, a jazz musician, and members of his jazz band. Probably the best bedroom in the apartment, with French windows overlooking a scenic view of the surrounding area, but BBGD understood the deal. Jazz musicians had no fixed income and Maxine was the only one that paid the rent; as such a rental income would be most welcome, if only for a short time. For he made it clear to her from the start that he was really looking for a self-contained apartment of his own. The advantage for BBGD was it brought him closer to the Centre and its director, Dennis Duerden.

While this advantage earned him a few projects, by far the best moments for the fledging professional actor was certainly when his mentor was in town, when BBGD could not easily be ignored. For any friend of WS, it seemed, was also a tolerated friend of Dennis D. Those were the sparse moments the director's face would relax and break into hearty smiles, as opposed to most times when his face was tortured with the Centre's budget, his hair standing on end, like porcupine's. But when he was happy among friends, his mouth constantly held a cigar or pipe, puffing away with abandon as opposed to frozen in the stasis of self-conscious nervousness; his gracious laugh showed a set of not-well organized front teeth creamed with tobacco stains. It was at such moments that his humanity and generosity extended to include BBGD, asking him to do a few radio readings for the Centre. Such moments included his one and only review of a newly published African novel, which, as admitted later to him by Maxine, Dennis apparently didn't like.

But BBGD had always accepted his limitations—he was no literary critic, the stuff of university graduates like Dennis and his cohort of friends. On the other hand, he was more comfortable with reading excerpts from other people's works, with a natural radio voice that was often recognized by the studio producer, a former BBC technical staff. In fact, the recognition, certainly an attribute to his Bruford training, affirmed his confidence in the not dissimilar but more professional acting projects at the BBC.

"What's the matter with Dennis today?" BBGD whispered to Maxine one morning. "He seemed flustered."

"Yah," Maxine responded, also in a whisper, "The Farfield Foundation director is visiting the Centre tomorrow. I think you should get yourself out of sight."

Whoever financed the Centre's artistic projects (be it in fiction, non-fiction, poetry, and visual arts, although visual art would seem to be the most visible since they were on display practically in every room), whoever was the source of Dennis Duerden's lavish spending, had hitherto been left unquestioned by BBGD. Whatever organization it was, he believed WS ought to know. And if the mentor approved, so should the mentee. He however noticed there was some political arm of it, one that was closely connected with the small radio studio the Centre operated, which mostly featured political developments in African states, especially those recently independent or anticipating independence. He also had some inkling that such organization was somehow connected with the U.S. As such, when Maxine intimated to him the reason for Dennis' display of flurry nerves, that it had to do with the visiting representative of the Centre's financial source, he surmised it also had to do with scrutinizing the books to make certain that all accounts were in order. That day Maxine got home very late, she and Dennis working well after office hours almost into the night. For, as implied, Dennis was a spendthrift when it came to entertaining artists, especially political ones, not to talk about the minor projects that involved minor personages such as BBGD, which of course also had to be paid for.

Thus was the big poetry project at the Royal Court funded, which obviously included the hiring of the theater space, and paying the reading artists, no less WS. And paying for the grand reception that followed.

It was at the rehearsal of these readings that BBGD had confrontation with WS. It wasn't really a rehearsal for WS, but he was present just to give a direction to the drummers he wanted to use to incite the beginning of the long poem, *Idanre*. Rather, the necessary rehearsal was for the readings that preceded the highlight of the evening, by lesser known readers. Among these, there were grades of expertise. BBGD easily singled himself out, so also was his friend Jumoke Debayo, both at a grade above all others. As a graduate of Rose Bruford, his sensitivity to poetry had excelled in many ways through felt emotions and spontaneous aptitude towards rhythm and conveyance of imagery to listening audience. His confidence had been bolstered by the praises he had received from his teachers through the way he had delivered Shakespeare, Keats, Spencer, Wordsworth, T.S. Eliot, and many others. And there was no reason to disbelieve them, since they pummeled him at every turn for everything else—rudiments of speech, teaching, etc. Thus, considering himself as an expert in his own right, he was quite eager to demonstrate his poetic talents at this reading.

The presence of his VIP mentor for a moment brought some nervous sweat to his temples. He wasn't in the orchestra when it came to BBGD's reading, as far as he could see, but the maturing mentee felt him to be somewhere. But since WS wasn't directly observing him, he was determined to rise above any deterrent and give an outstanding rendition, if only to show off to the poet being honored his level of competence and professionalism. That was exactly what he thought he did, a performance meriting, if nothing else, a nod of approval.

"No, no, no, BB," the interruption came from behind him, from the wings on to stage, the familiar tenor voice stabbing the back of his head like a sharp object as soon as he finished. There was hardly any time for him to come out of the emotional frame he had used to capture the imagery and rhythm of the poem he delivered. The deep breath he needed to make the transition from metaphysical reaches to physical present was busted by the critical voice that he knew so well. He stood transfixed for a moment before he turned slowly to regard the intruder—his mentor, his very own mentor!

"What?" he squinted, somewhat annoyed but respectful, at the VIP assailant.

"BB, you are too grandiose and pompous. The poem doesn't require it. Feel the words, feel the rhythm."

"I didn't?"

"No. You're too flamboyant."

From which superlatives the air of inferiority descended without sympathy on the formerly self-assured reader, so much so that he snapped:

"There, read it," thrusting the bound manuscript at arm's length at the unguarded mentor. "Why don't you read the way it should!"

Hush ensued for a few seconds through the whole theater. What came over him that he must address the distinguished VIP in such a fashion? An abomination! Has he lost his mind? Apologize, apologize at once and let this matter rest. Accept your mistake, and rude behavior; surely the VIP knows better than you. He could feel the pressure from the eyes that glared at him.

But BBGD stood his ground. From his own point of view, there was no need for the disgrace he felt he encountered in front of everybody. No matter how much his reading was off, and he didn't believe it was, he felt he also deserved some respect, thinking of the amount of preparation and emotional charge that went with the delivery of the poem.

"No need," WS rejected the offer with a wave of his hand. "I was only trying to help." At which point he left the stage, a reaction some people felt was filled with anger, distancing any previously existing relationship between the poet and the upstart.

BBGD knew better than that. Much later on when they met, both mentor and mentee aired out their thinking as it should have been done in the first place. The problem seemed to have been his interpretation of the African poem, which was slightly in conflict with his reading of mostly British experiences at Bruford. As such, the mentee, in deference to the mentor, compromised his rendition, just in time for the formal presentation the

91

following evening. The event even drew to the Court one or two former teachers of his at Bru's, who complimented him afterwards.

But that wouldn't be the only confrontation.

*****

The rehearsals of *The Lion and the Jewel* at the Royal Court had undergone some significant changes. First, it was change of the director. Auditions and casting happened about two weeks before *Macbeth* closed. BBGD had well been cast for the character of Lakunle. It was always good to know what your next acting job would be before the end of a show, and to play a central character at that. An envied chance that might not replicate itself for a long time, that is, for a nascent professional actor. *Macbeth* had been a very fortunate chance production for him also, since it had Sir Alec Guinness and Simone Signore as Macbeth and Lady Macbeth. In fact, he had been very lucky since his graduation at Bruford. Three productions of prominence happened one after the other, one influencing the other. First was the production of WS's *The Trials of Brother Jero*, at Hampstead Theater Club, in which he played Chume. Bill Gaskill, the artistic director of the Royal Court, saw that production, which got him thinking about the possibility of having African witches in *Macbeth*, using the three principal actors in *Jero*, that is, Zakes Mokae, Jumoke Debayo, and the Rose Bruford graduate. Then, by the time Macbeth started, it became evident that plans were underway to do *The Lion and the Jewel*, to be directed by a rookie director, one of Gaskill's friends, Desmond O'Donovan.

From the beginning of the rehearsals, it was clear that the rookie couldn't handle the play, which also betrayed the uncomfortable status of some actors in certain roles. About two or so weeks into chaotic rehearsals, urgent decisions had to be made. Bill Gaskill decided to take over the directing, and the contracts of two actors had to be cancelled and their roles re-cast. As BBGD was also having problems with his role under the rookie, he thought for a moment that all the hoopla might be because of him. But he was reassured by Bill, not in so many words, that it wasn't his role they were after. And so, rehearsals continued, intensely for two more weeks, with a major change— Baroka to be played by the South African Lionel Ngakane instead of the Nigerian Willie Payne. It was a decision not favored by some in a cast of mostly Nigerians. But it was a better choice on the whole.

BBGD and the cast had heard that Mr. Soyinka would be coming to see the show at some point. While he was delighted that he would see his mentor once again, which always meant some dinner and chit-chat about new developments at home; the portrayer of Lakunle, the lead, felt some reservation and trepidation about this. Granted, the playwright had been part of his development as an actor since the 1960 Masks and through Rose Bru. BBGD, on the other hand, had not been part of the playwright's new group, The Orisun Theater Company, about whom he'd heard so much, especially his satiric sketches, *Before the Blackout*, which ran guerilla forays frequently on to the steps of the House of Parliament in Lagos and Ibadan. He was envious about not being part of that experience, although not about the rigorous ways he had heard the director discipline his company. News strained his ears that Kongi had become somewhat ruthless with his actors, a far cry from the respect he experienced during his tenure with the 1960 Masks. Even at moments he should have had a deserving and severe reprimand, such as the incident of the Grundig tape recorder, BBGD was grateful that no harsh words slapped across his face, which would have crippled his confidence in his mentor. Therefore, the seemingly new WS made him a little nervous.

It was at the final dress rehearsal that the playwright appeared. In fact, the cast didn't see him until after the show—everybody was told to remain on stage, for a few comments from the playwright. That created BBGD's self-conscious dread. There were some moments in the play that he was still having difficulties with. Paramount was the delivery of the long speeches—he was simply not satisfied. A case in point was the assemblage of vocabulary that his character Lakunle declaimed, to befuddle, impress and tutor the naïve, "native" intelligence of Sidi, the woman he loves and wishes to marry, although without paying the bride-price, which he considers:

> *A savage custom, barbaric, outdated*
> *Rejected, denounced, accursed,*
> *Excommunicated, archaic, degrading,*
> *Humiliating, unspeakable, redundant,*
> *Retrogressive, remarkable, unpalatable.*

That particular night he was experimenting with yet another way of delivery, which really didn't go too well—although he felt much of that might be due to the response of audience. They simply were not with him, he felt. As such, knowing how his mentor felt about rhythm and resonance of language, he was almost sure those moments could not have missed his critical and sensitive ears. But he thought whatever comment was due to him, would be made more as a tête-à-tête, when they were both alone. In this mindset, he was looking forward to seeing him, and as usual probably getting a meal or two from him before he left London.

93

When he came on stage, BBGD stood his ground by the proscenium wall, still recuperating from the post-performance critical self-study he indulged his mind. When their eyes met, BBGD creased a quiet smile but immediately cast his eyes to the ground, as if a sudden guilt had just admonished his mind.

The playwright, without praising anybody, went on to explain his response in general, much of which somehow escaped BBGD because he wasn't really listening. Next moment, all he heard was:

"And you, BB," which immediately arrested him. He cast a glance in the direction of what sounded like a reproach, finally holding his face on the person that launched the seeming attack in order to consider his possible grievances. "You're not relating very well with Jumoke in that scene"—meaning the woman who played Sadiku. Since, there were many scenes he had with Sadiku, he had the right to be curious. Ah yes, now he somehow recalled a sentence from the earlier general criticism, words that now tried to make connections with the present comment. Something to do with actors not being curious enough. As he felt at the time that it didn't really apply to him, he must have naturally dismissed it from his critical thoughts.

"Which scene?" he queried.

"The scene with the drummers, when Sadiku was asking you for money."

"Yah?"

"You were too standoffish, far too standoffish."

And what did you expect me to do, BBGD thought to himself. What should Lakunle have done to a woman he hated, and who seemed to be instrumental to the disappearance of the woman he loved, a woman who had no good words for him at every turn?

"What do you want me to do?" BBGD felt the criticism came rather late in the rehearsal process. There they were, he thought, at the last dress rehearsal, tired from an exhausting performance, and preparing themselves for the opening of the play the following day, what could be better off than going home to rest. Yet, the playwright must now find fault with what they should have cleared up a while back. Knowing he might be too self-conscious and should be more open, he nevertheless considered WS's observation was somewhat antagonistic. He knew it, the playwright knew it, everybody he felt should know it. But here we go again, recalling by association the experience at the poetry session some months past.

"Can they set up that scene so I could explain it to him?" the playwright turned to the director.

"Certainly."

Oh God, now he's going to show him up in front of all these people, a professional actor that he is, BBGD mused, placing himself against most of the other actors whom he considered amateurs. An insult! He felt the only people that probably matched his professional skills were Jumoke, his friend, and Lionel Ngakane, the South African who took over the role of Baroka. Even he, in terms of his inadequate knowledge of the Yoruba tradition of the play, was lacking cultural instincts BBGD commanded.

The scene and moment took off. The drummers drummed with the lead drummer provoking him for money. Sadiku was told to invade the stingy jacket pocket of Lakunle, to try and discover some coins for the aspiring drummer, which, on impulse, initiated more effortful reaction from Lakunle to keep Sadiku's hand off his pockets. Sadiku in fact managed to get a coin out, much at the expense of Lakunle's hopelessness and anger at failure to retrieve his hard-earned coin.

"That's what I'm talking about," the playwright seemed to be pleased with his insight. "Curiosity. Look for moments like that. Stretch the limits of your acting."

Fine, he got it. But was that his curiosity or Sadiku's, he queried but left it unvoiced. Give and take, isn't that one of the hallmarks of acting? But is that it? Is that the only scene they needed to do? BBGD didn't appreciate using the scene with him as a guinea pig to demonstrate the playwright's criticism. However, he felt he was used to demonstrate the general fact probably because he was the only person in the cast most close to the playwright. Upon reconsideration, he felt thankful for the illumination, upon which he capitalized.

"Meet me at the Centre tomorrow, and I'll tell you one or two other things." This was what his mentor should have said in the first place, rather than the seeming embarrassment he inflicted on him in front of all the cast and director. However, he agreed he might have been oversensitive.

As with the poetry session, people came to him afterwards to upbraid him about the lack of respect he displayed to the emerging distinguished African playwright. As usual, he didn't feel quite the same way they saw it. He insisted he could take criticism, which all actors should be open to. Only it had to be more tactful than what he would refer to as an indiscreet exposition of probable limitations of a sensitive actor. But again, all was well and no hard feelings lingered over to the following day, when he knew he could resolve any other matter with his mentor, preferably over possible lunch at some bistro in Mayfair or a restaurant in Soho.

As Dirgeman in *A Dance of the Forests*

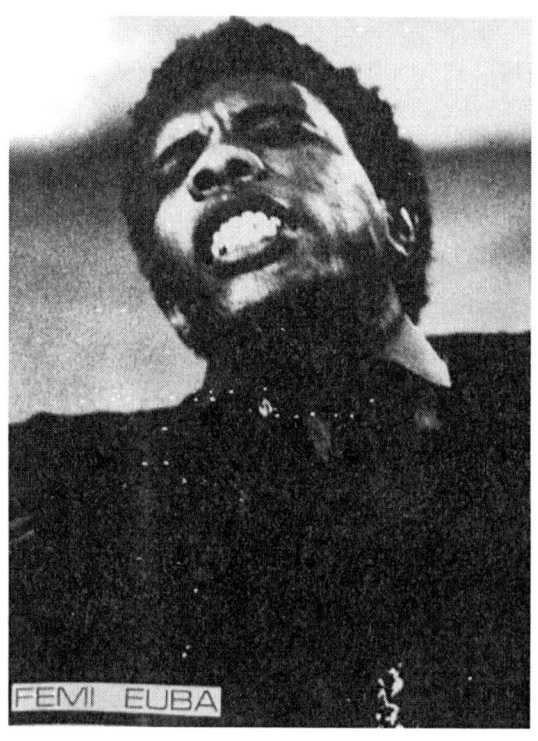

As Chume in *The Trials of Brother Jero*

As Lakunle in *The Lion and the Jewel*

LIONEL NGAKANE as Baroka, and FEMI EUBA as Lakunle in *The Lion and the Jewel*

Cartooned Lakunle in *The Spectator*

As Lakunle wooing Sidi

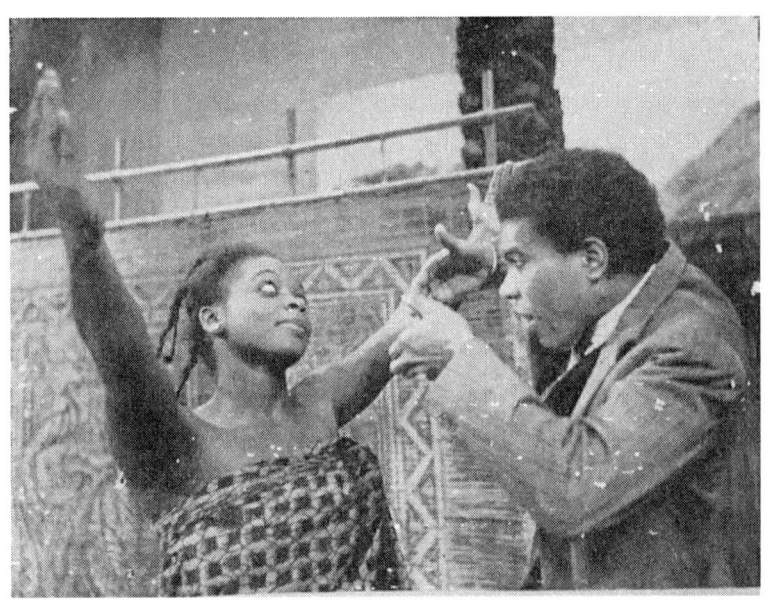

Lakunle miming as photographer

Scenes Five

In-Between Creative Growths: Forays into Playwriting

The Transcription Centre was located at No. 36 Dover Street in the Mayfair area of London. It was a kind of African artists' collective project, where artists from African nations came and went whenever they were in the UK. Run, unknown to most of them at the time, as a CIA operative under the aegis of the Farfield Foundation, it identified emerging artists (novelists, poets, playwrights, visual artists, etc.) that spoke to the various concerns of the recently independent nations. On the surface its objectives were legitimate—that of promotion of new voices from formerly disenfranchised peoples through the colonizing autonomy of the colonial masters. However, there was an undercurrent political objective serving the funding agencies—to keep them informed of any radicals against the status quo, still very much controlled by colonialism.

BBGD, like many others, was quite uninformed by all this; but then, he was probably the least of the artists to be worried about, since he did not really consider himself much of anything. He got to know of the existence of the Centre through his mentor, whom he adored and who was worthy of emulation as a playwright, poet and polemicist. He had just graduated from the Rose Bruford at the time. Through his former connections with WS, which had thrived through his training years, he was simply following orders—to meet his mentor at the Transcription Centre whenever he was around.

However, although not a known artist, he could boast of a few radio plays, which he had written for the BBC African Service while still at Bruford. Within these plays he was unconsciously trying a voice different from his mentor's, but was very much influenced by the other WS of Stratford-upon-Avon, and other Restoration writers such as Moliere. He first had direct glimpse of the French playwright of comedy of manners in Nigeria a few years back. Through his mentor, he had participated in *That Scoundrel Suberu*, an adaptation of Moliere's *That Scoundrel Scapin*, a project which toured many parts of the country.

At Rose Bruford, in one of his first projects, the head acting teacher, a former West End director, asked them to come up with a short scene to try out their directing skills. The first play that came to his mind was *A Dance of the Forests*, which was the only play he felt he was very familiar with and within his knowledge and reach. At first, he thought he had brought a copy with him to England, but rummaging through his things he was disappointed to find out he was mistaken. The play was just not in sight. It had not been published by then, but even if it was published, he would prefer a production copy, full of notes and markings that might give him some confidence to give his actors direction. He desperately wrote his mentor to send him a copy, a pursuit which, in an afterthought, was a little senseless; the assignment was due before he would get any response from Nigeria.

Thinking more about it, he calmly admonished his naivety. For how could his young student peers, and even his teacher, understand an African play and its characters, let alone its complexity, which even he still had problems with. That was how he came upon the idea of *That Scoundrel Suberu*, which he should have thought of all along as a much more logical and doable project. He regretted not having that script with him either, but since it was an adaptation of *That Scoundrel Scapin*, he felt it was something he could very easily pull off, by locating the play and selecting a comfortable scene from it. And what short scene could be more comfortable than the one that served well his rookie sensibilities?

Even though the small library at Bruford might have had a copy, he preferred, rather, to explore the only library he was very familiar with, the one that preoccupied his first year of studies in London, the Bayswater branch of the London Municipal Library near his former hostel, the Methodist International House. It was the library that was to provide ideas for the content of the essays he helped Ebun Odutola to write for her class assignments at Bruford, and provided ideas for his own essays when the time came.

Deciding on *Scapin* was really an asset. First, a close reading of the Moliere play made him discover the adaptation skills applied to the original by the Nigerian authors (university students at the time). More important, through the parallels he was inevitably drawing in his mind, he began to realize the similarities between the neoclassical comedic characters of Moliere and the characters that fascinated him in his cultural background in Nigeria, especially in Lagos. They were characters he was to copiously draw from in his BBC radio plays. He could similarly draw parallels with characters in the Shakespeare comedies he had read so far. A modest few really, but sufficient for his psyche to draw nuanced similarities and transpose the language of his Yoruba characters into English. While he was quite aware of the fact that

Pidgin English was liberally employed in *Suberu*, he noticed that it was used by characters that would normally speak in pidgin, for instance the servants, as opposed to the traditional characters of the status quo. These were the Yoruba characters whose voice, tongue and nuances he would try to transpose and dialoguize in English.

By the time he wrote his first play, *The Yam Debt*, in his first year at Bruford, he had begun to be familiar with the Comedia dell'Arte characters that had influenced both Moliere and Shakespeare. This fascinating source clinched for him the intuitive and nuanced identity of his characters and their dialogue.

Somehow, he was not as fascinated by the characters in the tragedies, although was often moved by them. Before he left Nigeria, he had read tragedies such as *Hamlet* and *Romeo and Juliet*, and seen at least one of these performed by the limited amateur skills of his high school peers and teachers. He had never felt inclined to perform in those productions, not because of the plays per se but because of his lack of confidence in acting. The plays he read in his classes were taught by the one and only Julius Ekpo. His colonial upbringing and emulation were so impeccable that it somehow made his overly respectful teaching of the Bard somewhat onerous and therefore boring to most students, and laughable to BBGD and a few others.

He caught up with the Elizabethan dramatist again at the Polytechnic in London, where he read *Macbeth*, *King Lear*, and *Twelfth Night*. There, he became even more attracted to the Stratford-upon-Avon genius upstart. Professor Hart's reading of *King Lear*, for instance, was more authentic and his somewhat morose delivery of Lear matched to the hilt the king's wallowing in self-pity in the storm scene. Even then, the tragic structure of the play, which he admired, did not conjure any parallel character for him from his culture, except of course that of the Fool. Same for the Greek tragedies, such as *Oedipus Rex* and *The Oresteia*. However, in contrast to these were Aristophanes' characters in plays such as *The Frogs*, a play that had fascinated him over the years and would much later compel an adaptation of it.

*****

"Have you read this man's play?" Br'er Wole asked his friend Yemi Lijadu, indicating a manuscript on top of a pile of files on Lijadu's office desk. They both had just come back from lunch in the cafeteria of the Nigerian Broadcasting Service, to which BBGD had tagged along. As he had trailed into the office with his benefactors, his eyes had also flashed in the direction of the item in question.

"Yes," responded Mr. Lijadu with his emulating stiff upper lip, "I browsed through somewhat. What do you think?"

BBGD was convinced the prompt counter-question was thrown to offset a similar question likely to be directed at him by his friend. Obviously, he hadn't thoroughly read the script, if at all, enough to tolerate any questions about it.

"It has some merit. I think his use of the stage is remarkable, and he has a sense of comedy. Must have been influenced by Aristophanes." His mentor's confident response demonstrated for BBGD his knowledge of world drama and theater. He came to that conclusion without really thinking why he did, except for the fact that the man had been in England, mingled with many theater practitioners, critics and scholars, which was far more than what his friend, Lijadu, had accomplished. That was quite enough for him; far more than enough for him. He looked forward to the day he would ask his mentor' for advice, that is, if he were to have the opportunity of furthering his education in the "land of milk and honey."

The mention of Aristophanes had stuck with him. He later asked WS about the Classical Greek playwright and got him to spell the word: A-R-I-S-T-O-P-H-A-N-E-S. "He was the greatest known among the extant Greek dramatists for satiric comedy," he was told.

"Do you have a copy of one his works?"

"I may have one or two somewhere. If not, I'm sure you'll find something at the university library." That is, whenever BBGD got back to Ibadan.

He did in fact locate one play on his mentor's book shelf in the living room of his Ibadan apartment—*The Frogs*. He was struck by the title and wondered what it was all about. Not very familiar with the Greeks and the Greek form, he struggled through the choruses, although he loved what Aristophanes did with the chorus of frogs. There were also many allusions in the play that he had to look up in the dense footnotes, but he got the thread of it. The idea of Dionysus going to Hades to look among the dead poets to find one he could bring back to revitalize the deteriorating Athenian culture. He enjoyed the rather scathing humor of Aristophanes. If that was what Br'er Wole found interesting about the play on Lijadu's desk, he would go along with that judgment, knowing of no other.

That very play surfaced again at Rose Bruford, among the Greek plays they read in the History of Theater class. He could not only boast of some knowledge of it, but also now was able to dig more deeply into it. The teacher, Mr. Hoffman, he found rather limited. Not entirely a fault of his, since the class only served as a background to the main training of the college, acting, and the teaching of speech and drama. And he had only an MA. But the course helped BBGD on his own to know more about the Greeks, the characters in the plays and the form, which resulted in a class project of another course. For the project, he chose to write a play involving Greek characters such as Socrates, Sophocles, Euripides, and Aristophanes. He couldn't for the life of him remember the title or what exactly the play was about. He must have lost the manuscript amid the various movements he had since made. He seemed to remember it was a funny piece, involving Aristophanes.

"Dig up an old unfamiliar book or thesis, deconstruct it, then use it to construct and argue your own thesis. That's the way to do it." BBGD couldn't remember the exact words he overheard of WS's conversation with one of his friends, probably Lijadu. He also couldn't quite recall the circumstances but the researcher seemed to be referencing his student mischiefs at Leeds University vis-à-vis his MA thesis.

That advice, or non-advice, stuck in BBGD's psyche and he exploited it to the full at Rose Bruford, either writing Ebun's and his own essays, or the play project for Peggy Sanders' class. Thus, he had found his favorite library at Baywater very useful, digging up old books he felt were unfamiliar to or above the heads of the teachers at Rose Bruford, then use their ideas and thoughts, the way he understood them, to lavishly write his essays, or influence the one play he wrote for Peggy Sanders' class.

"A very interesting and well-written play," remarked Ms. Sanders. "But how did you come by these ideas?"

"Mine." BBGD's response was met with a surprised but doubtful look from Sanders.

"I know. But what books did you research for your ideas? I'm just fascinated and curious, that's all."

"Some books I picked up in the library."

"Here?"

"No. In London."

"Maybe you can give me a list of some of them sometime. Anyway, a very interesting play."

BBGD had no intentions of providing Ms. Saunders with any list and the teacher really never pursued it beyond their conversation. However, news reached Rose Bruford, the principal, about the Nigerian student's creative endeavor and proven scholarly interests.

*****

Various political demonstrations happened along Piccadilly Square and on to Green Park past Eagle Star Insurance Company where BBGD worked as an Insurance clerk. It was a job that came in handy when no acting jobs were in sight. Radio acting from time to time at the BBC World Service in the Bush House also was a saving grace but that did not interfere with the Insurance job since it happened on weekends.

"There goes another demonstration," Mike, his co-worker, also temporary, indicated. "Aren't you going to join them?"

The demonstrations were in opposition to the Nigerian-Biafran civil war that was raging in Nigeria, bringing the conflict to the consciousness of the British government—to do what, BBGD could not exactly figure out. At any rate, most people were in support of the Biafrans, who were presented as poor victims that deserved a right to exist. It was a misinformation some British public fell for.

"No, I'm not joining them."

"Why? It's your country?"

"So?"

To go into explanations with Mike was an endeavor he found rather tedious and emotionally tasking; it would take a lot of wasted energy, for which he had no stamina. At any rate, he had always considered himself apolitical. As such, he had not really immersed himself sufficiently in the details of the conflict, except that it was what prevented him from going home when he graduated from Bruford. He had always, like most Nigerians, thought of home as the best place to go back to settle and work. There he would have found himself a good job as an acting instructor in one of the universities, especially where his mentor was currently Head of Drama in Lagos. Then came the war and his parents advised him to hold off coming home. Actually that became an advantage rather than an obstruction. He took it as his fate to remain in London to gain the much-needed professional experience. He had wondered what would have happened without the experiences he gained on the London stage and at the BBC as a radio playwright and actor.

But the particular demonstration in question was very different. He knew that more than anybody else, for it concerned what had been reported in the papers, the imprisonment of his mentor. He had intimated his relationship with Wole Soyinka to no one, Michael Bloom included.

"It was about your country man, that poet and playwright."

"I know."

"Do you know him?"

"Somewhat."

He wished Mike would not prolong his inquiry, for even though it was a situation that concerned him very much, he preferred to agonize in silence than to spit out his anger.

"Yes. But wasn't he the author of the play you did recently?"

"Yah."

"It's here in the papers," Mike pointed, indicating the front-page news in one of the dailies. "They said he might have sided with the Biafrans. That was why they imprisoned him. Do you think that's true?"

"Well, I don't know the facts, but I doubt it."

"So if you doubt it, you should be out there, demonstrating against the injustice."

"First of all, I am not that demonstrative, at least politically. Secondly, I'm not sure going out there to demonstrate does anything. And not going doesn't prove my lack of concern."

"You know the guy, don't you?" Michael had not been a person to give over easily; BBGD wished he would this one. The office mate was probably the only one around in that office that he considered at par with his level of intellectuality; they had often made connections at various dimensions of that level. At times they had conceded, at others they in fact had agreed to disagree. Case in point was the day he showed him a poem he had written to get his reaction, which turned out not to be a good one.

"Yes. But I don't understand what you're trying to say," Michael said after skimming through the piece.

"What do you mean?" BBGD was on the defensive.

"I mean, some of these words…they make the poem almost impenetrable and obscure."

BBGD felt slightly offended, thinking he had written something powerful. Yes, but isn't that what a poem should do, and that the reader should try to unravel that obscurity? He said this to himself.

"A poem should be lucid and accessible," Mike went on to demolish his thinking.

Well, maybe he just couldn't penetrate it because of cultural differences— he went on further to console himself.

"I'm sorry to disappoint you, but I just don't understand it," Mike concluded without sympathy.

BBGD realized his defenses were transparent, so he tried to neutralize them to end the process. "Okay thanks. I'll work on it."

The poem was trying to express his feelings during a flight on an airplane. As a matter of fact, it was an imitated version of a Soyinka poem, he confessed to himself. He had read the WS poem several times, and some of the thoughts in it had also eluded him at first. He had thought that was how a poem should challenge the reader. Accessing it eventually, he felt if he was able to penetrate it, so should any other reader. Relating to the poems he and his Bruford peers recited in class (Keats, Shelley, Wordsworth, etc.), he remembered how some of them were difficult to understand at first. He had to read them several times before he could interpret and project his interpretation to the class. It was an objective their teachers instilled in them. But he realized there might have been other things operative that made it difficult for him to penetrate the poems, such as the culture and location of the poems, about which he had to research. Even then, with no time for reflection by the listener, the mood and rhythm of a poem should be able to carry and engage, if they were correctly rendered. In fact, such delivery was something he was told he had talents for. So, what then?

One of the words that probably obfuscated the meaning of the poem, and Mike pointed this out, was "exacerbation," a word that had fascinated him in the Soyinka poem. He was determined to use it in his own poem no matter what. He had looked it up in the dictionary, as he was wont to do, especially with the words WS had used in his novels and poems. It was a ritual habit he had acquired, investigating very inspiring and workable word-images that not only spoke to his sense of curiosity but also elevated his intellectual reaches. He had however realized a difference between him and his mentor in the use of words. One seemed to have used it with natural ease from his storehouse of knowledge; the other used it with some vulnerable strain, out of sheer fascination, and from limited and inadequate resources. But then, perhaps younger Soyinka did something similar a few years back. He would like to think writers, in general, had some processes in common.

After some rethinking, he saw what Mike might be getting at; nevertheless, he stuck to his guns, not giving his critic any undue advantage.

*****

BBGD came to know Cosmo Pieterse, the late South African, African Studies scholar, through their artistic affiliations with the BBC African Service, and particularly through the Ijinle Theater Company under the directorship of Athol Fugard. He had walked into the Transcription Centre one fine day after office hours at the Eagle Star Insurance and chanced upon an ongoing meeting. How Dennis Duerden, who set it up, didn't invite him formally was beyond him. Dennis knew he was an actor, although, obviously not of any recognition in his eyes. Still, that was no reason for his oversight. It was possible, of course, that the intentions of the meeting were slightly different at first. The focus could be on the South African playwright-director, who had been brought over under the auspices of the Centre to promote his plays, which would obviously require South African actors. But then the late Jumoke Adebayo, a very good friend of his, was at that first meeting, and possibly one or two other West Africans he knew as well through the BBC African Theater. Anyway, no matter what, he chanced upon the meeting.

He would have gone past the room if his eyes hadn't caught Jumoke Adebayo, making him to halt for a second. Jumoke immediately beckoned him to come in and introduced him to Athol.

"Here's another actor you might want to meet."

"What are you all doing here?" His curiosity was directed at Jumoke.

"We are trying to inaugurate a theater company."

"Yes, we would like to have you," Athol immediately chipped in. "Why don't you join us?"

BBGD pretended reluctance, since he wasn't formerly invited, but then went on to join the group. He was formally introduced to Athol Fugard, and then Zakes Mokae, Cosmo Pieterse, and Bloke Modisane, all compatriots of Athol.

After tossing a few suggestions around for the company's name, they settled on the Ijinle, suggested by Ms. Adebayo. Fugard liked it because of its implications in Yoruba as a foundational organization. It was also suggested at that first meeting that its first production would be Fugard's *Blood Knot*, which apparently was written for Zakes Mokae, who had worked with the author-director back in South Africa. Since there were noticeably Nigerians in the group, and *Blood Knot* only had two characters, it was also suggested that Athol's play should have a companion, to run alternately in the productions. They decided on Wole Soyinka's two short plays, *The Trials of Brother Jero* and *The Strong Breed*. The productions were being earmarked for the Hampstead Theater Club space.

Made available for workshops and rehearsals was the Round House, a former warehouse that was being renovated gradually at the time. They met mostly on weekends. About two or three months were spend just on workouts and improvisational exercises, so the company could get coordinated before embarking on the scripts. BBGD was quite familiar with the nature of these exercises, through being with WS in Nigeria and, more important, as a Rose Bruford trained actor. He was quite at home, although felt it was a waste of his time. Without an anticipated production, he probably would have opted out— for him the workshop period went on for far too long. However, he realized quite a few of the actors, especially the ones that were later drafted in, were not as trained in or familiar with acting. He was glad that Athol recognized the professionals from the amateurs, but this recognition was to produce its problems later.

BBGD had written a few plays for the BBC African Service at the time he met Cosmo Pieterse, such as *The Game* and *Down by the Lagoon*. He had also written a strange, "cerebral" (a word later used by a German Professor at the University of Ife) but rather inventive play for the television, *Abiku*, and a rough draft of a full length, *The Union*. As a matter of fact, the South African might have performed in one or two of the radio plays and it was these initial accomplishments that caught his attention in terms of publication.

"I like these plays and I think we should try and publish them," he said, with *The Game* and *Abiku* especially in mind.

"You think so?" BBGD replied with some reservations.

"Yes, I think so. I think they could be published together. With your permission, I could submit them to Heinemann for their Educational Books series."

BBGD gave him permission and handed him the scripts. He knew about Heinemann and their series, which indeed included a number of African works he knew. He began to imagine his plays among them and was quite joyful about the possibility. He felt he had missed the first wave of Western interest in African Literature, which included works by Achebe and certainly by his mentor. Much of this trend began while he was still in Nigeria. And although the interest was still very much there, those in that first surge seemed to have set up a model by which to evaluate the next. He certainly could not compare his level of writing with WS's, although he hoped he could attain that level as he developed as a writer. But he felt *Abiku* and *The Union* seemed to be groping there.

In terms of publication, he thought the only limitation for *Abiku* was the fact it was written with television in mind; he would like to see it as such—on TV. He would also like to see *The Union* on stage rather than first getting it published, for the play seemed unwieldy in places and needed revisions that a production or workshop could provide. In fact, he had shown it to one of his peers at the Rose Bruford College, who enthusiastically presented it to her father, a literary agent. After a few weeks, the manuscript came back to him with a comment from Leslie's father. Certainly not negative, but it, perhaps conveniently, lamented the fact that theater had moved away from the kind of declamatory rendering that the play possessed, that is, away from that kind of Shakespearean or Classical Greek formality. The movement away implied the more preferred contemporary sparse, non-sequitur dialogue such as Beckett's and Pinter's. BBGD understood the agent's implications, but also realized the fact that plays with large cast were often rejected for production, with the exception of those by well-known playwrights like Shakespeare, and emerging African playwrights like Wole Soyinka, whose nascent works, producers felt, were worth promoting.

Problem of unfamiliarity with the terrain was also a deterrent, which Leslie's father seemed to have also implied. BBGD's position on that had always been: "If Africans could labor over Shakespeare and English setting to get familiar with it, surely certainly should the English or Western theatrical establishment over unfamiliar but interesting works set in Africa." The imbalance was obnoxiously remarkable and his position was probably justified, since these literary agents and producers were capable of saying anything on their own turf,

It was on this question of terrain that he felt Athol Fugard, being a South African (although white) might be more sensitive to *The Union* in a positive way. Thus, he gave him the script to read. He was also encouraged to give the Afrikaner the play as a possible production for the new Ijinle Company. To his surprise, after a week or two, Athol gave him back the script although with an encouraging remark in terms of the writing: "Yes, the play has promise, and it could be considered for production later. Let's wait and see."

The rehearsals for *Blood Knot*, *The Trials of Brother Jero*, and *The Strong Breed* had gone on for some weeks. *Blood Knot*, the longest play, was going to play for some nights and the other two plays would show for the rest of the production. Since Zakes and Athol had before played the only two characters of *Blood Knot* in South Africa, it did not need much rehearsals. At any rate, both Athol and Zakes could work separately in their own time. The two shorter Soyinka plays, each had quite a number of characters; as such they were the main focus of the rehearsals.

About two weeks before the opening, there was dissension in the company, which welled up and boiled over all of a sudden. Some amateur members of the company had grouped around a ring leader, who found out that the three professionals in the company, Jumoke Adebayo, Zakes Mokae, and BBGD were being paid by the Transcription Centre. The group leader had recently come from Nigeria but had been in Soyinka's Orisun Theater Company. In that respect, he considered himself also a professional and therefore convinced the group that the only way to get attention and therefore express an equitable right was to go on rehearsal strike. The sudden initial loss of actors at rehearsals got the attention all right. The director, explaining the reason for the loss, let the three professionals get a whiff of the situation. He then had a meeting with the dissenters.

Before the altercation, BBGD had been rehearsing key roles in the two plays. He had almost mastered the first, Chume in *The Trials*, and was getting the hang of Eman in *The Strong Breed*, the play that the strike critically affected. One of dissenters was playing opposite him as his wife; without her, the development of his character was almost hopeless. For this unnecessary interruption, he was simply beside himself and didn't fail to make his feelings felt.

Three or four rehearsals went by without her or any of the others, and the production was in danger of not opening. In the meantime Athol was talking between the dissenters and the Transcription Centre to no avail. Dennis Duerden, its director, stood his ground not to pay them, but was also trying to resolve the issue the best he could. Then it seemed the group was broken up and some of its members were willing to come back, knowing the implications of their continued absence. Athol then had a critical meeting with BBGD and the other professionals.

"Well, they want to come back," Athol confirmed. "The question is whether you all want them back at this stage, given the limited time we have. *The Trials* is intact and almost ready; *The Strong Breed* needs a great deal of work, which is possible with rigorous rehearsals." He made BBGD aware that it was mostly his call and he, the director, was willing to work with him and get him through before opening.

BBGD did not quite like being put on the spot, so to speak, although he understood why the director turned to him. He had begun to get an idea of the play but he was far from being comfortable with the part. He would prefer the director had simply made the decision of letting the dissenters back and working diligently with him. He probably would have accepted the challenge and responsibility. He toiled over the issue and what he still had to accomplish in less than two weeks—really two weekends, when they could get everybody to rehearse. His characters were his first professional roles and he knew he had to be at his best, especially on the opening night. He was quite comfortable with Chume in *The Trials*, given the incident that happened one rehearsal night, when Athol remarked he gave a virtuoso performance. Looking back at the decision he made, he regarded himself as young and naïve, innocent and new to the fact of professionalism. For, he got chicken and decided with the director that it was wise to drop *The Strong Breed*.

In hindsight, he felt it was probably a bad decision. He had allowed his anger with the dissenters to get the better of him with, subconsciously, a bit of vengeful streak. The rebels, he felt, needed to be taught a lesson, especially their ring leader, who was playing an important role in that play. He remembered the woman that was to play his wife came to beg him so the two shows could go on as planned. Jumoke Adebayo also reasoned with him, although she realized the burden that was on him. In spite of this, his decision was negative and Athol accepted it without any hesitation. If he had deliberated with care on the implications of what came to be a substitute for *The Strong*

111

Breed, he probably would have reconsidered. *The Trials* was double-billed with Chris MacGregor's South African Jazz Band. Obviously good on its own terms, but the jazz band, in reality, was not consistent with the theatrical Nigerian play. The audience, who did not fail to see this dichotomy, felt let down. When BBGD realized his probable mistake, it was too late; his decision could not be undone.

His naïve decision in fact had played into a probable objective of Athol. On the one hand his acceptance of BBGD's decision might have been innocent. However, an ulterior motive could be evident. As a developing playwright who was also trying to get a footing on the international scene, he might not have wanted to be upstaged, a consequence that the Soyinka plays might have affected. A double-bill with a jarring jazz band would seem to diminish the due recognition of a Nigerian playwright, who had to share that recognition not just with a South African playwright but a South African Jazz band. For to all appearances, the project was South African.

BBGD's rationalizing and deliberating postmortem did not quell his mind. For quite some time, he felt the guilt, especially given the audience dissatisfaction, not with the production of *Jero*, but with what the program used to double-bill it. He wished they could have seen him in two contrasting performances that would probably have launched his debut more remarkably. He was young and naïve, but he had to move on.

"I heard…from Heinemann," Cosmo Pieterse indicated during a break in the rehearsal of a radio play at the BBC, sometime after the production of *The Trials*. He wanted BBGD's plays to be published together to make one of Heinemann's educational series. "The editor was very interested. But he felt you still need to develop as a playwright before Heinemann could give you such a prominence. I don't agree with him of course, because I still feel those plays could stand on their own."

Before BBGD could get dismayed over the rejection, Cosmo struck an alternative ray of hope. "However, I'm striving to put *The Game* and *Abiku* in separate collections. I think this would work. In fact, I'm certain it would work."

"You mean, in a collection of other African plays?" BBGD creased a smile for the hope, although wished he could see his plays published on their own.

"I still wish to keep *The Union* though, if you don't mind. I think it can still be published on its own."

BBGD thanked Cosmo for his efforts and decided to leave the script with him, perchance his intentions succeeded. He was of two minds about this. A play is meant for the stage, and as such he would have preferred seeing it on stage. However, publishing the play, he felt, might be a good alternative and faster way of bringing attention to the work. It would have been better if Athol Fugard had taken up the play and at least do a workshop of it, so he could hear it and do necessary revisions on it. Such a workshop would have been possible through the Transcription Centre if the playwright/director had backed up the proposition; he only needed to tell Dennis Duerden who brought him to London. That was why BBGD was convinced it had to do with the problem of diverting attention from the promotion of Athol's own plays.

Yet, one must wonder how the Afrikaner worked underground with black actors in South Africa to evolve a workable play, except that the effort to collaborate also favored his playwriting. BBGD was convinced it was a kind of strategic exploitation of the black that promoted his work. In London, Athol did not have apartheid to capitalize on black actors. There was no need for off-the-government-radar workshops. It was a matter of not getting upstaged in the promotion of any play other than his own. The unfamiliarity with the terrain of *The Union* also might have to do with it. But it would not be unthinkable, BBGD was convinced, to locate in Zulu culture a dramatic incident similar to that in the play, a situation which the Afrikaner, indeed the climate of Apartheid, had no interest in, or sought to destroy.

*****

He was present at the rehearsal and production of *The Detainee*, a radio play written by WS. The play was inspired by the imprisonment of Obafemi Awolowo, the leader of the opposition party to the ruling government of Tafawa Balewa, the first Prime Minister of Nigeria. The opposition leader was accused of plotting to overthrow the national government. The play dramatized life in prison as suffered by Mr. Awolowo, with its two characters, Konu played by Soyinka himself, and Zimole, played by his friend, Banjo Solaru.

The play, even with its humorous moments, had moved BBGD immensely. It projected Awolowo as an astute and witty political leader that was unjustly imprisoned. BBGD didn't fully understand the ramifications of the political charges levied against the stalwart, for whom there was no court hearing. But he felt the playwright well demonstrated the injustices of the imprisonment. The play's treatment also revealed WS as a dogged lifelong supporter and campaigner for the leader and his efforts to expose a corrupt system.

BBGD had always admired his mentor's political activism, but did not see himself in that direction nor did he feel he had such a clout. As a creative piece, he felt *The Detainee* was worthy of emulation, but as a political engagement, he could only admire it at a remove, disinclined to negotiate an effective activist perspective.

When he was in Nigeria, before he came to the UK, he had witnessed the undercurrents of political campaigns, some of which were backed with competitive thuggery by the campaigning parties, what he was later to compare with American mud-slings and "marrow-slush" diggers, his coinage. He was fascinated by all these, including the stump speeches on soap boxes and the broadcasts projected through loudspeakers on top of moving trucks and cars. Apparently, these political cacophonies were mere highlights of the things to come after Independence; their destructive surges didn't begin to erupt until after he left for further studies abroad.

In London, as a non-eyewitness of these violent and inhuman conditions resulting in so many loss of lives, he could not imagine enough the senselessness and recklessness that had gripped his country and Africa as a whole. At any rate, he was much consumed by new academic and creative challenges among new friends, and news that brushed his ears about the critical developments at home created no immediate stir.

Something happened in two successive hits that jumpstarted his political consciousness and gradually imposed on his creative senses. The first was when he read and heard on the news media that a certain person held up at gunpoint the victory speech of the apparently illegal Premier of Western Nigeria, Samuel Ladoke Akintola (alias SLA). It was alleged that the gunman was the activist Wole Soyinka. At that first break into his consciousness, he dismissed the news, for he could not perceive his mentor was capable of such an act, unless the incident was simply a humorous scare-tactic of a jokester that he knew WS could be.

Then upon hearing the playwright had disappeared from his residence and was being sought by the authorities, BBGD became more engaged and was on tenterhooks for some days. But when WS turned himself in and denied the accusation, he affirmed his belief and conclusions that the incident was a political ploy to label his mentor a criminal. On second thoughts, judging by the little he knew about the vicious political leader that stole the elections, he went on to acquit whoever committed the justified crime, even if it were WS.

The second time the political hit occurred, its impact on BBGD was more critical and serious. It was during the Nigerian civil war when the playwright-activist was accused of siding with the enemy, the secessionist Biafra. It was an apparent false accusation of treason that landed him in the dangerous life of prison for almost two years, in the maximum security of General Gowon, the war Head of State. The attention the incident got in the West activated many demonstration marches in London, some against the treatment of Biafrans by the Nigerian opponent, some against the war itself. In general, the demonstrations urged the British government to use its influence to stop the war; but more important for BBGD was the rallying drive to release of the poet-playwright from prison. It was one of those marches passing through Piccadilly Square and in front of the Eagle Star Insurance building that made Michael Bloom incite BBGD to join the protesters. He had tried to conceal, in front of the co-worker, his position and relationship with the obvious victim of the unjust imprisonment, and thereby had repressed his emotional affect. But the incident touched him to a political hilt as to what to do, that is, aside from joining the march, which his strong disposition would not allow him to do.

The Detainee effortlessly resurfaced and nudged his creative mind. Somehow the play seemed to suggest a certain premonition of the fate of its author. Judging by his extraordinary wit, the prisoner, Konu, fitted the playwright's character, like a habit worn, more than the character of the politician he had implied. "Like a habit worn," a phrase BBGD probably coined from the work of the other WS, the Bard of Stratford-upon-Avon; he would come back to it and explain it in greater detail in *Poetics of the Creative Process*, the playwriting text he later wrote. But, moved by the play, BBGD felt compelled that his mentor deserved something similar from him, a response that was effective if not equally political, a small but functional way to make his voice of protest be heard.

He resisted re-reading *The Detainee* for many reasons. For one, he did not want to be influenced too much, which might impede his creativity; however, he realized some influence would normally creep in, which would be natural as opposed to forced. At any rate, some of the allusions in the play eluded him, since he was far away from the political scene in Nigeria. He had gathered only what he could from newspapers, or stories from friends. He had also gathered some facts, all too briefly, from the horse's mouth when he saw him at the BBC recording studio and afterwards went out to have dinner with him and Mr. Banjo.

BBGD wanted his play to be as tight as *The Detainee* with two main characters, but that was about all of his conscious influence. At the time, much of the intellectual dialogue going on between Konu and Zimole went well above his head, just as he would imagine with, perhaps, much of the shortwave radio listeners. For the in-jokes and referents between the two characters would probably be difficult to conceive by the listener in a radio set-up. But he admired the writing, which encouraged him to think of different circumstances and strategies for his own characters. The result was his play *Tortoise*, and the action between the witty prisoner, whose death seemed to be a matter of fate, and the rather bombastic prison guard, Kuru.

He had read about what the Nigerian government had accused his mentor of—siding with the enemy by arranging to deploy arms to the leader of the Biafrans, whose friend he was. BBGD had found that allegation very hard to believe. If anything, according to some reports, and WS's testimony, he was trying to find ways and means of resolving the war between the two factions. That rendering would be more like the truth. What he couldn't understand was why there were no persistent protests from the prisoner's supposed friends, intellectual as well as political, an endeavor that should support his innocence and therefore demand his prompt release. However, BBGD could not be too certain about what had been or was being done, especially in secret, such that had come to inform the international public and writers to sign a petition for his release. Also, more importantly, he realized the military was operating with different set of rules, which might have made things very difficult for anybody that had wanted to open their protesting mouth wide enough to get caught. He concluded that was why his mentor was singular and different. As activist, WS would do anything for a friend he believed in, even if it meant risking his life. Case in point was his voice and action of protest against the government, on account of the politician he implied in *The Detainee*.

He wanted to reflect all the dramatic stirrings of his mind in *Tortoise*. As a playwright, he had learnt that no idea could become realized by brooding for too long on it. He had to confront the two main characters he had in mind on the blank page before the action of the drama could evolve. As it happened, borrowing an idea from Brothers Capek's *The Insect Play*, he used two oppositional armies of ants to represent the two warring parties of the civil war. They functioned, with a tongue-in-cheek humor, all in the imaginary and rather delirious mind of the prisoner, probably through his hunger strike. In antagonistic conflict with his thoughts grew Kuru, the constantly interrupting buffoon of a prison guard, whose boss has refused to grant the intellectual prisoner his request for a novel, or such mind-enlightening and therapeutic books. Instead, he has been provided children's books. The delirium builds to a hallucination sequence where his former friends (represented by Poet and Politik) jeer at what they imply as the egotistic intellectualism of the prisoner's clever mind (like Tortoise's, the Yoruba folkloric character) and therefore deny him the much-needed support. Through such cleverness, jolted by the prisoner's reverie, it seems the guard would finally fall prey to his wits and grant him his request of writing implements, in lieu of the novel. It is at that point that the hysterical laughter of the gun-happy guard mistakenly pulls the trigger and kills his prisoner.

BBGD had toiled with that ending, but fearing such accidents could happen to his imprisoned mentor, he justified it and hoped it would never happen.

Although he couldn't keep the play to two characters, he was satisfied with the outcome of a writing that took only about a week to write, incorporating all his thoughts. He realized it was the prisoner's hallucination that had brought all the other characters within the tightness of the main action. It was a necessary extension that also demonstrated his dramatic influences from his expanded knowledge of Greek drama at Rose Bruford, through the works of authors such as Euripides and Aristophanes.

*****

The production of *The Trials of Brother Jero*, limited as it was in terms of BBGD's performance versatility, went on to offer unexpected rewards. News came from Athol Fugard that the Royal Court Theater had included *The Lion and the Jewel* in its 1968-69 season, although not to be directed by Athol Fugard, who had to go back to South Africa. But first, Bill Gaskill, the Artistic Director of the Royal Court, who saw *The Trials* was drawn to the idea of using Africans in Shakespeare's *Macbeth*, in which the late Sir Alec Guinness was to play Macbeth and the French actress, the late Simone Signoret, Lady Macbeth. They went to have a formal audition at the Theater and got offered the roles of the witches—Jumoke Debayo as the First Witch, BBGD as the Second and Zakes Mokae as the Third. Additionally, both Zakes and BBGD were to play the Second and Third Murderer respectively. Before that production ended, BBGD got offered the role of Lakunle and Jumoke Debayo, Sadiku in *The Lion*, and rehearsals were underway.

Through these productions, *The Trials*, *Macbeth*, and *The Lion*, BBGD easily saw his future in professional theater in London, especially as the civil war in Nigeria continued to rage, preventing him from going home any time soon.

Scenes Six

"Happy That I Am Black:" Fields of Discrimination

One of the drama exercises WS tendered to the small number of friends that first constituted the 1960 Masks was his poem *The Telephone Conversation.* BBGD at the time didn't quite understand the significance of its experience, except that it was a funny piece that was written by its author when he was in England. As a matter of fact, he had read it somewhere before, probably as a feature in the *Daily Times* or *Sunday Times*; but not understanding it, he did not give it much thought. At the drama workshop, he wasn't asked to participate in the reading of the poem, probably because of his naivety or shyness—and he thanked his stars he wasn't asked. But he listened to the others, the poet's more immediate peers, such as Yemi Lijadu and Ralph Opara, both working as Heads of Drama and Talks, respectively, at the Nigerian Broadcasting Service, where the informal workshop of exercises often took place.

Hearing it many times in succession of course made a lot of difference. With each repetition and discussion, he was able to understand it more and more, although the full monty still escaped him. He would remain mystified until he got to London, when he became conversant with the experience, partly through entering some of the telephone booths in Bayswater and seeing the writings and phone numbers all over the inside walls. What he understood at the workshop gave him a general idea—thanks to the different renditions of the piece—involving a telephone conversation between a black African and a white British presence. That much he got. The significance of "HOW DARK? ARE YOU LIGHT/ OR VERY DARK?" was totally beyond his experience. But, given the various inflections demanded by the poem, he later realized that it worked very well as a dialogic acting exercise. He presumed all those who read simply assumed everybody else knew what was going on. And perhaps some didn't quite grasp it but just went on to laugh hilariously at the images being rendered.

BBGD was not curious enough to ask the writer or his friends about it, but not because he felt he would not be told. It was simply because of his own inhibitions, ignorance, and inadequacy—shortcomings that he felt he should have some control over rather than betray them, as he sometimes did. Certainly he wouldn't have asked in front of somebody like Yemi Lijadu, whose smirk looks and response BBGD had already conjectured: "Yes, you wouldn't know that, would you, old boy? This experience is meant only for your seniors! You needed to have been in England to know what it's all about." But had the joker himself been to that country and had the experience? BBGD would very much like to know; he doubted it.

The poem, with its various renditions, especially one given by the poet himself, was to remain very much with him through his London days and beyond, its implications mutating to other forms or patterns of the same idea.

BBGD could easily make telephone calls from his student-hostel, The Methodist International House, in Bayswater. He didn't often have many calls to make anyway. In fact, aside from his friend, Ayo Craig, living some tube miles away in Kentish Town, he had no reason to call anybody. Rather, he had quite enough to fill up his leisure and conversational moments at the hostel, talking to various student-tenants like him, especially the women, and sometimes playing Scrabble with them. But he had stumbled on this particular kiosk near the hostel by accident.

One Sunday, after church and a hearty lunch of pork roast, baked potatoes and green beans, some homesick student, of rich Nigerian parents, had held up the hostel's phone booth, waiting for a call from Nigeria to come through in order continue her conversation, presumably with Mum and Dad. It had to be at the time he was expecting a call from Ayo, to discuss whether they should meet in Bayswater, Kentish Town, or somewhere else. Ayo might have tried to call him during the Nigerian call and, with no luck, might also be waiting to hear from BBGD, equally with no success. He was quite flustered when the Nigerian call came through for the student that he decided to go outside to give Ayo a call.

Down the road from the hostel, away from Bayswater Road and almost at the corner of Inverness Terrace and Westbourne Park Road was a telephone kiosk he had discovered. He had passed by a few times on his way to the Westbourne Park Odeon cinema. He decided he would rather go and slot a few pennies to make the call than wait for, God knows when, the Nigerian student to finish talking to her parents, whose money after all was being squandered for the call rather than hers.

It was the first time he would enter one of these red boxes. A cautious, nervous pull at the door availed his nostrils at once to a mixed whiff of tobacco, beer and, urine smell. Urine?! How could that possibly be, in this prime city of

Her Majesty's kingdom? Especially so, since back in high school they had always been taught by one teacher or the other about hygiene and the barbaric nature of peeing in public places other than the specified latrines—a violation which happened anyway but which he somewhat took for granted. For why not, if the pressure happened at desperate times, at some corner with dirt or grass, or areas with small bushes or open gutters. Sure enough, such colonial imperatives went out the window of legal obedience after Independence—that is, about two or three years after the pretentious settling in of the neo-colonials, after which they began to show their true colors and the country went berserk. As far as he knew, only a lunatic, during the colonial era, would think of a telephone kiosk as a veritable place for unburdening the involuntary pressures of his or her bladder.

Thus came his first unexpected but informative shock in, no less, the capital of the old colonial home country. Equally startling was the littered inside walls of the kiosk, graffitied with racist barbs, such as "Nigger go home," "Blacks not wanted here," and invitational notes to call certain numbers. Two especially caught his eye, "Majorie is available, call…" "Need a blowjob? I'm round the corner, call…" "Are you a voyeur? Call…"

He figured out the invitations in general, but a "blowjob" was something he was not familiar with. What is a blowjob? Something involving the blacksmith's bellows or a blowtorch? It didn't seem to make any sense. Blow what? And what goes on with a voyeur… A voyage of sorts…? He couldn't wait to ask Ayo; his friend had been in London some months before him, and also more experienced in these things.

However, one thing that had dawned on him, and he was sure of it, was that the kiosk was similar to the one represented in WS's poem. In fact, he had instantly recalled it at the first surveying and gloating that his eyes had applied around the kiosk as he entered. It all made physical sense, adding to the depth of his experience of the poem. What of course needed to be done was to call any of those numbers, to have the total experience. But he couldn't bring his cowardly mind to act upon that curiosity. He would rather wait for more enlightenment from his friend.

"Ayo… Yah, some Nija-woman was hugging the phone for a call from her parents… You were just about to leave home? Great… Okay, I'll be waiting… No, I'm calling from a telephone kiosk…not far from the hostel…just wanted to know if you're coming… Yah, yah, yah, they're all waiting for you in the nurses' quarter. Yah, look for me in their lounge…probably playing Scrabble with some of them… Okay, see you soon."

The hostel was full of ironies, and the nurses' quarter was one of them. You entered the building through a thick Victorian oak-framed glass door. One of the students might open the door, especially if a visitor was expected. Otherwise, it would be one of the two house matrons, or Miss Porter, the old director herself, who immediately asked for your quest. To the immediate left inside was a visitor's book that you had to sign, establishing your presence and objective within the hostel. Then the next door on the left, a few feet away along the hallway, was the entrance to the nurses' quarter, the door of which opened into the lounge upon descending two or three steps. Far right end of the lounge was a door that led to the rooms.

The quarter was inhabited not only by temporary tenant-nurses; a few somewhat mature female vacationers also occupied the rooms. Being more mature than regular students, the quarter-tenants had a kind of flexibility as to their movements, although the matrons, certainly Miss Porter, didn't expect any of the rooms to be invaded by the opposite sex. Or, if they knew of such invasions, as sometimes happened, they might choose to pretend not to know, or at least reprimand the violator. For, who indeed, one might consider, could prevent what went on between two consenting adults, since an offending male visitor could swiftly disappear from the often-unwatched lounge into his intended hostess room? The important thing was not to catch or be caught red-handed.

The main lounge of the hostel, further on to the right of the hallway, could boast of no such concealment. It was wide open and always within the eye-reach of the matrons, who placed their office directly opposite, and next to the main stairs that led up to the student rooms on the second and third floors. Even then, things sometimes went on between consenting students within the hostel, things that the matrons didn't know or pretended not to know. By contrast, the nurses' quarter presented far better possibilities, which both students and nurses often took great advantage of.

BBGD would rather find himself in the nurses' lounge than the main one. Ayo met him there as they agreed over the phone, and as usual, he was playing Scrabble with three other people, one of them a nurse from Bermuda. As soon as Ayo came in, his roving eyes were on the woman.

"*Omo Forgor!*" they accosted each other with their customary appellation. Translated roughly with its implied meaning—Kid Forger (that is, dissembler apropos women). Scrabbled eyes lifted for a moment from the board and the small bracket-tray of letter-pellets. Not recognizing the intruder as a fellow hostel tenant, they simply fell back on their preoccupation.

"A new *Ajereke* is she? Is she?" Ayo, without any compunction, went on to suggest the likely origins of the nurse in Yoruba language, assuming she was from somewhere in the West Indies.

121

Again the Scrabble team cast an involuntary glance, this time at the dictates of their ears because of their unfamiliarity with the uttered language of the intruder, a language that was no doubt far removed from the attuned spoken language in the hostel. But, again, they nonchalantly refocused their attention on to the game.

"Yah," BBGD emitted a reluctant grunt, swiftly casting his eyes around, as if to ascertain nobody else understood the language. On principle he disliked this frequent attitude of his compatriots, like Ayo, who insisted on using their language to conceal meaning or secret information from unintended ears. Case in point was the derogatory word Ayo used that labelled the West Indians as sugarcane eaters. He was always forced into an embarrassing position among such other friends or acquaintances. People should say what they needed to say in a language understood by everybody around; otherwise what is not intended for other ears should be left unsaid until time and place allowed—that was always his polite position.

"Draw an extra chair here and let me finish this game," he motioned, keeping his eyes on his letter-pellets. Ayo looked around, went on to grab a chair and came back to plant himself between his friend and the nurse.

BBGD hoped Ayo would not attempt to fan and disturb the elegant lady's ears with inquisitive questions, such that would advance familiarity and hasten the eventual invitation to the cinema house and hopefully to various exploits of intimacy. He hoped his friend would be patient to hear his own assessment of the lady before jumping into an awkward move that might be very embarrassing. And he would entertain no prodding in Yoruba, either.

Her name was Maquella and was on vacation from the British island of Bermuda. First time ever BBGD had been struck consciously by such a name, a woman's and from that part of the islands. Something of the country immediately rang a bell, from their high school geography class. But as far as the name Maquella was concerned, that was a first. No name like that had ever crossed his path let alone his ears. But with due respect, the rhythm of the name rang well in his ears. Associating it with the face and body, he felt it was fitting, and, placed against her light-skinned beauty, it was all the more somewhat enchanting. That latter factor was what drew his attention towards her in the first place, that is, the very day he saw her, presumably in the lounge the second day she arrived.

As such, BBGD himself had had designs on her, a situation that Ayo would need to know and respect, whenever he had the time to tell him. Even then, he knew when his friend learnt this fact of the circumstance, it would not be the end of the story. Hence, he was prepared.

"Well, how was it?" Ayo almost immediately pestered him further when BBGD dropped the coin. As naïve as he was with intimacy, he knew exactly what Ayo was gaming towards. No, he hadn't tried to seduce her, and Ayo knew he was always very slow about that—an approach or attitude for which he sometimes blamed his restricted upbringing. But he also put some blame on WS, from whom he could have learnt but did not, probably compelled by the awareness of his parents' imperatives.

"Omo Forgor, what are you waiting for?" predictably, Ayo demanded. "Okay, how many times have you gone out with her?"

"Twice."

"So, what more do you want?"

"Let me do things my own way."

"Yah, until she goes back to Bermuda."

Come to think on it, that word rang another bell apart from his encounter of it in the Geography class. There was a British warship that bore that name— the HMS Bermuda—one of the few World War II vessels that somehow found themselves in the Port of Lagos, and was proudly opened to the confounded wonder and bedazzlement of the public at the superiority of the British race.

They got to the telephone kiosk before the sparse autumn light faded to dark. BBGD had arrested his friend's curiosity, although Ayo, as the more experienced, seemed to have had some knowledge of the situation. The tiresome "Go back home, Nigger" ads were few and were easily ignored, as their eyes roved to something more striking. Apparently posted by "The Countess" who would like a visit from "Johnny," whoever that was, BBGD queried.

"People like us," Ayo pointed out. "You know, 'Johnny just come,'" referring to the familiar phrase that, back home, called attention to the ignorant sailor or white man just landed in town.

"How so?" BBGD was not convinced.

"Just think about it. We are like the ignorant visitor just arrived in London and looking for, you know."

The ad went on to state her features: "Blonde, sweet, and hot. A few minutes away."

"Shall we try it?" Ayo located the phone number, scrawled at the bottom of her name. Before BBGD could say anything definitive, contemplating with a few staccatoed "Hmmm…errr…" Ayo had fed the box with two pennies, and started dialing, making any "Okay" from BBGD redundant.

A few rings on the other side finally clicked a connection.

"Hello," a soft alluring voice answered. "Dollie here."

Ayo flick a nervous look at BBGD, and queried in a whisper, "Dollie?" Then quickly returning to the mouth-piece, with a stammer: "Is-is-is that the Countess?"

"Speaking…" The voice, detecting an unwanted accent at the other end, suddenly became unsure. "W-Who are you?" Ayo, not exactly knowing what to say was silent for a few seconds. "Are you responding to the ad in a telephone kiosk?" The voice wanted to make more determination.

"Y-Yes," Ayo became encouraged. "W-Where are you located?" he added.

It was enough words to sense the intruder's speech pattern. "Are you Negroid?"

"N-no." Ayo refused to classify himself with the word that they had, in high school, associated with the American Negro. "I am African," he proudly affirmed.

The telephone without any ambiguity clicked off to the disengaged drone.

"What…?" Ayo flicked a mystified glance at BBGD.

"She hung up?" BBGD asked.

"I'm not sure. I'm going to call her back."

"You want to waste another money?"

Ayo fed the box again with two more pennies. Again a connection was made.

"Hello?" answered again the soft voice.

"Is that the Countess?" It was a mistake Ayo could not have avoided making, for his speech pattern, again, became evident. But this time, instead of a response, the phone clicked off with more emphasis, as if to tell the caller to buzz off.

Illumination had suddenly dawned on BBGD even before the second call. The whole meaning of his mentor's poem creased a knowing smile on his face. But that knowledge was to grow incrementally and to dog him through his acting career in England, beginning with his training at the Rose Bruford College, what with all the names he acquired, such as nig-nog, darkie, and woolly-head.

*****

It had become increasing clear to his tutors at Lamorbey Park, perhaps a veritable pseudonym for the training college, indicating the beautiful grounds on which it sat. It had become relatively clear that BBGD had some acting talent lurking within him and their British curiosity was fascinated by and wanted to explore it. This of course did not mean they were willing to let this captivation compromise their notions of his speech, which seemed to be registering a strong "African" pattern, both in diction and delivery. It was a blemish that must be eradicated, or at least coerced into semblances of the Queen's English within the three years of his training. As he would find, it was a challenge they apparently failed to surmount, try as BBGD strove to convince them.

Reports of this talent went to Bru herself, and she seemed to take special interests in watching him during her mime (really movement) classes. Sometimes, her watch was so obvious that it became somewhat embarrassing for the young student to contain, even though he enjoyed the attention.

"Stop," her Quaker voice would halt present exercise and students into the stillness that simultaneously pervaded the air. The hiatus made the nostrils more sensitive to the light odors coming from energized private parts that might have been left untreated to showers that morning. "Henry," she would continue, as if he had been the culprit, "I want you to move across the room the way you did just then. I want you all to watch him."

And BBGD did, although he didn't see what the hoopla was all about, the sense of urgency that she called attention to. As far as he knew, whatever was striking in his movement, or its appearance, he had executed without any effort. Or, as Bru would like to point out, the deceptive effortlessness was full of the required urgency the exercise needed. For it was a stage practice that everybody should emulate, the nimbleness of his African feet.

At other times, the hash-tagged embarrassment was calling attention to the too serious face of BBGD: "Smile, come on smile, show us your white African teeth."

He had often wondered, with ironic amusement, whether this reminder was, in reality, to signify the signified—the desirable whiteness that British teeth nakedly lacked! He would reluctantly break his lips into a teeth-smile, not because he needed to respond to the command of Bru-authority, but because the very idea always tickled him to the ribs. Yes, he felt proud of the fact that he had taken care of his teeth, every morning and evening with Kolynos, although he preferred the traditional chewing stick, which, back home, he had applied along with the colonial import. But he had always doubted the implied whiteness, which he felt was often exaggerated, unless of course it was being compared with some of the ragged teeth he had seen spiking British gums. What tickled him the most was the boasted fact of being British. Back home the colonials preached clean teeth, displaying sparkles of white teeth with Kolynos on billboards, at the cinema and on television screens. Yet, coming to the home country, that whiteness had failed to meet his expectations—an ironic matter of "physician heal thyself"?

Much worse was the fact of body hygiene that pummeled the ears of pupils of his colonial upbringing, a datum which proved an ironic contrast to what he experienced in England and among his Rose Bruford colleagues. Perhaps, as they often argued, it was the case of the weather, the cold climes that made bathing every morning an unnecessary exercise. But even then…

BBGD fell into that trap, but made sure he took care of his armpits and privates. Not so the colleagues he shared digs with. They got up, washed their faces, made semblances of brushing their teeth, undid their pajamas only to go into the same underwear and school clothes, combed their hair, and then into the dining room for breakfast and then out to school. Actually, in the first digs he lived, they had to feed the meter with pennies for the hot water to shower, which sometimes made showering every morning very difficult. He understood that. But he felt it was a disadvantage carried to extremity by some of his peers and other encounters.

"You have a deceptive harsh face," Bru raised a concern to BBGD once in her office. He had come for the end-of-term assessment of his performance. "All your teachers seem to agree on this. You should smile more. Come on, smile, smile…"

BBGD obeyed, as usual quite amused.

"Yes, yes," she applauded, lacing a quiet, somewhat sarcastic smile on her cheeks. "That's how I want to see your face light up, with your nice white African teeth. It makes all the difference."

Lamorbey Park. Acres of land, partitioned in sections by low cut-stone fences, at the center of which sat the Rose Bruford College (now the Rose Bruford College of Theater & Performance), a property of the Kent educational system leased to the college. BBGD, like most students, lived within walking distance from the park gates. Through these, he travelled every school day along the pathway of hedges and trees that led to the open center-area, well-manicured and landscaped around the 18th century Manor house which overlooked Lamorbey Lake. In Spring and Summer, the beauty of the lake was accentuated by pigeons, swimming ducks and white swans, suggesting a peacefulness and serenity that made meditation and learning a joyful experience.

Rose Bru's foresight must be commended, for making the location accessible to a teaching and acting education. BBGD was quick to learn that it was a place festooned with acting inspiration, and where words of the dialogue could easily be transported to and retained in memory. That truth was maintained, even with the distraction of sandwich lunches that brought many students to lie, recline, kiss and sunbathe on the manicured lawn. He wrote to his mentor about this, and the fact that he probably chose wisely, opting for the acting training instead of the literary commitments of an academic institution. That was his first intention and the reason why he pursued the GRE at the North Western Polytechnic. He opted for Bru after one year of the two-year university preparation when an opportunity presented itself to gain a Nigerian scholarship in drama, which his brother advised he should apply for at once. Having a previous communication with the college in Nigeria, during his nascent years of acting with the 1960 Masks, helped. He simply reestablished communication with Lamorbey Park. Ms. Hendricks, the registrar, remembered his letters. It was also easy for the college to accept him with a ready source of training budget in form of his scholarship.

It was during such times, in his second year, that he basked in the serene atmosphere of the manicured lawn overlooking the lake. There he was, taking that advantage to allow the serene treasures of the lake to secure the lines of Othello into his head, whispered, analyzed, synthesized and given various interpretations of utterance. Mrs. Baker, his year-two acting instructor, had tolerated her curiosity to win her over to choose Othello for the acting challenges of her potentially talented student, for the end-of-term productions. Leo Baker, her husband and the Director of Acting, was one of the old West End directors. Both husband and wife came two or three times a week from their London apartment to engage the students with their professional abilities.

"Yes," Betsy Baker had affirmed, customarily sounding the "s" with light upper-class spread between her English teeth "Yes, I think Othello will be wonderful for you."

Moi? The inner response was at first both overwhelming and terrifying. Overwhelming in a rather joyful way, but terrifying because of the challenge it posed, especially so, since the other two African students became envious. Alton, the South African, to all appearances was the college's favorite African student. Apart from the fact that his country was of particular interest to Britain both in terms of Apartheid and its diamond and game resources, he seemed to have come with a history of professional theater behind him. It was the production of King Kong that had brought him to London in the first place, after which he was given a ready asylum. Then later on, he had secured a British government scholarship to study at Rose Bruford. Thus, by instincts, BBGD's friend might have felt the role of Othello should have come to him.

"Tsho-tsho-loza…tsho-tsho-lozaa…kulezondawo…" struck, in BBGD's head, the Zulu songs and gum-boot dances that made Alton Kumalo an admirable student among his peers and teachers at Bru. End-of-year celebrations usually made the students turn to the three African students to display their African talent in the nature of rhythmic movement, "weird" songs, and "wild" dances. BBGD couldn't be brought to participate in such endeavors, the jungle antics they had imagined, no matter how much they implored him.

Apart from the fact of his anathema of bringing unnecessary attention to himself, and he had always claimed to be an inhibited introvert, he simply knew of no such "wild" dances expected of him by students and faculty. Even if he knew, he had no intentions of making a fool of himself, since he had never been given to such dances in the past. Not even to his traditional Yoruba dances, which he never regarded as wild—even the rigorous body-twists and shoulder punctuations demanded by the batá drums of Sango, the Yoruba thunder-god. Rather, he had regarded himself out of reach of those graceful rhythmic traditional movements that undulated the buttocks of women and tweaked their legs in complex foot-working patterns. The type of wild capers that his peers desired had been informed by Hollywood movies such that he himself had seen, dances usually attributed more to the "bush Negroes" of the Central, East and Southern Africa, rarely the West, let alone the Yoruba culture. But perhaps the nearest to "wild" he had physically seen were some of the dances from Eastern Nigeria, usually featured in the yearly Arts Festivals in Lagos, organized by the British colonial government. Even then, those dances, as far as BBGD was concerned, were more intricately graceful; hardly jungle-wild. In fact, his mentor incorporated such a dance, the Atilogwu, in the production of his commissioned first full-length play, *A Dance of the Forests*, in which BBGD had performed. He remembered his admiration of the dancers then, mesmerized by the intricacies of their movements, as their stringed kernel anklets jigged the ground to produce emphatic jingling rustles. Those were hardly "wild!"

The nearest BBGD had participated in the display of his Africanness, to feast the gloating eyes of Bruford's students and faculty, was when he succumbed to the implorations of his peers to wear something African to a Sunday reception by the lake. That was in his first naive year. The "costume" he wore (*sokoto, buba* and *agbada*-overall, with melding shades of black and red) was the only one he had brought from home but since buried in the drawer. He had with cautioning reluctance dug it up, wore it with combatting hesitation, and had eventually appeared, rather with uncomfortable awareness, on Lamorbey lawn with it, on a rare sunny hot day. The amusement of the gloaters was immediate:

"How wonderful!"
"What colorful fabric!"
"Wild colors."
"Is this your traditional costume?"

"You look different!"

"But isn't it wonderful?"

"Looks like a museum piece."

"What dance do they perform in these?"

"Can you please show us?"

"Please, please, show us"

"Don't you feel hot in these?"

The barrage was overwhelming and it proved BBGD's misgivings. That was the first and last of his attempt to strike a national pose among the Brus.

"Haply, that I am black
And hath not those soft speeches that chamberers have…"

BBGD was to recall again and again the fine lines of modest Othello's speeches from the scenes he performed. They set a tragic and ironic coda to the otherwise humorous and human experiences of discrimination he encountered with the white race along the paths of his career. On the modest space of the Rose Bruford's Barn Theater, he had made the connection between WS's "Telephone Conversation" and Othello's self-conscious agony. With his performance he had felt right, illuminated, compelled, supportive, somewhat vindicated. The compliments that had come to him from his peers and acting teachers, even if some of them sounded somewhat disingenuous, were satisfying in terms of the genuine passion he had felt for his Othello.

*****

The Trials of Brother Jero, directed by Athol Fugard, seen for the first time in London as a full production on a professional stage. Acclaimed by the theater critics, it was an eye-opener to many directors, that is, seeing the African as a veritable actor, and not as a savage or a commodity for servitude and all its implications. That notion of the African seemed to have been at the back of the minds of directors and casting agents, that is, in their frequent use of a black man on stage, as spear-carriers, servants, etc. As such, black man had been cast rarely in principal roles let alone as central characters. There might have been attempts in the past, here and there, at casting black in important roles—after all, one or two plays of Soyinka were workshopped or featured for one night at the Royal Court—but it was nothing consistent. Nothing like the production of *The Trials*, with a black or African ensemble, produced and critiqued on a somewhat large scale, and seen by a large audience over a period of a week or so. As implied, the production probably would not have happened were it not for the Transcription Centre and the presence of

Athol Fugard, a white South African, whose nascent career the organization really wanted to bring to the limelight in London. Hitherto, the Afrikaner's plays in South Africa had been in collaboration with black South Africans and therefore had been underground.

In terms of artistry, London audiences were able to see the capacities of the African as playwright and actor, whose personalities pitched beyond being that of subject or servant of the colonial master. One or two critics even compared the Nigerian WS to the English WS. They saw in their writing, along with those of other prominent white playwrights, such a Yeats, Singe and Beckett, similar inventive manipulation of the English language, rescuing that language from staleness and giving it fresher and invigorating countenance. Furthermore, the production of *The Trials* allowed the directors to begin thinking of experimenting with the black or African in Shakespeare plays, even if much of what their eyes could still see, imaged on the English stage, were supernumeraries and spear-carrying servants.

Some in the establishment foresaw, in their creative gaze, the rather dim objective and possibility of bringing into some degree of prominence the experience of underdeveloped black apprentice under the tutelage of his far-more developed white master. That seemed to be the direction of that distant light, seen through the dark tunnel, which informed the Royal Shakespeare Company to call for a general audition of prospective black actors. BBGD was unaware of this opportunity till too late, basking in the limelight of his Chume in *The Trials*. He knew nothing of it until the auditions were well over and his supposed friends, Alton Kumalo and Oscar James, had received the company's contracts for five years—much to his chagrin and envy.

"Why didn't I know anything about this?" he demanded some accountability from his agent.

"I didn't think it would be worth your while," she tried to console him, then went further to explain: "You're playing a principal role. To go from this to being a spear-carrier or servant—that's all they were interested in, I guarantee you."

The explanation did not quell his curiosity. He felt he should have been notified just the same and let the decision of making the audition rest with him. However, thinking more about it and the opportunity that came after his role of Chume, he knew that would have put him in a difficult position he often found himself—at the crossroads of fate with two equally good and possible desires tensing his mind. He was almost sure he would have hastily gone along with signing the RSC five-year contract, and heaven knows what jeopardy that would have caused regarding the other possibility.

Through Athol Fugard, Bill Gaskill, of the Royal Court Theater, got in touch with Mae Bleazard, for BBGD to audition for the role of a witch in *Macbeth*. While this did not compare with a five-year contract with the RSC, it was probably a less demeaning role than a spear-carrier, although he insisted his talents would probably have changed the minds of RSC directors to give him a more rewarding role. However, the production of *Macbeth* was also a VIP endeavor, to feature Sir Alec Guinness in the title role and Simone Signore as Lady Macbeth, which happened to be also an experimentation intention of the Royal Court. The deal with BBGD included the other principal actors of *The Trials*, Zakes Mokae and Jumoke Debayo, all making up the three Shakespeare's witches. Contrasting the roles for Zakes and BBGD were the First and Second Murderers. The Royal Court daring and challenge, probably never before seen on the British Stage, was exciting and worth it, even though the critics balked at the experimentation.

"You must be Femi Euba," came the resonating voice of Sir Alec as he glided up to the two actors that had just entered the rehearsal room rather gingerly. The celebrity actor's face was particularly focused on BBGD, who could only assume that the accosting was well directed. But how was this possible? Where had the eminent actor seen him before?

"Y-Yes." BBGD was bowled over on the inside, which resulted in his querulous look.

"Didn't you audition for *The Comedians*?"

"Y-Yes." Illumination began to dawn on BBGD, although still clouded in mystery. Yes, he did audition for the movie, apparently for the black lead, and he had heard that Sir Alec was going to feature in it. But, as far as he was concerned, he hadn't thought much about it, since the possibility of being chosen was beyond his wildest dreams.

"The director's a friend of mine," Sir Alec continued, his unblinking eyes gleaming with superior knowledge and certainty. "He liked your audition. He would be coming to see you on opening night."

"Oh, that's great... Thanks." That was all BBGD's bewilderment could afford him.

"Looking forward to working with you guys," Sir Alec concluded, and then gave a rather grand turning to glide to another group of actors. His conclusive acknowledgement had also taken in Zakes, who had been standing there throughout Sir Alec's bombshell.

"Wow, Femi, that's good news," Zakes grunted with obvious envy.

"Yes, I'm just very surprised." BBGD was still nursing the pleasant shock.

"What are you surprised about? Sir Alec must know something that you don't know."

"I guess."

BBGD was doubly surprised at the extent to which the news had spread within a few minutes. Even before the first read through of the play, two other actors in the company, somewhat veteran, came to welcome him to the first rehearsal and then congratulated him about the impending principal role, which now appeared to be a forgone conclusion. But "Why is this?" was the question that continued to nudge him. He failed to see himself as that special actor being sought for, although he knew nothing about how actors were chosen for a film role.

The audition and screen test that he did was nothing special. The director introduced himself, thrust a script at him and indicated the section he was to look through for a few minutes; he also told him a bit about the character. When he was ready, he was told to deliver, which he did but, as far as he was concerned, rather unsatisfactorily. Not having seen the script before he didn't even know he was auditioning for the black male lead. The only connection he made was that the movie was set in Haiti and the lines he looked at and uttered had words familiar to him, such as Ogun, the Yoruba cultural god of iron and metallurgy, implicated in the script as "Ogun Ferrai." From the little he knew about Yoruba survivals in the New World, he was intrigued by how the god had crossed the Atlantic and persisted in Haiti.

What then may this portend? Was the director fascinated by BBGD's Yoruba ancestry, by which he could lend the role a good interpretation? Is this how luck jumps into unforeseen laps of actors meant for greatness?

Came the first night of *Macbeth*; through the rehearsal period BBGD had built up his hopes with nervous anticipation and tenderness. By the opening, it had become general knowledge that he was going to play the leading black male in *The Comedians*. He felt particularly good about his performance that night. Just like the first night of *The Trials*—although Athol Fugard had remarked his performance that night was unlike the one he gave about a week before. Regarding that for the moment, he seemed to have an idea of what Athol meant—the intoxication brought about by what happened by accident, lifting his performance to certain heights. Chume, the character had come on stage carrying his termagant wife, Amope, on bicycle. In his anger the spokes of the bike suddenly disengaged which landed them both on the ground. But that incident and his character's frustrations involuntarily propelled him from that moment on to another level of experience. He was unaware of how he handled it but felt good about the rightness of it. Dumping his wife at her seller-location, the intoxication had persisted as he went on in haste to prophet Jero, begged the perverted man of God to let him beat his wife, and then knelt in prayers that Jero asserted. Then, gratified by the prophet's approval, the euphoria and leverage had incited his joy of eating dinner at home and telling his wife to "shut your big mouth before I shut it up for you!" All his actions, compelled by that bicycle accident, had resulted in, apparently, a dazzling performance. According to one of his acting teachers at Bru's such inspirational moments happened when creativity and invention took over to render a virtuoso performance. Such performances he had heard differentiated a star (in the real sense of the usage) from an ordinary actor, so to speak.

Something similar happened, apparently, during the first night of *Macbeth* playing the second Witch. In fact, Bill Gaskill, the director, afterwards remarked it. The production was experimentally Brechtian. As such, various dolls, emerging from the witches' cauldron that was sunk beneath the stage level, were used by the witches to prescribe Macbeth's inquiry of the future. Bill had commented on the way BBGD manipulated the handheld dolls and his various contrasting expressions used to convey their messages. Personally, he wasn't absolutely satisfied with that first night's performance, a perfectionist that he was (an attribute he later came to realize); however, he felt adequately good about the fact that nothing terrible happened on stage, and that what he did should please the film director.

But nobody in the semblance of the director showed up in his dressing room afterwards or even asked for him. He had filled himself with nervous anticipation about meeting the man as soon as the curtains fell, but nobody showed up. What happened? Maybe the director did not come after all— although he was almost certain he would have come, at the least, to see Sir Alec on such a night? What could have happened?

The following evening, the somewhat wounded actor, like an apprehensive dog, approached Sir Alec's dressing room. He knocked and was told to enter. The distinguished actor was sitting in his chair, tweaking his beard. On his dressing table was a bottle and a glass of whiskey.

"Sorry to bother you, Sir Alec," BBGD felt his words betrayed some timidity, but summoned up his courage to continue. "Did the film director come yesterday?"

"Didn't he see you?" His voice was calm and nonchalant, looking straight at the fledging actor with a particular noncommittal expression.

"No, he didn't."

Expecting a more direct and hopeful answer, he failed to receive any. The knight gave none. His response was a simple shrug that tried, without success, to project a feeling of dismay. Then he added: "Maybe he'll come again to see you."

BBGD was hardly satisfied with that response. As he walked out of the star's dressing room, he felt something was amiss. But what? He gathered from one of the other experienced actors that maybe the film director had dropped the idea of using him for the black lead, but that he would probably use him for one of the lesser roles. Actually he wasn't in particular hell-bent on the leading role, since he had no such ambitions that early in his career. As such he was quite happy with any role given him. But he wanted answers to quell his querulous and confused mind. For curiosity's sake, he really would like to know what happened. Did it have to do with the nature of his voice, and speech, for which he had always felt inadequate since Rose Bruford?

Till the end of the show, nobody ever came to see him about the movie, and Sir Alec never said anything more about it. Not even when BBGD approached him to thank him for the bottle of aged whiskey he gave every member of the cast:

"Thanks for the whiskey, Sir Alec."

"It probably is of no use to you. I assume you don't drink at all."

"No, but I'll keep it."

"I'll think of something else to give you," he said, with a supposed interest in the young actor's welfare. The prospect brushed his ears but he queried its sincerity as he left the dressing room.

Just so, till the time the superstar left the show, which was two of the four intended weeks of the run (the rest left for his understudy to complete), he never offered anything else. While BBGD didn't hold him up on it, what concerned him more was the fact that, with even the possibility of having a smaller role in the anticipated movie, nobody had shown up to enlighten him more about the matter or what to do. Worse than this, Zakes Mokae, who never experienced any of the hoopla that surrounded him, got a role and so did many other African actors he knew, they all got something. Even though most of those roles turned out to be very small and incidental, the thought of their being given at all only raised more suspicions in BBGD's already saturated mind. *The Comedians*, when it came out and he saw it, confirmed his enigma, much to his chagrin.

One theory he quickly concocted to calm his head, and perhaps his agent had to do with it, was that the director was reluctant to offer somebody of his caliber smaller roles, somebody formerly earmarked for the black lead. But sneaking feelings became evident, the more he grew to expand his knowledge about the acting profession. In fact, there was an incident that confronted him not long after, which confirmed the thought. A television director was interested in giving him a role in a television drama. That much the man transmitted to him when they were introduced. However, the man also wanted him to come to his house for a party. That was when he was intimated with the fact of the director being gay and with the kind of parties he usually threw, which provided BBGD's misgivings. He did not show up at the party and nothing about the role was communicated to him until he saw the director again:

"You didn't come to my party," the man smiled with certain amusement.

"I know about your parties," BBGD grinned with certain boldness.

"Oho! Don't worry, I'll get you yet!"

The response immediately initiated some racing thoughts. Was that all to be said? No more mention of the role? Was there even any role intended? And, regarding *The Comedians*, was the situation similar? Was there any role intended in the first place, a role which finally went to an African American living in the US? Or, if there was such a role in the beginning, was there something he was supposed to have done, as a black actor, some gesture or favor in kind after that initial propping up of the role to him by Sir Alec? Something frivolous he should have done but was too naïve to doing in order to get him the role? Such questions, regarding Sir Alec and the director of the film, were to dog him for years to come, even when he finally became familiar with the practices of the world of professional entertainment, and the demands implicated or expected in the ascendancy to stardom. And perhaps this was one of the reasons he decided to, rather, follow his nose into the academic world.

*****

"I've seen you on stage, and therefore know about your qualities," Jonathan Miller reassured BBGD. The medical doctor-turned-director must be referring to his recent performance of *The Lion and the Jewel* at the Royal Court. "I just wanted you to read for me."

After he was briefly informed about the forthcoming production of *Benito Cereno*, for which audition his agent had sent him, the director tossed him a copy of the play with a selected scene for him to consider for a few minutes: "Look at the character of Babu," he added and left BBGD to his thoughts.

As he had concluded time and again, he detested this kind of auditioning, when he knew nothing about the script until the moment of audition. He had learnt a week or two before about production coming up at the National, and, perhaps, he should have done some research of it, probably in the library, and/or read the play beforehand, if published, so as to know what to encounter. Although there wasn't much time between when he was asked to audition and the present, he granted he was naïve to these circumstances of the profession and the way to handle them.

From the little he gathered; it was about a slave rebellion on board of a slave ship bound for the New World. Since the slaves were Africans, he didn't think he had to think of changing his voice or speech pattern. It crossed his mind that an exaggeration of the African talk might be required of him, but he didn't think it was wise to impose that at this time. At any rate, the play was written in verse and in veritable English, albeit by an American poet, Robert Lowell.

"Ready?" Miller asked to confirm the shift of BBGD's eyes from the printer page to the director. "Okay whenever you're ready."

He stumbled through the reading with his nerves acting crazy. He read it two or three times with Miller giving him directions after each time as to what he wanted. And then the usual followed, "Very well, I'll get back to your agent about it."

He felt he didn't do his best, but for some reasons entertained some belief in what the guy said about knowledge of his capabilities on stage. The audition, he thought, was just a formality. But that was just it—another one of those unfortunate experiences he had to write off with some regrets.

He was somewhat curious to know the person who got the part when the show opened, and so he went to see it. No greater an actor than he was, but a West Indian no less, and much darker in complexion than him—all of which pointed to the conception of the director, if not of the playwright. Babu as a slave had to be close to being jet black, and to look like a rebel African, in contrast to the character of a mulatto who, was more favored because of his color and therefore used against the black rebellious slaves. Perhaps BBGD's complexion would not have contrasted well with the mulatto. He did like the performance of the Caribbean actor, but felt he might have given the character a better interpretation as an African. For, surely the slaves, at sea and en route to the New World, were still African and not yet Caribbean, or African American as the case might have been.

*****

"Dey's gettin' ready to take Jerusalem down dere. Dat was my big fine city." That somber reflection by the Lawd God to his archangel Gabriel in Marc Connelly's *Green Pastures*, for some strange reasons sometimes came upon him, especially when he felt some injustice had been dealt him personally. At times, it came as a sequel to Othello's "Haply that I am Black." Thinking more about it, he didn't find the quote quite an appropriate addendum, at least not as precise as another one that sometimes teased his mind—"I am a man more sinned against than sinning." Of course, the disparate

136

history of both pacifiers of his tumultuous thoughts could easily be documented.

The latter, Lear's consoling self-pity of his outrage against his "pelican daughters," was obviously the earlier, and nearer to the time he first began to experience touches of racism, initiated by WS's "Telephone Conversation." Shakespeare's *King Lear* was one of the English Literature requirements for the make-up of his scholarly deficiency, at the Northwestern Polytechnic in London's Kentish Town. The necessary make-up was needed for him to enter a British University—he had neither a Higher School Certificate nor the so-called GCE before he left home. But, regarding Lear's speech that often ended BBGD's gratification of consolement, there was the English professor, Mr. Hart, a rather huge middle-aged man with a pale bulldog face and a weary walrus moustache. He always preferred to read aloud all Lear's speeches, perhaps to demonstrate his knowledge of Shakespeare's metrical system to his mostly foreign students—although Naomi, the English student who always sat beside BBGD seemed to have a counter opinion of that knowledge. Be that as it may, on the particular day Hart struck upon that speech ending in "I'm a man more sinned against than sinning," he seemed to have cast his sorrowful eyes in the direction of Naomi Richards and BBGD as if to hit their maligning thoughts with that line. BBGD of course was guiltless; if anything, he had allowed the lines to sink into his mind, in agreement with Lear about the injustice brought upon him. For Naomi, that didn't seem to be the case. She seemed to have challenged Hart's moroseness and apparent directed glance with a whispered snigger: "Pathetic old fool."

But who is the fool? BBGD's thoughts queried, casting a quick glance at Naomi… Lear or Professor Hart…or him for that matter, for believing in Hart's reading? He couldn't summon enough gall to verbally ask, and that would be foolish. For, perhaps such a question had better be left alone unasked for fear of certain embarrassment. Certainly it would be if the apparent sarcasm turned out to imply him, the ignorant gullible African who knew nothing about Shakespeare and the body language and witty innuendos of her British people. But then, the thinking had extended, as associations usually manifested, to what Naomi had previously intimated: "Have you noticed how Hart usually directed his gaze at us?"

"Yah, yah. Why?" BBGD was anxious to find out.

"Don't be fooled by it, my dear. That was directed at you." Naomi was nonchalant.

"Really? But why?"

"That gaze is loaded, my dear." BBGD was always curious about Naomi's "my dear" qualification. Yes, she seemed to have offered an unwritten language of friendship by coming to sit with him in every Literature class, but he had felt nothing warm enough to make him engage further than that—which had rendered any implication quite superficial. In fact, her rather cold gray eyes seemed wicked enough to offset any thought of intimacy that he would rather hold her at a cautious arm's length. So, what may she mean?

"I could read faces," Naomi pursued.

"Oh yeah?"

"Believe me, he doesn't have your African interests at heart. He thinks you're wasting your time in this class. He thinks you can never make a good grade, no matter what. That's what he thinks."

"Oh yeah." He didn't know how to respond other than to let out that redundant rejoinder.

"Believe me, you don't know these people. But you'll show him, won't you? You'll prove him, wrong, won't you?"

All BBGD could say was, "Of course."

As he got to know Naomi better, and her English innuendos, he had wondered on whose court she was—his or Hart's. He had not failed the course, although he couldn't prove his abilities at the GCE either, since he had to abandon the Polytechnic's two-year coaching to pursue the Rose Bruford acting training.

"Dey's getting ready to take Jerusalem down dere…"

Thinking again more about this philosophical tool of consolement, BBGD concluded that the Lawd Gawd's sentiments about the raging battle of Jericho had to do, more appropriately, with the insult they had wanted to dump on him at the Rose Bruford regarding his diploma. He had been part of the third-year exit skit that the class of '65 intended to entertain both faculty and students. He was part of it until he realized the intentions of the establishment to award him an inferior certificate, because of his deficiency in teaching and, perhaps more contentious, in the Queen's English demanded for voice and speech. As such, he decided to abandon all end-of-year activities, including the spoof on the faculty.

"Come on, Henry," his class peers had implored, "we can't do it without you."

Their persistent persuasive plea had always met with his negative, obstinate and silent shaking of the head. But they knew what had happened, and both Roger and Tony, his more tolerated colleagues (in spite of their "nig-nog" appellations), had every intention of addressing it in the skit.

"Okay, come and watch the show at any rate."

"No." He remained strategically adamant.

However they addressed it, he never had the opportunity to experience it at first hand since he wasn't present. Long before the event ended, he had decided to absent himself from his digs, just in case his peers came over to make a last-minute plea, or even to tell him how it all went.

He had sat in silence at the movie theater, not able to concentrate on the particular film he was watching. At any rate, he had not chosen any particular film of interest to watch. As such, his mind kept drifting, punctured by thoughts of the skit, which they promised to make more satiric on his behalf.

"Dey's getting ready to take Jerusalem down there. Dat was my big fine city!" The line struck in singular chord with his thoughts, for reasons he couldn't quite figure out. It kept thumping in counterpoint to his thoughts of the injustice dealt him by the Rose Bruford establishment. Vaguely now, he could understand it as an arguable complement of "Haply that I'm black."

Scenes Seven

The Reluctant Professional Actor: The Ife Years—1976-86

BBGD and WS came back home about the same time, Summer of 1976. They both arrived to take up appointments at the University of Ife, later to be changed to Obafemi Awolowo University. BBGD had always thought the original name sounded better than the new one. At any rate, the so-called Unife, during those fun thriving years, certainly distinguished itself as number one university in the country, as opposed to the academic and intellectual drain, and the deterioration of the facilities that gradually beset the university as Obafemi Awolowo.

WS came back from exile (in Ghana and in Great Britain) first to coordinate and assume position as Head of Comparative Literature. But soon, after a year or two, he became the Head of Dramatic Arts, to which he really belonged. The sudden change, which appeared to be a coup to replace Ola Rotimi the Head of Dramatic Arts for so many years, was a story by itself. The takeover caused an inevitable discomfort and altercation between the two theater personages, and this led to the eventual resignation of Ola Rotimi from the university. Regarding the matter, BBGD had resisted taking sides and would rather such discussions be left alone. But he was delighted to be back working with his mentor, as colleagues no less.

The passage of time between when he left for Britain and from there to the US, and the present, a matter of twelve years, seemed short. Yet, the so many things that had happened during those years, and in the life experiences of either of them, certainly made it seem an eternity. Not that the experiences of the younger artist could compare in any way with those of the older, experiences that included periods of the Nigerian civil war, during which his mentor served two grueling years of incarceration. Those excruciating moments, about which he read in WS's prison text, *The Man Died*, were nothing BBGD could ever imagine. He had rushed to get a copy of the book when it came out, and as he read it his eyes almost gorged out of their sockets, in empathy.

There was also no comparison in terms of theatrical development. He had wished he were in Nigeria during the so-called guerilla theater, when the company he knew and of which he was a foundation member had changed names, from The 1960 Masks to the Orisun Theater. Appropriately so called, *orisun*, the Yoruba word meaning a place where (water) springs, would seem to better fit the cultural focus of a newly independent African nation. He was somewhat envious of that new crop of actors that performed the guerilla skits that constituted the scripts of *Before the Blackout* and *After the Blackout*, respectively. More than this, he couldn't help biting his lips reading about the company's production of *Kongi's Harvest*, the first major production after *A Dance of the Forests* in which he participated. The production was in many ways politically notorious as much as it was celebratory, dubbing its writer with the title name and central character, Kongi.

> *Koooongi o, Kongi e*
> *Koooongi o, Kongi e!*

Stories filled his ears, coming back from the US to assume a position as Professional Artist-in-Residence. He arrived, confident with a prideful attitude of some professionalism, backed by a solid acting training at Bruford and some six years of professional theater on the London Stage. Stories abound of the iron-fisted method his mentor used in drilling his actors, stories that confounded him. For they were experiences he never knew and would never have believed, except that they came from those that experienced them. Stories about how WS came to acquire the name of the dictator, Kongi, the Head of State in *Kongi's Harvest*.

Actually the first time he heard of the Kongi's discipline was in the U.S., from a fellow foundation member of the 1960 Masks, who had lingered to become a member of the Orisun Theater. According to him, he had suffered a kick from the angry young playwright for some actor misbehavior, a foot-kick that sent him rolling from the stage into the auditorium. At the time, the story seemed far-fetched, until his first time back home, at the University of Ibadan, when he heard similar stories. BBGD had worked briefly at Ibadan for only a year, then went back to the US for another year before he came back home again, this time to the University of Ife to work with Kongi. All he could surmise was that the political years of instability must have put the playwright-director on edge, working on his nerves, sometimes, into untypical frenzy. Maybe.

At Ife, the London years seemed so far away, even though he had met his mentor between those years, albeit so briefly. He saw him when he came out of prison, at the Royal Festival Hall where WS was invited to read some of his poems. It was an opportune occasion BBGD could never have missed. He wanted to see the man in person, if only with his eyes, to celebrate his mysterious survival in prison. He wasn't sure of the poet's schedule after the reading and whether he would be able to see let alone chat with him afterwards. If possible, he wanted to make it a surprise encounter, but he realized that might be a one-chance-in-ten gamble. As luck would have it, there was the man coming out alone from the stage door, where BBGD had gone to cast a hopeful eye. There was WS in person, coming down the stairs and on to the hard concrete passages of the Embankment.

"H'm! Bem-Bem-GuDu," accosted WS, even before he landed, as his eyes struck his once-upon-a-time rookie actor. As usual with most of their verbal engagements, it was those first moments when the air was full of promises of exhaustive, timeless conversation; but almost after, those initial promising thrusts would gradually thistle and disappear into thin air, like the three querulous witches in *Macbeth*.

"What are you doing here?" he added, delighted to see the now-professional actor.

"Well...?"

"Great, I'm hungry, let's go and have something to eat," before BBGD could supply an appropriate response to explain his presence.

The invitation-surprise, which shouldn't be a surprise at all, laced elation on the actor's brow at the thought that, of all the people that would have loved to have dinner with the celebrated poet, BBGD was the chosen one the trickster-god of fate had devised for WS to make things happen—borrowing from one of *Esu*'s praise chants. The effortless dinner invitation described a generosity that BBGD was accustomed to, but which always left him baffled just the same with excitement. This time was more special precisely because he hadn't seen the political activist since his incarceration. They immediately took a cab to Soho, and lavished the evening with wine and à la carte at the poet's favorite Indian restaurant. As usual, his mentor did most of the talking with only questions and short remarks here and there coming from BBGD. This time, the speechless awe he felt seemed justified, if only by the ghostlike figure that possessed and dumfounded his eyes.

Not long after that encounter, BBGD had departed for the U.S. At Yale University, where he had somehow mysteriously found himself, he had concentrated on playwriting, abandoning any possibilities or opportunities to act on stage. At first, he had intimated Robert Brustein, the Dean, with his professional experiences in London and of his possible interests in the Yale Repertory Theater productions, for which the Artistic Director encouraged him to audition. But, came each time the opportunity to audition, he reneged. Reasons for this was somewhat muddled in him. On the one hand, he didn't feel there was any part suitable for him to audition for; on the other hand, he felt he probably would have had to start all over again, since nobody knew him in the US. He felt all he would probably be offered would be something insignificant, like a servant, or a spear carrier, or part of a crowd—all the roles he had resisted in England, effortlessly, especially since he had played principal parts such as those in Soyinka's dramas. And then he felt he should really concentrate on what he had come to do at Yale, playwriting. But, over and above this, he was somewhat nervous—all to do with his persistent actor's inhibitions, and the responsibilities acting posed on him.

The only acting he did in the US happened well after Yale. Then he was working at the Ethel Walker School, a college-preparatory high-school for girls. One of the directors at the Hartford Stage, whom he had previously met and worked with in a project for the school system, had called him to audition for Derek Walcott's *Dream on Monkey Mountain*, to be directed by somebody else. The same director-friend was later to cast him in *A Raisin in the Sun*, to play the part of Asagai, but at that time, he had comfortably used his conflicting intended visit to Nigeria to decline the offer. It was a decision he had regretted afterwards, even though going to Nigeria to accept a job at the University of Ibadan was an offer he almost couldn't resist. Thinking about it after the fact, he really could have stayed to do that production, and still have gone to Nigeria afterwards. However, with his head still in the US, and as that god of fate would have it, after one year at Ibadan, he had deflected back to the Ethel Walker School, a rather tempting site of certain freedom from responsibilities. There, the students and faculty seemed to have worshipped him. He ate almost all meals with them in the dining hall, and lived in a chalet overlooking about 800 acres of land, the private school's property. Furthermore, he was able to drive to New York as often as he wished, and rode on horses with the students most Saturday mornings.

Even then, acting in *Dream* (as Pamphillion, a small but funny part) was not enough to bring his confidence back to acting as he had pursued it in England. First of all, his leaving for the US for the first time, in 1970, had to do with his original thoughts when he left Nigeria, to pursue drama in an academic setup. All his accomplishments at the Royal Court and the BBC, could not persuade him to do otherwise. At the back of his mind was still his ambition to parallel the accomplishments of his mentor, which included the literary. As such, acting as a profession had no sufficient hold on him, not enough for him to pursue it full blown. He had always wanted to do much more even when at the Rose Bruford College. And so, when the opportunity came, either to go to Yale to pursue playwriting, or stay in London to become a member of the National Theater Company, he didn't have to struggle too much before he chose Yale. The decision was made all the more easy for him because of the fellowship he was awarded by the University of Ife in Nigeria, through the connections of his mentor and his brother, Akin Euba.

He often felt that if Soyinka had been present in Nigeria at the time of his appointment at the University of Ibadan, he would have stayed, especially since that presence was instrumental in bringing him back home again a year later, although there were other reasons. For one, he had been haunted by the guilt that he didn't give Nigeria enough chance to reconnect him to its terrain. Then was the matter of his aging parents in some fourteen years he was abroad, not counting the chance two week visit he made in 1972. As such, when another opportunity came in 1976, with the added possibility of reconnecting with his mentor, he snatched it. At any rate, by that time the lure of his staying in the US had been somewhat shattered. When he returned from Ibadan to the Ethel Walker School, he no longer had the privileges he thought he had at the school. He still enjoyed his meals and teaching with the students, but he wasn't able to regain his former lodging, the chalet overlooking the inspirational woods, which had been given to another faculty during his absence. He had no other choice but to accept one of the units in the faculty and staff complex—really more for staff than faculty. It felt like being downgraded from a VIP status to that of the hoi polloi.

*****

Ola Rotimi, at Unife, had headed the Department of Dramatic Arts for several years before BBGD and WS got there. During those years, Rotimi had trained a company of actors for performances of his plays. That was his singular objective for his productions, to do his own plays with his so-called Ori-Olokun Theater players, in a theater space a mile or so outside the university. In fact, he had absorbed these actors into the university system, which paid them like members of staff. The advantage well-complimented their professionalism.

In a way, Rotimi's idea was not a bad one. Having actors for the sole purpose of promoting a playwright's work to the university community as well as to the nation was not unthinkable. After all, it was a good way of not only developing the playwright's works but also exposing his talents to the world as a significant African playwright in his own right. For Rotimi, the idea had gradually accomplished a legitimacy. But, to continue to do this for a long time was probably a bad idea, and eventually this obvious self-promotion received insatiable frowns among the university community, although at first it was not addressed directly.

Ola Rotimi was still the head of the department when BBGD arrived at the scene. WS, alias Kongi, had also arrived, but to avoid unnecessary conflicts, he was put in charge of the newly created department of Comparative Literature, although he was given a free use of Ola Rotimi's company whenever desired. In fact, arriving at Ife, the playwright from exile had anticipated his new play, *Death and the King's Horseman*, for production. It was after that production that the university community frowned on Rotimi's self-interests more formally, and the discontent became wide open. So, inevitably, the question of who should better serve the university as head of the department of Dramatic Arts arose. In the eventual ruckus, Ola Rotimi had to resign and went to take up another head of theater position at the University of Port Harcourt. His apparent demotion and disappearance from Ife, however, raised counter frowns of displeasure from some who had seen the growth of the Ori Olokun Theater Company under the strict aegis of the former head.

BBGD's appointment was under that old regime. In fact, when he came home for a visit, in 1972, he had met Rotimi at Ibadan and had been fascinated by his company, ingenuity and craftsmanship. He had been invited to see the playwright's ongoing travelling production of *The Gods Are Not to Blame*, staged at a location that lacked direct electricity. BBGD had been captivated by the makeshift stage, lit with fluorescent-fashioned floodlights against kerosene-tin reflectors. It was a commendable invention that was designed to overcome the challenges and handicaps posed by sprawls of rural, unsophisticated, non-literate theater communities across the nation. The audience came, watched, and participated with delight, and after the show, Ola Rotimi spoke of his magnificent devices and achievements and invited BBGD to come home to join in the effort to take theater to the people. In fact, the incident took BBGD back to his formative years with WS and the tour he did with the University of Ibadan Players with *That Scoundrel Suberu*, then there were similar challenges and attempts to combat them, although not as innovative as Rotimi's.

When he got appointed to Dramatic Arts at Unife under the headship of Rotimi, he was willing to take up the challenges with the playwright-director, but he was also hoping he could work with his mentor whenever possible. BBGD had made this known to Kongi, promising to assist him in any way he could, although, perhaps, not as an actor. For, along with acting, his diploma at Bruford assumed his capabilities as a speech specialist—an ability he had not been able to put to test a great deal in the US.

Kongi had not changed his audition procedures since the 1960 Masks. BBGD realized this with the director's forthcoming production of *Death and the King's Horse man*. All actors, including students, Rotimi's professional actors, and wishful faculty, all gathered in "the Pit," the arena theater space of the Dramatic Arts department, used for various events such as rehearsals, lectures, assembly, actual productions, etc.

The Pit was not to be confused with the Ori-Olokun theater space that Ola Rotimi conceived somewhere in town, outside the university, a venue cleverly structured with traditional dramatic values in mind. The courtyard space anticipated and could accommodate demands for household setting constituting different family or ethnic groups, as well as dancing, village crowd, etc. It was a location supported by the university and had served Rotimi's productions for many years. But, finally, probably due to the agitation of Rotimi and the special entrepreneurial interest of the enterprising Vice Chancellor, Professor Oluwasanmi, a theater complex was planned and built on campus, apparently to European standards. This was happening at the time BBGD and Kongi appeared on campus.

Although the new theater was earmarked for theater performances, such productions, as it turned out to be, were probably the last item on their list for the facility's usage. The university administration had in mind other events which they considered more important, such as concerts, faculty and/or student assembly, Inaugural lectures, etc. But as it was nearing completion at the time of the production of *Death*, the play was planned as a proper and fitting event with which to libate the new theater. This implementation perhaps had to do with Kongi's persuasion.

As a rehearsal space for the anticipated production, the Pit arena-theater served Kongi's audition procedures well, with the prospective cast and personnel sitting around the square-area of the pit, and a table set in front of the playwright-director.

"I'd rather help in the production process than have an acting role," BBGD thought he had made that clear when asked whether he wished to participate. Or did Kongi just assumed he would help in other ways as well as acting? Perhaps, but he was sure he insisted on not participating as actor. With his vigorous background in voice and speech from Bruford, he felt he could far better serve the production with that specialty. However, more than this, and the fact of the years he was absent from professional acting—about six or so years—was his reasoning on that very professionalism. He felt, perhaps somewhat naively, a professional of his caliber should not defile his background doing a show with students, or with Rotimi's not formally trained although disciplined actors. Fixed in his mind, no doubt influenced by his various encounters abroad, was the notion that professionals and amateurs did not mix well on stage. One such encounter that supported his claim was Athol Fugard's attempt to negotiate that relationship in the production of *The Trials of Brother Jero* in London, a production that was to double bill with *The Strong Breed*, which unfortunately got cancelled, all because of the disastrous marriage of professionals and "a bunch of amateurs." A more recent experience was the problems he had with that mix when he directed *The Winti Train* at the University of Hartford in Connecticut. However, further knowledge and rethinking of that conviction would make him later reconsider his position.

At the first rehearsal of *Death*, the whole play was read as usual with no assigned parts, so that everybody read what came his or her way. Kongi himself was reading the directions as necessary. BBGD, as his presumed assistant, sat next to the director, thereby giving himself a privilege he felt he could assume. Thus, backed by this assumed understanding, he declined to read the first and second time round when it was his turn to pick up the baton; he simply waved the dialogue to the person next to him. He felt some guilt on both occasions, since all the other faculty present were reading. But more to that fact of guilt was the impact of Kongi's querulous cold side-glances on him each time around. As such, when another round came up, he felt defeated and therefore he conceded to read—forced, as it were, to comply with the status quo. However, he didn't think that compliance compromised his stance; he regarded it as a kind of assistance lent to help the flow of the reading.

"Are you sure you don't want to act?" Kongi asked him after the audition process.

"As I said, I think I can serve better by helping you with the production," BBGD insisted, convinced by his rationale. The heightened, almost Shakespearean rendering of the play's dialogue, he anticipated, would present speech challenges to the actors enough to warrant his expertise as a speech specialist and experienced actor.

Kongi at first seemed to agree with him in general about this; nothing more was said about the matter, until a few days before actual rehearsal began with assigned characters.

"I know you said you'd rather help, but I can't cast Olunde. So, you're going to have to do it." Kongi's tone was rather definitive, leaving BBGD speechless for a few seconds. But the playwright/director continued to bear his customary crushing stare on the presuming assistant for a response. "You can still help with the speeches of the actors," he added.

"Oh…alright." BBGD was not quite compelled, but it seemed there was nothing more he could say on the matter. But far be it from him to let out his real concern, the matter of professional versus amateur. He felt that basket would not hold water in front of his former mentor.

"Good." Kongi smiled as if relieved from a major obstacle. He turned to go, then stopped abruptly and turned back to BBGD. "By the way, OBJ is coming this evening. Why don't you come for dinner? Around 8 o'clock."

That camaraderic afterthought somewhat sealed the deal for BBGD on two fronts. It was a reminder of WS's generosity as regards the superfluity of dining and wining with him, a preoccupation that was to reinvent itself and continue to develop more at Ife as an affirmation of collegiality. Secondly, the mention of OBJ instantly evoked memories of family ties that superseded Kongi, relationship between BBGD's family and that of the now prominent Insurance CEO, Femi Johnson, alias OBJ. BBGD didn't know exactly how OBJ and WS's friendship began, although he surmised it originated within the social circles of Ibadan after BBGD left the 1960 Masks for England. Obviously, it had happened by the time that theater company changed its name to the Orisun Theater in which OBJ participated. He played a role in the new company's first major production after *A Dance*, the production of that same play, *Kongi's Harvest*, that earned Soyinka his nickname. Apparently OBJ gave an outstanding performance as Secretary General to Kongi, the character.

On the contrary, BBGD's relationship with OBJ dated back to childhood. Femi Johnson's father and BBGD's were best friends perhaps long before they were born. Stories abound about that friendship, not through OBJ directly but his junior brother, Lanre, of BBGD's age; both were teenage best friends until his death in Germany when BBGD was in England. But, a direct unfortunate incident with OBJ had lingered with him.

His memory of how he decided to get into the boxing team at Baptist Senior High had become very dim. Why he chose that sport of all the activities was beyond his comprehension. It was probably a kind of unquestioned curiosity for him. But there he was one unfortunate day matched to spar with Femi Johnson, his senior and probably too tall and muscular for his age. He should have refused to partner with that imposing stature, but he never thought the incident could result in the way it did. He never thought this person, who should act like a senior brother to him, would be very serious about sparring with him. But at the clanging of the bell, this hefty young man hastily came at him and landed a severe punch on the right side of his head, which sent BBGD spinning and staggering backwards, and, losing his control, found himself crashing on to the concrete ground. And to make matters worse, there was his assailant laughing his head off, very unsympathetic to his weaker opponent's condition and nodding his head as if to say, "Serves you right, BBGD."

He very slowly got up, a bit dazed, controlling his tears as much as he could as he tottered out of the ring. That was his first and only attempt at what he had considered a dangerous sport from then on. Johnson may have apologized much later, but BBGD never forgave him for as long as the incident remained conscious in his head. However, while the humiliation suffered had stayed with him, he didn't dare tell anyone at home, especially his father, who probably would have chided him with a few strokes of the cane, just for participating in the sport without first asking him if he could. All that happened years before BBGD encountered WS, and after that encounter, years before the playwright became friends with OBJ.

The rehearsals and production of *Death and the King's Horseman* proved to vindicate BBGD's notions. The professional-amateur mix did not work, or at least was difficult to achieve an even and unified production. He played Olunde next to the person that played Jane Pilkings. This was most unfortunate. As in happened, it involved an attempt and strife, mostly from his side, to make sense with her about what was going on in one of the longest and most important scenes in the play—the Olunde-Jane banter/debate about cultural responsibilities versus the somewhat naïve foreign or Western understanding of those cultural imperatives. No matter how hard he tried to obey and achieve that simple actor's adage, give and take, he found himself having to give all the time, and getting nothing in return, and therefore making it difficult for him to explore and develop his character. Furthermore, he doubted whether the other person, Ms. Martins, either understood Mrs. Pilkings or got anything he, the experienced actor, provided and challenged her with.

It was an excruciating experience. How the actor in the first place got Kongi fooled with an appearance of having some talents was hard to figure out; she simply had none. Was it the fact of her simulation (superficial however) of a British accent because she was born overseas—suggested by her name Tokunbo? The question was how many years did her parents spend in Britain after she was born before they came back home? Not that this guaranteed much of anything in terms of acting experience, which she went on to prove to be blatantly nonexistent. Regarding the acquisition of some semblance of Britishness, there was a British lecturer in the English department, Mrs. Margaret Folarin, who helped in the process. But what that experience turned out to be, at least with Tokunbo Martins, was a phony accent that persistently sent grating sensations to BBGD's ears and almost drove him crazy. He felt this very much influenced and explained the rather low-keyed acting his performance offered. There he was, for the first time in some six years (not counting his incidental performance at the Hartford Stage) trying to re-establish himself as a well-trained actor, with some background of professional experience from his London years, there he was trying to prove himself to his former mentor that he still had it in him. To his dismay, he was unable to do so with any efficient capacity.

Then came the fiasco of the problematic opening night, of what turned out to be the one and only performance of the production. The builders of the new theater had striven to put final touches to the building but up till the very last minute. In fact, rumors persisted the work might not be completed on time, and that the A/C and the sound system were still causing some problems. The building looked impressive on the outside, colorful, a fact that was challenged as questionable by Kongi. Apparently, the outside of a theater building was not supposed to compete with its inside, where emphasis on magnificence would be more appropriate. Examples of this credo pointed to London theaters. Especially so was the newly built Royal National Theater on the South Bank overlooking the Thames, the whole arts complex of which included the Royal Festival Hall and the Hayward Gallery.

This aspect led to some other issues of concern, boosted by the evident "frequently asked questions," such as: Did they build a theater or an opera house, or concert hall for that matter? Actually that particular question was easily answered since the university administration did not specifically have "theater" in mind. But then, "Who are these builders?" "Do they know anything about theater?" "Was there any feasibility study for the project?" "When contract was awarded, were credentials of the builders demanded, or illustrations of their work submitted?" "What specifications, if any, did the relevant university authority demand?" None of these questions provided a direct straightforward, intelligible answer, if at all. What became evident was the fact that the architect and builders knew what they were about, but with a very revealing addendum. There was indeed a feasibility study by some members of that the university administration that went to Europe. Apparently, they saw an interesting building that looked like what they wanted and then came back to act on its emulation. But exactly what that building was, if indeed a theater, was difficult to pinpoint. Certainly not what any theater person had any knowledge of.

One certainty gave support to the speculations. It was the evident fact of the goings-on in the world of corruption that was rampart and had become a standard part of the system in Nigeria and beyond. Contracts were awarded on account of what was expected in kind: usually ten percent of the negotiated amount. Hence the outcome of negotiation from the awarder to the successful awardee depended on who could comply the most with those important terms of contract. But then the full picture of the negotiated amount need be understood. The "price" was often complicated by the stages of negotiation, which could start from the clearly visible to the amorphous invisible, from the low office to the high one, from the officiating incorrigible negotiator, the OIN so to speak, to the dictating CEO or CFO, in between whom might be many levels of negotiating stairs to climb and positions to encounter, as many as ten or even twenty to say the least.

In this particular case of the theater building, a fact to remember was the obvious, that it was being built at a time of plenty from dug-up resources of liquid gold. Which meant the sky was the limit and everybody involved, no matter how many, should be fairly comfortable with the monetary demands each imposed. That confidence was grounded on the assurance of abundance that originated from a Head of State, Yakubu Gowon, who was quoted to say: "The problem is not the money, but how to spend it."

Thus, the problems of the new theater started from over-budgeting. That is, in terms of a corrupt environment, what was projected was far more than below-the-budget amount that actually landed in the hands of the architects and builders. As such, the problems of deadline for completion of project arose, due to problems of insufficient funds, which probably had to be renegotiated. All of this complicated the much-needed timely use of the space for rehearsals and actual performance, which ultimately was limited to only one or two days before the opening night. There was hardly enough time to test any of the problems of the facility against those of acting, director, designers and performance. There was no specific ground plan, and the areas for usage (backstage, balconies, entrances and exits, etc.) new to the actors were mostly assigned or re-blocked on the spot within the limited time till the opening performance.

Everybody was delighted by the good news that there would be central air after all, since that alleviated the problem of the audience having to deal with heat, and the accessibility of the rich but difficult language of the spoken text. But what missed the ululating sensibilities of praise-singers of the anticipated comfort was that the A/C mechanism might in fact hinder audience reception, depending on the degree-level of coolness and the noise that system might render.

BBGD couldn't understand it at first, the many unfavorable comments flaunted at him after performance. He knew his delivery was competing against something; what it was, was difficult to assess during moments of his performance.

"What's going on, BB? It's difficult to hear you, and I was sitting close." That comment from Kongi was echoed by many. "And the acting was dead, man. Dead."

BBGD thought he tried hard to enunciate and project, and so the comments were very baffling and disturbing. His internalized reaction echoed the case of an old professional actor that was trying to stage a comeback after many years of absence, only to find out that he was after all a bad or ham actor.

"I can't understand it. It felt as if something in the air was blocking my speeches from penetrating the audience."

"Nonsense. Nobody could hear you." Kongi was unrelenting.

"And that woman was terrible."

"I know that. But it's up to you as a professional actor to help that."

"As if I didn't know that! Easier said than done," BBGD mused the response only to himself, unwilling to prolong the unyielding stance of the director.

Tickling himself with the thought, he reflected on a statement made in the play by the police officer, Amusa, his reaction to the desecration of the Egungun masks worn by the Pilkings: "Sir, it is a matter of death. How can man talk against death to a person in uniform of death?" Reconstructed for his own amusement: How can one successfully convince the writer of the play that it was his play's words that failed to penetrate the audience, blocked, apparently, by the rather hostile drone and airwaves of the A/C? Like simple-Amusa in his own simple way contrasted it: "Is like talking against government to person in uniform of police." A ticklish smile laced his face as he recalled the preciseness of the actor playing a perfect Amusa on stage. Nevertheless, he wondered why his voice failed to go through while those of others succeeded. Quite a food for thought that could only be answered by *Esu*, the trickster-god of fate, he considered.

Ultimately, he was undeterred and stubbornly stuck to his belief. The central air was in full blast. He could hear it. This might have caused in him some stage terrors that weakened his delivery, which he thought he was striving hard to project. His conviction was consistent with the facts he gathered much later. The air was turned on about an hour or so before the performance. For such a huge space, it should have been turned on one or two days prior—which of course was not possible, for the contractors were working round the clock. Thus, he concluded by the scientific fact that it was hot air rising. Complicated by the heat of the bodies that filled the space, the culprit air rose and hovered between the actors and the audience, making it difficult for his voice to penetrate some areas. Whether this was true or not, it sounded logical enough for BBGD to wave off the complaints about his acting.

"Why you though? Other actors also might not have been heard. Why the focus on you?" As for that ticklish thought attempting to gnaw his insides, he simply dismissed it as if waving off an annoying fly that was tantalizing his vision.

"Agh!" followed by what to him was a convincing argument: "The debate between Olunde and Jane Pilkings was probably the most noticeable. Precisely because it was an important debate in which stakes were claimed on either side. Not able to participate in the debate sufficiently, the director officiating for the audience picked on the person that was supposed to, as a professional, make it easy for them. They picked and vaunted their emotions on him, and damn the consequences!"

Back to *Esu-Odara*, that confusionist trickster-god, he felt it was also very possible that his fateful-fatal impositions had to do with it, playing tricks on his devotee, so to speak. To what effect one may well ask? Was the god's fatal blow meant for his devotee for him to be more aware of the acting flaws around him or the potential of his voice? If this was the case, he could have tried to overcome any of the obstacles in the following performances, except that was not to be. There were no other performances of the play scheduled after that night. The director decided to scrap the production for good or ill.

Be that as it may, even Kongi, like any human being, could err. He felt comfortable with that conclusion, recollecting the conflicts he had with his former mentor in London. But more immediate was on account of an incident that happened during the rehearsals of *Death*.

He had acquired or been exposed to different methods and mannerisms of acting, vocal or gestural when he was in London, especially watching various actors from the Royal Shakespeare Company. With such experiences in his stockyard, he was capable of experimenting with his acting choices. So, one day at rehearsals, he had pondered laboriously over how to deliver the Olunde's line, "Eater of leftovers," with which the character rejected his father for failing to do his death-duties to the king and the community. BBGD therefore decided to experiment with it by letting himself go with his delivery. He expected the emotional thrust he summoned up to extend his Olunde's stare of disgust at his father's failing to come up with the right tonal response. Thus, putting himself to the task and risk, he let it out. What came out was a kind of pitched and strained tone at the edge of life itself, which apparently raised a horrified frown from Kongi. He managed to catch that reaction in a slit second as he cast his gaze, unwittingly, in the playwright's direction.

"What was that?" came the director's query afterwards.

"What?"

"The way you delivered that line. 'Eater of leftovers.'"

"That was the summation of the pain I felt."

"Well, cut it out. It needs to be delivered plainly and emotionless." And the director-playwright went on to demonstrate how it should sound.

BBGD felt the demonstration wasn't necessary but contained himself. "I was experimenting anyway," he made an afterthought defense, which didn't seem to make any impression on the director.

"Cut it out."

He felt Kongi's abrupt closure was quite unnecessary, and rather authoritative. Thinking more about it, his rendering probably sprang from an internalized emotion, absorbed through similar outburst he had experienced, probably from one of the Shakespearean actors he had admired on stage. However, what he did, he was convinced, was genuine and did not need the kind of reprimand from WS. For, has an actor no right to experimentation? From his experiences on stage, he had since discovered he was such an actor that was given to constant experimenting and discarding until he felt comfortable; most times he was not satisfied and the experimentation continued even till the end of the show.

He instantly recalled a case in point that gave him credence. It was during the production of *The Lion and the Je*wel and how he fought with some lines of Lakunle. For instance, there was that string of hyperbolic, highfalutin words that Lakunle apparently culled from the dictionary, which he used to boast of his intelligence only to be made fun of by Sidi, whom he was trying to woo without the traditional bride price. The stage manager of the production had watched BBGD struggle with the lines every evening. At the end of the show, bringing his attention to the fact, the stage manager remarked with amazement how the actor never said those words the same way till the end of the show. Recalling this, BBGD felt the need to cock his face squarely at Kongi and ask: "Does an actor not have the right to experimentation?"

But he decided against such a confrontational strategy with the director, any director for that matter. Rather, he just curled up a cheeky smile and walked away, leaving his apparent "adversary" to interpret it whichever way. He would rather consider the "Cut it out" harmless, and simply a mistrust of a director-playwright, who had in his head too set an idea of how certain lines of his play should be rendered.

It would not be the first or last time WS would be protective of his lines. And it would not be the first and last time that BBGD felt the playwright-director was wrong. But perhaps the incident of *Death* was singular in the fact that it was a difficult moment for both mentor and mentee, in the attempt to get back to understanding and acknowledging each other's work ethic, especially now they were colleagues. Both however realized that if the show were to go on, Tokunbo Martins would have to be replaced as Jane Pilkings. Unfortunately, that performance was to be the only one for that production.

"Yah, he redeemed himself in *Opera Wonyosi*," WS was to recall some years later to his friend and former mentee at Cambridge University, Henry Louis (Skip) Gates. The African American Professor had asked BBGD to write about his experiences of that one performance, to be published in a collection to mark WS's 50th birthday. BBGD had been somewhat reluctant.

"I know why he was reluctant," WS decided to offer his judgment, beaming remembrance at BBGD as they all sat in an Italian restaurant in New Haven. "He was terrible in that production." Before BBGD could raise a defense, he had added, "But he redeemed himself in *Opera Wonyosi* all right."

*****

Precisely because of the *Death* experience, he had once again, at first, declined to participate as actor in *Opera Wonyosi*, but again promised to help wherever possible in terms of voice and speech.

"Fine, but I will get back to you if I need you as an actor." The playwright/director's usual cunning smile fell on BBGD's face as if to say "In fact, I know I will get back to you. But so be it for now." The shrug that accompanied the response was very clear to the reluctant professional.

Kongi's return was shorter than he had anticipated. It was immediately after the audition process in which the rookie colleague inevitably had participated, although this time he kept some distance away from the director's table. As he rose from his seat to depart, he caught Kongi's eye, which held him to a stop, followed by a friendly beckoning hand to summon him to his presence.

"Come to the house." The director must have changed his mind in terms of strategy, BBGD thought as he approached. But it was possible the change had to do with an impending interruption from one of the other colleagues. However, he had already sensed what that invitation might mean. A brief talk about the rehearsal process over a glass of wine and then the real objective of the call.

In fact, two other colleagues came to participate in the camaraderic influence of wine, and it wasn't until BBGD had dowsed himself with two or three glasses of his favorite red wine and wanted to go home that Kongi had the time to tell him what he had in mind. As the director walked him to the veranda door: "By the way, I'd like for you to consider that character of Colonel Moses."

BBGD had appreciated the respect his distinguished colleague had given to him. For all their disagreements and conflicts over *Death and the King's Horseman*, he felt he was treated like a professional. He felt his former mentor needed an urgent response and his agreement to playing the role before he devised a cast list. He knew he could not refuse to entertain the role.

For years to come, Colonel Moses almost took over the BBGD appellation. He was not only accosted by friends and colleagues who saw the show but by Kongi himself. He welcomed being accosted as such since he knew it was justified and all in good faith. The role felt right, and he created it with all the sensitivity and intuition the role deserved, adding to it a gesture that clinched the nickname. It was a clicking sound he made with the heels of his military shoes, a salute by which the Sergeant needed to establish his hypocritical authority. It was obvious that the character, of course through BBGD the actor, was influenced by his knowledge of the Red Army. But the interpretation felt right and suited the image of its representation. It also imbued the nature of the Police State that characterized the autocratic imposition of the Nigeria government, in a play reimagined by WS as an astute adaptation of Bertolt Brecht's *Threepenny Opera*. Judging by the comments that came to him from Kongi through his other colleagues, the distinctive traits imposed on the role by the actor was not lost to the director.

"Just look at BBGD," stated a colleague relaying Kongi's admiration of the clicked heels, "He had mastered that role to the hilt!"

The scene was none other than when the Colonel, under the guise of being efficient, paid a fact-finding visit to the premises of Jonathan Anikura, the proprietor of a kind of business school for beggars. Clicking his heels, with head half-bowed, into a dignified pose in salutation to Anikura, he ceremoniously refused the offer of a glass of champagne, which he however accepted seconds later with effortless persuasion. Anikura then went on to arrest the sympathies of his corruptible visitor by ordering the appearance of his student-beggars. At once, as instructed, the student beggars surrounded the Colonel where he sat with his glass of champagne, thus dismantling his comfort and arrogance with their stage-managed physical afflictions. It was the scene that showed up, the corrupt, oily-faced, supercilious, victimizing, power-hungry character and officialdom of the Colonel.

It was as if the role was created for him—and perhaps Kongi did, since it was a Nigerian character, although close to Brecht's corrupt police chief in *Threepenny*. As such, he felt the character was handed to him, as it were, on a silver platter. He also gave the amateur students and Ola Rotimi's former professionals something to ponder on regarding his acting capacities, thanks to his training at the Rose Bruford College. At rehearsals they were always baffled and dazzled by the acting of "our *oga*-professor," the way he handled props that were not physically present. The champagne-filled glass was a case in point, the way he held it, sipped from it and always placed it at the right spot on the right side table with amazing conviction and credibility. One day they all came to confront and asked him about this. He responded with a lecture and demonstration on the art of Mime, compelled by the hours he had spent at Bru's with his student peers, doing exercises such as feeling, with various drinks, the sizes and weights of various glasses and cups. Taking the cue from the curious actors, he decided to incorporate some of the exercises in his acting classes as an essential component of the training.

"Yes, he certainly redeemed himself," Kongi punctuated with sumptuous finality as he lifted the wine bottle to refill BBGD's glass, as if to celebrate the occasion more formally.

"Okay, my man, write me that essay," Skip demanded, his eyes glowing at the prospects.

"I will, I will," BBGD assured him, rolling the last strands of spaghetti in his plate with his fork into his spoon.

*****

Biko's Inquest was a different kettle of fish. Kongi wanted to include in the production as many professors as possible to take up the more mature roles in the play. Thus, Yemi Ogunbiyi played the judge, Olu Akomolafe played one of the prosecuting attorneys, and BBGD played Von Lieres the expansive pontificating prosecutor. And there was the rumor about the possibility of its travel to the US to correlate with an award being given the distinguished playwright. In fact, the African American organizers, Hazel Bryant and her associate, of the Alliance Theater Company, came all the way from the US to see the show. It happened to be the night BBGD forgot his lawyer's wig in his house.

As soon as he realized the error, a few minutes before the show began, he was faced with a frantic dilemma—to quickly drive back home, some five minutes away, or go on stage without a wig, both of which had risks. Five minutes of driving-time could become ten, depending on unexpected setbacks, which was probably unlikely but possible just the same. On the other hand, to go on stage without the wig would obviously receive a serious admonition from Kongi, which he would rather avoid. Only a night before, he got everybody on edge, including the director. It was during his character's longwinded rigmarole when, all of a sudden, he saw a blank. So, there he was hand held high in space, head cocked in the air towards the audience, eyes wide-open, lips frozen apart, as he fought desperately to remember the next lines, which fortunately came back to his head, just in time before he lost the engagement of the audience. Kongi's admonition for that was quite enough, even though it was left unspoken until BBGD himself brought the situation up. "Yes, I was wondering what had happened," was the director's disapproving grunt. "Got even me nervous."

Knowing he had about half hour to play with, he decided to take the risk to drive home, which of course sent all his character preparation to smithereens. He knew he had violated a serious acting hazard, but thought he could deal with it in good time. He intimated the stage manager with his intentions, who should have cautioned his objective if he knew any better. But who was he, a student, to object to his professor's intentions?

"Oga," the stage manager leaned across to whisper, as BBGD came back and was making for the dressing room to catch his breath, "Kongi was looking for you. I said you went home to pick up your wig." He knew then he was in for a big reproach. It had to be his unfortunate luck that the director came backstage, to check for what, or whom, was anybody guess. But he was almost sure of what probably happened. One of the faculty members in the cast, somebody like Kongi's favorite surrogate as chair, Yemi Ogunbiyi, might have alerted him, that is, when the busybody deputy somehow got wind of his disappearance.

"That was a stupid thing to do, and you a professional should know better." Kongi's admonishment finally came after the show. By then his anger seemed to have quelled, perhaps because it was a good show anyway, even if it was no thanks to the risk-taking actor.

"I didn't want to look conspicuous without the wig on," BBGD explained although he knew his explanation was fruitless.

"Anything could have happened, going home to pick it up. And then we would have been in bigger trouble."

He decided not to pursue the matter further, because any defense at this stage was after the hazardous fact. He was thankful enough that he wasn't chewed up in front of his other colleagues but came to his house to clear the air, although he questioned out of curiosity the real reason for the appearance of the director at his doorstep. Not that he mistrusted the man's discreetness, which was gracious of him, but he felt the matter could have waited till the following day. He had disappeared in a hurry after the show, precisely to avoid an encounter, which however had to be brought to his house. Because of what, he wondered? Strike while the iron was hot, perhaps? Knowing Kongi well enough, that would seem highly unlikely. As such, the way the admonition was directed, with certain calmness, made the victim all the more curious to suspect other intentions.

Just as he thought, the caller abruptly got up and started to go, then stopped. "Oh, by the way, we're having some drinks with our guests in my house. You haven't met them, have you?"

"No, not yet," he responded. He knew they came into town that afternoon but hadn't seen their faces.

"Well, you can come and meet them." That, of course, BBGD concluded, was the main reason for the short call. "Take your time though, Yemi has gone to pick them up at the guest house," he added.

Ah yes, Yemi Ogunbiyi, he mused to himself. Ever since the boisterous, enthusiastic young scholar appeared on the scene, having gained his PhD at the New York University, he felt he had lost ground to him as Kongi's right-hand man. Not that he seriously considered himself as such, but he had thought his years of relationship with Kongi at least should speak for themselves to earn him something of the sort. However, what had always crushed that notion for him was those very years of his absence since the 1960 Masks, some fourteen years to be exact. During those years there had been The Orisun Theater, the dramatist-poet's incarceration, and his years in self-exile. Within those years must have been numerous relationships, including his students, of which Ogunbiyi might have been one, and certainly Biodun Jeyifo, who had also returned from abroad with a PhD and as an up and coming scholar. Compared with them, BBGD with just an MFA had sometimes felt somewhat inadequate, especially with the University of Ife's bias for a doctoral degree.

Actually, he got along with Ogunbiyi, even when WS eventually relinquished his headship to him, something that BBGD gradually had seen coming. The surrogate had often substituted for WS in that position on days the chair was away, somewhere. He did not feel any envy for the position since he would rather create than administer. However, he took his feeling of inadequacy as a challenge for him not to rest on his oars or be content with just a professional degree, even though it was a terminal. He very much wanted to earn a more academic degree and be recognized as a scholar as well, even if for the sake of satisfying an ambition he set out for himself before diverting to Rose Bruford and to being an actor. In fact, after his acting training while still in London, he had tried to pursue that ambition once or twice. Then that desire had to be modified, because of a circumstantial opportunity, to pursue an MFA in playwriting at Yale. The accomplishment of an MFA for the mean time served as a positive alternative, until he came to work in an academic environment first in Ibadan and then at Ife. It was then his needs as a scholar

159

came back to be prominent in the face of the conflicting situations he found himself in.

Times there were when he thought of himself as an intellectual-artist, a designation he would rather claim for Kongi than a scholar. At such moments he felt a little more comfortable, seeing himself and his former mentor as compatriots, so to speak. It was then he mostly felt the Head of Dramatic Arts should have won his trust more profoundly. If that had happened, those seemingly vacuous years could have done much to ameliorate his discontent. Yet, the moments of inadequacy had persisted, and his longstanding ambition had come to nudge his ego to disquieting consciousness.

He felt a comforting moment the night of Kongi's brief visit after his unprofessional behavior performing Von Lieres. The director, he felt, went out of his way to come and invite him to his house to meet the New Yorkers. What initially seemed to be a gentle admonishment turned out to be only a red-herring to his visitor's real intentions. Such moments, and there were quite a few, were gratifying to him. They always gave him an incredible assurance that there was something special and still to be treasured in his relationship with his mentor-turn-colleague, even if he was aware that relationship was not of the scholarly, politically conscious type as that of Yemi, or BJ for that matter.

As usual, it was more than drinks at WS's. His cook-steward had prepared vermicelli spaghetti rolled in light tomato stew, something the director knew the African Americans would have a taste for. Along with this were peppered goat meat and pheasant, and fried plantains. And, of course there was wine galore, especially red, which the host knew was BBGD's favorite.

"I understand you directed a show recently," one of the visitors threw her curiosity across the table to him.

"Yes, *Madame Tinubu*, written by one of our Ife faculty. A very challenging piece."

"Also very well directed, we were told."

"Thank you."

"We would have loved to see it. Is there a way we could?"

"No." His response was firm, but went on to explain: "It was a massive cast. And of course, the set has been struck. Besides, it would take quite a number of rehearsals."

"Pity."

He later understood they would have loved to see it as a possible consideration for the US tour. Much as he was excited at the thought, he didn't understand it as a possibility. He thought plans for the *Biko's Inquest* were quite conclusive, in terms of bringing an African production to promote the consciousness of the US audience. Although now that he thought of it, *Madame Tinubu* could fit that bill, but then *Biko*, to his understanding, was already a foregone conclusion.

"Look, it doesn't matter to me, we could take that production if you like." Kongi's position came as a surprise to him, but then he continued to the visitors: "It's just that we're dealing with a huge cast here. We have to think in terms of budget—I don't think your producers could handle that with *Madame Tinubu*."

BBGD had thought of that anyway, so he agreed. But it was a nice gesture that again confirmed the extraordinary dimension of WS in terms of his willingness to accommodate his former favorite mentee-turn-colleague. He wasn't in town when the *Tinubu* production opened at Ife, but apparently saw a touring performance of it in Lagos. BBGD wasn't aware of the fact; he could only go by the brief conversation they had in Lagos when he breezed by the theater. The production crew were rehearsing light and sound cues at the time. But he had no reason to doubt his presence at the actual performance, which he now seemed to confirm at the dinner. His high approval of the production, for the first time, seemed genuine, and therefore was gratifying to the young director.

However, what had elated the junior lecturer, or professional-in-residence as he was designated for a brief period, what had made the production a worthy accomplishment was the comment made by a Visiting African American Professor in the English Department. In fact, as he thought of it, the visiting professor might have kindled the US visitors' curiosity of *Madam Tinubu* in the first place.

"That was a superb production, man," the professor intimated BBGD when they met. "Directing seems to be your forte, hold on to it."

"Thanks."

"Man, that production could match any professional production in the U.S. When I get back home, I'm going to see whether some grant is available to bring the production."

Well, that didn't happen, but the thoughts, he was convinced, were genuine. For the first time he felt enabled to consider himself as a director of note, which Kongi's accommodation and approval only sanctioned. It was moments of such accommodation that stabilize their relationship, overriding any conflicts that sometimes came their way. Case in point was the New York tour of the *Biko's Inquest* and director's response to his needs over the unexpected lodging conditions he faced. He had been excited about the tour, not so much because it was a welcome opportunity for networking and to become known on the New York professional stage. In all honesty, it came as an unexpected stroke of luck to reconnect with a relationship that showed promises of development.

Ever since he had returned to Nigeria after his MFA in Playwriting and Dramatic Literature and his stint at the Ethel Walker School, he had nurtured a prospective eye for a more formal return to the land of opportunity, to pursue his original quest for a PhD degree. His application for a green card at Ethel Walker didn't quite work out. Probably nobody to blame for that other than him, at least in part.

His return to Nigeria to work again with WS seemed promising at first, and temporarily put on hold his pursuit of a higher degree, until he realized being a professional in a Nigerian university wasn't really that prospective, especially with their doctorate emphasis. One had to be a Soyinka, or probably a Rotimi, a stature he probably could develop. But it was a gamble he wasn't willing to take.

With the PhD pursuit at the back of his mind, he had made regular summer visits back to New Haven. Through these sojourns he developed a relationship with Henry Louis (Skip) Gates, Jr., who happened to be a mentee of WS at Cambridge University when the poet/playwright was in self-exile. Through him, about four years later, an opportunity arose to return to Yale, to do Master's in Afro-Am Studies. For that, he had secured a leave-of-absence from his position in the Dramatic Arts department at Ife, where WS had become the Chair.

The degree in Afro-Am was another terminal master's; he knew that from the start. But he thought that could be a stepping stone to his real quest. He tried to gain admission twice—in his first and second/final year—into American Studies as a logical and easier step to take in terms of his goal. To his surprise his attempts to do so failed both times. Perhaps he should have taken the advice of the chair, John Blassingame, who indulged in quoting him the well-known adage, "Don't put all your eggs in one basket." Come to find out later that the African American History professor was part the cause of his failure to gain admission. According to Skip, he did not give a very good recommendation. Skip went on to imply that Blassingame's action was probably a vendetta, for something BBGD was innocent of. For a period of about a year, he, with hardly any effort, dated an adjunct professor in the department; apparently, she was a former concubine of Blassingame. BBGD was completely bowled over when he learnt about this, by which time he had lost his interest in the woman any way. But only too late.

He was faced with the possibility of going back home to resume his position with just his masters, or taking up a research fellowship that Skip offered him until he could reapply for admission the following year. It appeared he would be able to get into Art History. A PhD in Art History was not exactly what he desired, but there was a promising compromise initiated by the presence of the distinguished Robert Ferris Thompson, the African Art Professor and a praise-singer of Nigeria's greatness in Art and Culture. Working under him, BBGD would be able to accommodate his research interests in *Esu-Elegbara*, the Yoruba trickster god of fate, which he wanted to pursue further for a possible PhD dissertation. Ultimately, he wavered on Skip's offer and allowed the pressure of his still-held position at Ife to supersede the opportune considerations that confronted him. He had regretted his decision to return to Nigeria almost immediately afterwards, but by the time he changed his mind, it was too late. After he had declined Skip's fellowship offer, it went almost instantly to somebody else, in whom John Blassingame had some interests. Another vendetta? It was a hard fact he had to learn about African American men, or perhaps men in general, considering the feeling of inadequacy that women impose on men in the dating game.

The relationship with Darlene, a ground airhostess stationed in Washington DC, developed a year before the *Biko's Inquest* tour, that is, about two years before he began a master's degree in African-Am Studies.

He had met Darlene on a summer visit to the US, at a reception celebrating Mary Lou Williams, the celebrated Jazz pianist/singer. Crossing each other's line of vision as they walked by in opposite directions, they had exchanged a rather coordinated eye-wink and had stopped to confirm their relative interests. Unfortunately, the relationship had to be left hanging as there was no opportunity to develop it beyond that evening. However, since Darlene was an air hostess, she was able to arrange a vacation visit to Nigeria for about a week. That visit was a disaster in many respects and it seemed the relationship was doomed. *The Biko's Inquest* production in New York however, presented an opportunity for BBGD to try to save it, what with the benefits it might present to resituate himself in the US.

The accommodation reserved for the actors in New York, although central and near the Lincoln Centre, was obviously unsatisfactory to BBGD's objectives—two actors were assigned to a room. Even though he was to share his room with another faculty member, it was hardly a convenient situation that involved his anticipated romantic exploits. WS, however, came to his aid.

"Listen, I'm staying in a reasonable hotel a few blocks away. I can help you arrange an accommodation there, if you like." He jumped at the director's suggestion as a godsend. He didn't mind paying for the room with much of his per diem.

In hindsight, the whole incident was probably not worth the fuss, let alone the expense and, certainly, the wasted time of missed opportunities. For instance, the stupid conflict that developed between him and Darlene made him miss an afternoon feast with Chuck Mike's family in Brooklyn, an event for which he never forgave the woman.

But, back to WS, as indicated repeatedly his gesture of consideration and accommodation was an example of his generosity. Flashes of such moments illuminating such attributes always made BBGD re-affirm his relationship with his former mentor, weighing the moments against those that raised conflicts between them—like the two or three times he almost threw the script at the distinguished playwright's face when they disagreed on an interpretation that he wasn't allowed to explore. And sometimes he felt he had been misunderstood and WS could have exercised a little bit of patience. The preparation towards the US tour was a case in point.

In addition to the *Biko's Inquest*, a kind of workshop was requested by the organizers, after which the anticipated award would formally be presented to the playwright. Kongi had chosen a section from *Death and the King's Horseman* for the workshop and had asked BBGD to take on the role of the Praise-Singer. The section chosen was that core moment in the play, the end of scene 3, when Elesin Oba, amid the drumming, dances himself gradually into the metaphysical world of the ancestors. The Praise-Singer is using the moment to quest the psyche of his master for knowledge of what lies beyond the physical space.

BBGD needed no persuasion. It was his favorite scene and was honored to be entrusted with such a difficult but powerful recitative. At any rate he couldn't imagine anybody among the cast of *Biko* capable of handling it other than him, but he was a little nervous about its power. He understood how the moment could get some actors so intoxicated that they went under. Kongi spoke of such experiences, of some of the women dancers in the production he directed at the Goodman Theater, in Chicago. He wasn't afraid of this. His concern was more about finding the balance between images that would help the intoxication and remaining in control of himself. But first, he had to deal with the tones and figures of the speech that constitute the monologue. He was also nervous about these, as was often the case when being directed by the playwright. It was on account of these combative issues that a slight misunderstanding arose between him and the playwright/director.

One day at Ife, during a preliminary rehearsal of the segment, BBGD stopped dead in midair at the cruising height of the emotional drive of the "plane" and, as the vehicle lost power, it had to crash. Fortunately, it was a test drive as the actor was still doing an explorative reading from the script; as such, the crash should really result in no casualties. BBGD knew this and that was why he could afford to submit to the power failure. Not so the director.

"What's that?" stricken by the need to understand an image, the actor innocently queried, albeit with a confused, screwed up face that Kongi must have misread.

"What's what?" the director's sensitivity, struck with impatience, was at an edge.

"The 'dark groom and master of life.' What's that?"

"Will you get on with it, and stop asking me stupid questions." It came out more like, "How dare you question my image?"

"Wow," BBGD immediately tried to clarify. "I was merely asking you about its meaning so I could realize it with the rest of the sentence. I wasn't sure."

"Oh," the playwright-director immediately softened. But rather than answering, he applied his customary counter question: "But what do you think it means?"

BBGD within seconds of his interruption had actually figured it out. He needed the break to assess and incorporate it, although, in hindsight, he admitted the moment he chose to do this was wrong to a certain extent. But things happen. Thinking further about it, he felt he couldn't have helped it and the matter, surely, was deeper than his surface rationale. For, somehow, between the capturing of images and their delivery, an actor all of a sudden could face sudden blank. At such a moment, the actor faces possible choices; to stop as he did, or to fake the delivery the rest of the way, and then ask his question afterwards. He, for some reasons, was incapable of faking it and subconsciously chose not to do so, especially since the reading was still in the early stages of rehearsal. More than this was another consideration. Given the fact that the narrative was only being read, it had to be infused with some emotional value nonetheless. It was that value that probably failed him. Thus, feeling let down and very asinine about the delivery, he had to stop and then as a protective fake a reason in terms of the meaning of the words. As it happened, he did not succeed in eliciting any sympathy from the director.

And it was also possible the playwright/director saw through this actor's makeup and, therefore, from his own point of view lost his patience. However, the defensive way that impatience came out was probably unnecessary and therefore wrong. For why would the playwright think his mentee, even if now a colleague, would wish to challenge or oppose the rich images he had always admired, the way they seem to have manifested so perfectly on the script? On either side, the attitude smacked of some insecurity, which probably was legitimate. It was an unfortunate incident that never should have received any intolerance. As usual, the conflict diminished nothing in their relationship, certainly not his admiration of the playwright. If anything at all, the conflict was short-lived, the momentary emptiness that seemed to halt their relationship was refueled by an immediate or the next flow of wine.

The workshop went well as it should, but BBGD got a little too intoxicated with the words and therefore a little out of control. This was made known to him by the drummers, who said they found themselves lost in the rhythm of the delivery and were trying to catch up with it. BBGD disputed this but was not certain what had happened. What probably was fact, come to think on it, was that he found himself competing with the rhythm and the loud volume of the drumming. As such, in an effort to project and engage the audience, he might have gotten intoxicated with his own delivery rather than with the images. It had happened before, during the celebration of poet-playwright's 50th birthday. He was given some verses in *Idanre* to read, against the background of drumming and tinkling of cymbals and "shakarees" of the *sekere*-maracas. That accompaniment was so loud that he got intoxicated with his delivery.

The award ceremony after the workshop also went well, only to be marred by an incident that happened two days after, something to do with miscommunication between the Ife-Theater company and the organizers of the visit. Return flight was booked one day later than hotel checkout time. The organizers refused to take responsibilities for the extra day. At first Kongi attempted to resolve the issue in a cordial matter but failed. He therefore chose to call their bluff by throwing them a magnanimous hardball. He called a press conference where he formally refused and returned the award given to him. After that, they conceded.

The drastic decision taken by the playwright was a minor solo political act that mirrored all the major ones in the past, some of which almost cost him his life. This attributive fiber of this singular personality was something of envy that had constantly amazed BBGD; he wished he possessed such Ogunian discipline and nerve but knew he couldn't. Apart from the fact that he was a-political, he felt that of all the accomplishments in which he had struggled to emulate his mentor (in poetry, playwriting, intellectual capacity, etc.), this one, which described an indomitable, seemingly fearless spirit was nothing he could aspire towards. He doubted if many could.

He began to believe what people had said, that WS was an Ogun incarnate. A former girlfriend of BBGD had once intimated that fact a few years back. Apparently her sister had once seen the "demigod" worship his surrogate "father" in the backyard of his house in Ibadan. However, BBGD was unwilling to take that story verbatim. It was possible that, for his research into indigenous African drama, the playwright had invited an Ogun priest to perform some ceremony he then tape-recorded or videoed. But that the man himself worshipped as a firm devotee or believer was probably a fantasy or an exaggeration. The story may also be an extension of what WS himself had stated, that his grandfather took him to an Ifa priest, like many traditional parents did, to confirm and initiate him as a devotee of Ogun. However that may be, the researcher/dramatist, with an artistic bind, had come to regard the god, patron of the arts, as his patron, but with an artistic remove. Or, Ogun was a divine personage that had come to interest him deeply, interest enough to allow the god's character and personality to frame his, so to speak. Thus, the playwright had quested and celebrated the god, directly in works such as *Idanre* and *Ogun Abibiman,* and indirectly in plays such as *A Dance of the Forests* and *The Road.* In such plays are characters that could be recognized as Ogunian in varying degrees, characters such as the Professor in *The Road*, Elesin-Oba in *Death and he King's Horseman*, Kamini in *Play of Giants*, etc., characters that display the temperament of Ogun but are somewhat limited.

BBGD came nearest to being possessed by an Ogunian spirit when he played Olunde in *Death.* As there was, unfortunately, only one performance of the production, he wasn't able to explore and inhabit the character to the full. At any rate, as he saw it, the eldest son took over his father's Ogunian spirit when the old man failed in his duties, for reasons BBGD the actor felt were nebulous. As such, he felt Olunde was not fully developed by the playwright. On the other hand, the actor should not expect such a development since the play is Elesin's.

As for having a political nerve, he would admit he was very weak in this. The nearest he was able to feel it on the pulse (or on the scotched bottom of the "pot that will eat fat," so to speak, recalling that beginning song in *Kongi's Harvest*) was when he played Chief Mujeyo, in WS's only full-length film, *Blues for a Prodigal.* That is, not counting the filmed *Kongi's Harvest*, which was written initially as a play. As with the playwright's political plays, the film was an example of the corruption that pervaded political life in Nigeria, circumstances that always got WS's critical satiric nerve on edge to take on singular feats that challenged the status quo.

*****

The Blues was BBGD's only full-length film endeavor. All he had been able to do, in his all too short professional years in London, were little scenes in short films and television productions. The hopes of being in *The Comedians* had been a non-starter.

Through Chief Mujeyo, the character he played in *The Blues*, he became more political conscious of the deteriorating situation in Nigeria. But, as he always stated with political concerns, he certainly wasn't a Soyinka in terms of activism nor could he deceive himself trying to be. He felt the only way possible for him to take action was to get out of the country and relocate in the US. He had made a few hesitant forays into the attempt, but always found himself crippled in trying to follow up by the thought of his aging parents.

He had good reasons to justify his desire to leave the country with impunity. He wasn't in the country at the height of its oil-riches; he did not participate in the pleasures that came with the riches, so why should he now suffer the problems that were now afflicting the country? Why should he pit himself against the seeming irreconcilable evil, brought about by economic greed, corruption and wastage? Why should he wallow in the academic and intellectual stagnation that had begun to manifest through the acute, blatant exploitation by the one percent of the people that had consumed and were still consuming the country's wealth?

Involving himself in the satiric objectives of the *Blues* was a kind of non-confrontational activism he seemed to be capable of. He became exposed, nakedly, to the impact of the corruption by playing the oil-faced, resource-looting Mujeyo. His hope was that his satiric delineation would send a message, if at all possible, to the powers that be.

What immediately became obvious to him was his inability to feel that impact in toto, due to the nature of filming in scenes, as opposed to developing a character on stage and performing it live without interruptions. Also, because of the repetitive "action" and "cut" process of the film crew, he was unable to summon up a consistent flow of energy from the point of action to a climax or from one dialogic moment to another. And since the audience was not present on the scene of action, apart from the director, the camera man and the film crew, he wasn't sure who exactly he was trying to engage and impact. As such, it all seemed so superficial and all that was memorable were individual scenes that however did not serve any political means other than self-gratification of character and actor. Scenes such as descending and alighting from the Chief's motorboat, which anyway ended up in a damaged knee tendon of the actor and was to result in a chronic pain. Or, the back-hand slapping of a crony, which took several hilarious shots. Or, going on a trip to a London location, which allowed the actor to visits his old friends. Other than these, there was nothing gained in his opinion in terms of political satire, except to rely on the scriptwriter-director's knowledge of what was happening from one clip to another.

The extent of his role and the graph the character described only became evident to him for the first time at the preview of the film. Until then, he had always regarded the character as minor, although probably significant. As such, during the showing he distanced himself as much as possible from all and sundry.

"You didn't tell me you had such an important role?" Andrea, his excited African American friend and lecturer in the English department, confronted him after the preview show.

"Well, I didn't want to spoil your fun." His response was rather reticent and modest.

"Yah, but you didn't even tell me you acted in it," she countered.

Until then, since the beginning of his new relationship with Andrea, he hadn't revealed that part of his life to her. All she knew about him was as a lecturer and developing playwright in the Dramatic Arts department. Their first encounter was when he asked her to help one student acquire the African American accent demanded by his play *The Gulf*, which he directed some weeks before the film's preview. Since then, with an objective of exploring a possible future opportunity in mind, he had developed some friendship with her.

That evening after the preview show, BBGD decided to treat her gloating eyes to the scintillating pleasure of visiting WS's house. For there on the dining table, to celebrate the occasion, were evidences of the hunting spoils of the playwright and his friend, OBJ. The sumptuous spread consisted of garnished pepper-fried cuts of deer meat, pheasants, squirrels, and goat meat, around dishes of vegetable stews (bitter leaf, okra, "ewedu"—a specie of hibiscus leaves), all accompanied with bowls of pounded yam, cooked rice and fried plantain cuts.

"B-B-G-D. Is that your nickname? What does it mean?" She had been baffled by the appellation that he was accosted with, first by OBJ, who was the only one that knew its history since childhood, and then complimented by WS, who in actual fact learnt that history from OBJ, perhaps incompletely.

"That will be telling," was BBGD's blunt reply and before she could pursue the matter, he introduced her to both hosts.

"Very good. Very good performance," OBJ complimented him.

"Not bad," WS supported with a warm smile. This may not be taken at face value, since compliments from the playwright didn't come easy.

"The man didn't even tell me he could act," Andrea tried to pursue her surprise.

Knowing the reticent nature of BBGD so well, both hosts just smiled, and left Andrea's curiosity hanging. In matters of relationship, it was an assumed rule in Kongi's circle that nobody interfered until all the facts were known, that is, if the member wished to have the requested information supplied. Andrea seemed an interesting attraction which he wanted to capture, but in such a sensitive matter, it was up to him to offer any details of it. He also had the sole charge of the intruder that came into the circle, whose members must know what his objective was before anybody could anticipate or initiate having any romantic interest. In this case not even Kongi, in whose house they congregated, had the technical right—although he had been known to establish his authority and priority when a female outsider was brought, vaguely claimless, into his environs.

However, as much they praised his acting, which, with Kongi's support, had a certain ring of truth to it, BBGD remained somewhat dissatisfied. It was a dissatisfaction he had always felt with every acting role he had taken up, but perhaps much more so with Chief Mujeyo, because of the very disjointed nature of the filming. Also, no filmscript had been provided before filming started; much of it was written and rewritten as they went along.

All these of course aggravated the problems he had often had with delivery and enunciation. There were words and phrases that sometimes seemed to trip him because of their somewhat inconsistent rhythm and flow, which cloyed his tongue and rendered his lips somewhat inflexible. He noted, watching the preview, two or three of such speeches, which needed more work and therefore needed to be redone for clarity. Surely this should have become obvious to the director and should have been redone. He wondered whether the tripping bothered the preview audience. Acting is one thing, but clarity of speech is another, even though one should complement the other. If good acting is complemented with muffled or swallowed speeches, what intelligibility could an actor render to anybody?

As the only political statement he had ever expressed visually, his character did not seem to have made any definitive impact on the audience for obvious reasons, but certainly that would not be because of his acting. That the film failed to make its proposed circulation could probably be attributed to the script and montage, which received negative criticism in some artistic circles. If they ever found his acting hampered by some speeches, it would have been in passing or as an afterthought.

BBGD had often wondered why WS's works had not been attracted to filming. He had constantly alerted the playwright of his acting interests in such filming should opportunity arise, with such plays as *Death and the King's Horseman*. But nothing had happened in that regard. He couldn't help thinking about the disastrous attempt to film *Kongi's Harvest* a few years back. He was in England at the time, studying, otherwise he would have certainly participated. A random flying to Nigeria for the filming would have been impossible. But he had wondered why attempts with any other plays never happened, if indeed ever proposed. Perhaps such plays that relied heavily on poetic imagery were difficult to film. But then Shakespeare's plays, which reveled without apologies in rich poetic imagery, found their way on to the celluloid through the imaginative response of some directors. Some of them, he realized, featured with questionable result and success.

All he could come up with as possible reasons was that WS's plays could only be handled by a very creative and committed filmmaker, who knew the script and culture inside out, and who should be trusted to handle the script with little or no interference from the playwright. Such a commitment, backed by substantial funds, seemed difficult for an African artist, even as distinguished as WS.

*****

In Ogun, the playwright-researcher had found the first actor, a superhuman character who dared the primordial amorphous reaches of being, in an effort to understand the specific potential of his creative impulses. According to myth, through combative will the god, as central character, was able to lead the other personages, the other divinities, across the chthonic realm to find and reconnect themselves on the other side with their human counterparts, with their human characteristics. In the process, he suffered almost annihilation. But through sheer force of will, really a singular tunnel vision characteristic of tragic heroes, he succeeded and reassembled (reintegrated) the disintegrated elements of his potential at the end of his experience, by which he had greater understanding of himself.

As artist, BBGD had gradually come to understand and appreciate possible parallels between his mentor's Ogunian tragic spirit and an actor, that is, as he dug into the depths of character study to come to an understanding of his particular role. But, as he always felt, something presupposed that spirit, the inevitable force that realized the accomplishment, or non-accomplishment of the character's objectives, what could be called the fate of the character. To understand this driving force is to come to terms with processes of characters (indeed life processes of all human beings), the roles the artist-playwright create for actors to inform audiences.

It was in an attempt to understand this process that BBGD encountered the divinity that Yoruba tradition poses to sanction the fate of humans, Esu-

Elegbara, the trickster fate-god[††††]. The god, by extension, implicates the fate of characters that playwrights create, and therefore the fate of the actor that tries to assume these roles. BBGD always felt indebted to WS for his perception of Ogun, even though that insight has become a point of departure for the interests they both entertained on their respective gods. Actually, BBGD did not see it as a departure at all; rather, one that is an informative extension of the other. He hoped WS would also see it that way.

Be that as it may, he had gone on to apply his theoretical argument to all central characters, especially those of WS's creation, such as the Professor in *The Road*, Kamini in *A Play of Giants*, Kongi in *Kongi's Harvest*, Bero in *Madmen and Specialists*, and Elesin-Oba in *Death and the King's Horseman*. Although he had a clearer perception of them as Ogunian artists, he found none as complete an artist as the god they surrogated. As such, they must remain Ogunian by the fact of the fate (Esu) that cripples all mankind in the effort to accomplish the balance Esu embodies. It is also the balance that gods and avatars strive to achieve in their ascendancy to deification and divinity. This thought and idea ultimately brought him back to the performance of *Oyedipo at Kolhuni*, WS's adaptation of Sophocles' *Oedipus at Colonus*. For the play seems to have dramatized the achievement and subsequent deification that expresses Oyedipo/Oedipus/Sango fate's (Esu's) balance. More about that experience later.

[††††] The research into the god latter produced the writer's scholarly books: *Archetypes, Imprecators and Victims of Fate: Origins and Developments of Satire in Black Drama* (Westport, CT: Greenwood Press, 1989); *Poetics of the Creative Process: An Organic Practicum for Playwriting* (Lanham, MD: University Press of America, 2005)

Scenes Eight

Artist of the Theater: Quests into Directing

Coming upon directing, for BBGD, would seem to be a discovery of an inborn creative talent dating back to high school in Baptist Academy, which he liked to dub simply Baptist High. He felt an academy meant several things, which Baptist Academy was not, except it suited the mindset and pleasures of the American mission that modelled it after the American system of high school. Anyway, he had no interest in acting; in fact he had an aversion for any memory work, an endeavor to which he ascribed acting. But then, he seemed quite at ease, or at large, with directing something, which seemed to fit his leadership qualities, as he later found out.

He couldn't quite remember how it happened. Of all the students in the class, he was the one chosen by the English teacher to direct a mock trial. When the possibility was suggested to him, he could see himself in such a role, so he accepted the challenge. How it all went, and what exactly he did that merited the art of directing was anybody guess. He simply couldn't put his finger on it as time went on, except that, there was a group picture of the event that he had somehow carried with him ever since. Coming upon it, some thirty years after, there were all the members of his cast. He could recognize some of them in varying degrees, especially his high school best friend, Wole Alakija (alias Jackie), who had on the lawyer's gown and wig borrowed from his father. Apparently, the show went very well, otherwise he would have remembered any negative critical feedbacks.

Similar kind of faith in him as a director also happened a few years after, when he was at the Northwestern Polytechnic in London. He had to go there to study for his GCE, a higher school certificate that would gain him admission into the university; he was anticipating Bristol, about which he learnt from his mentor before he left Nigeria. At the Poly he had met Naomi Richards, who initiated the directing idea. As he would realize later, Naomi's act of faith in him was not blind, but subtly garlanded with ulterior motives.

"Hey Henry, I've been thinking," she said one glorious day, all smiles and seemingly warmhearted. "We need a drama club here, so why don't you and I start one?"

"Really?" He cast a sharp surprised look at her. They were, as almost always, sitting together at the small special Literature class (a kind of Honors class) created by Dr. Dante Rossetti, the chair of English. She had also pushed him to go and ask Dr. Rossetti whether he could be in that class.

"Why not? I think it'd be exciting!" Her contrasting, rather cold gray eyes almost betrayed an insincerity that BBGD failed to capture at the time. "You've been in a theater company in Nigeria, haven't you; I bet you were very good too."

"Well…"

"Don't be modest, I can see it." Before he could betray his still shaky theatrical experience, she had already framed him and concluded. "I've spoken with Rossetti about the drama club; he's quite agreeable."

"Well, I guess that would be delightful," he said, as he summoned up his expansive ego.

"I've thought about our first production." She leaned over to him with cold-glowing affection to whisper it, *"Romeo and Juliet."* Dr. Rossetti had just then come into the lecture room, as usual with pipe in his mouth, treating them all with a smokeless puff of "What a fine afternoon!" his beaming cheerful eyes panning across his students. His birdlike head features, sporting a pipe and sitting on his tall somewhat skinny frame, somehow suggested enormous intelligence and wisdom, which he engaged with stiff-upper-lip, modest control.

"I've asked John Ivey to be Romeo and I'll be Juliet…"

"Who's John Ivey?"

"The guy that always comes in so late in Dr. Hart's class. He's also done some theater, I believe. But he'll be a perfect Romeo. I'll introduce you to him later."

Dr. Rossetti had started introducing his seminar topic.

"And you can be the director," Naomi finally dropped the bombshell.

"Me?" BBGD hadn't quite conceived the whole idea of theater club and his place in it, let alone directing unfamiliar faces in a not quite familiar, white environment. Although the polytechnic had a noticeable international flair, he was the only black person in Hart's Literature class and, of course Rossetti's special seminar class. Also, he had only been about two months in the country.

"Yes, yes, you. I think you'll be a marvelous director." How Naomi conceived and confirmed that in her head was hard to figure out. She didn't know anything about BBGD's theatrical experience apart from what he had told her, which was not much. Simply, he was in Soyinka's 1960 Masks in Nigeria where he acted a few roles. Although he probably feathered his expansive ego a little bit saying that, he never quite got into any details as to what plays or roles he played.

Dr. Rossetti now pointed his bird-face towards the two with humorous charge. BBGD caught him just in time to discourage anymore conversation with Naomi, however whispered.

"Okay, let's talk further after class."

Rossetti had gone on to list an African novel in his introduction. Thankfully BBGD was half-listening to what ended in a punchline, with the professor's eyes directed at him: "Do any of you know which novel I was referring to?"

It was BBGD's luck that day, because he was probably the only one who knew the answer to the question, precisely why it was directed to him. He was thankful that he had managed to catch the name of the writer of the reference from the hardly moving lips of the professor: Alan Paton.

"Cry the Beloved Country," he brimmed with pride, to which Rossetti shook his head with admiration. He had come upon and browsed the novel only a few years before, back in the British Council library in Lagos. It was about Apartheid South Africa, of which he knew little beyond the boycotts and the recent tragedy of mass killing of blacks in Sharpeville Johannesburg.

He vaguely imagined what the situation would have been like had he not stood up to the challenge and come up with an answer that was expected of him. He decided not to even think about it, the idea of being a nincompoop or the ignoramus. That cloud would have descended on his head from the vantage point of Dr. Rossetti. Since he joined the class, he had striven not to let down the race, but to try and confront its intellectual challenge, whenever he could, by posturing a well-informed ego. When he first approached Rossetti about joining class the professor was a bit reluctant, but after a few test questions about BBGD's colonial-fashioned intellect, he finally conceded. Then the English chair became more convinced after the first essay BBGD submitted for the class assignment, the idea that "Man needs gods."

Naomi posted the notice about the drama club and a handful of interested students met with her and BBGD, including John Ivey. At the meeting he felt a little intimidated by the questions Ivey asked regarding Naomi's announcement of BBGD as the director that had some theater experience. To be fair, BBGD may have himself betrayed some inadequacy about the announcement. He tried as much as possible to surmount this, but Ivey may have caught it by his peculiar deep, dark gaze. However, the true test of conviction came at the first rehearsal, when BBGD began to block cold and dry. At every move he suggested, Ivey imposed questions about the justification for the move and was unwilling to accept the director's hesitant defense. Rather, the actor suggested the way he felt he should respond to the Shakespeare's lines. Naomi as Juliet seemed to be on the side of Ivey, while at the same time tried to calm and fence off the rising tension.

Shakespeare's lines. BBGD did not pretend he understood them better than a native of the culture. He had probably at that point not read as much Shakespeare as they had. But somehow, he had a sense of the particular Elizabethan culture and the Bard's lines and all he could go by was his instincts. He did not begin to understand that intuitive attribute until much later by way of so many developments. These would include, the positive comments of his Bruford instructors in poetry and acting classes; particularly comments with regard to his response to Shakespeare. Also, to be taken into account was his enchantment with the Bard through watching several of his plays at the Aldwych and at Stratford-upon-Avon; the intrusion of Shakespeare's rhythm, syntax, and choice of idiom in the dialogue of his own plays; and his final confrontation with himself to investigate his sensory response. Regarding Shakespeare seeping unto his plays, Professor Gilman at Yale was to make a joke at his expense in class.

It was after that first rehearsal that Naomi made it known to him that John Ivey wanted to be the director, and BBGD could do nothing but give in. In fact, that seemed to be the collapse of the drama club. He couldn't remember any other planned rehearsals after that, although it could be, they had other rehearsals in which he refused to participate. But, to his knowledge, there was no resulting performance of the play. His relationship with Naomi also seemed to have suffered a sharp decline after that, for he couldn't remember any other specific dialogue with her thereafter. But it was possible that a vacation happening after that first rehearsal helped the decline, making it impossible to go on or start afresh. At any rate, as it turned out, his time at the Poly was limited to one year.

Come to think on it, Dante Rossetti could have had something to do with it. He had heard of the drama club and BBGD's involvement with it. He had gone for conference with the professor about his essay—perhaps the one reflecting on the suggested topic, "Man Needs Gods." After the professor finished with his comments, his bird-face held BBGD at a glance with unblinking eyes as he made a few puffs at his pipe.

"Heard you're directing *Romeo and Juliet* with Ms. Richards," he asked, speaking through his nose and piped stiff lips.

"Yes," BBGD made a quiet response, head bowed. He was unable to hold up to the English Head's fixed and non-committal gaze.

"Why don't you face your studies, my boy," was his blunt advice, with a few more puffs at his pipe. Then he got more specific: "Be careful. Face your studies and don't be distracted by Ms. Richards."

Dr. Rossetti, obviously, was pitching beyond the drama club. BBGD felt the judgment of the professor was somewhat correct; his habitual sitting in class with Naomi may have betrayed some ulterior intentions. Of all his encounters at school and his hostel, the Methodist International House, she was the first English woman he felt somewhat close to. Even though there was something deceptive about her beauty and cold gray eyes, he had indeed entertained getting romantically closer with her. Rossetti's subtle advice, a shower of wisdom not to be ignored, suddenly overcame his thoughts and drenched his body with caution. The advice also probably awoke a subliminal caution, which implicated his colonial upbringing and his parent's negative attitude to white wives brought back home by Nigerian husbands. BBGD was to resist that attitude as far as he could throughout his various encounters with whiteness in England and the US. His resistance probably struck a vulnerable nerve in the US when he became more aware, exposed nakedly to the racist nature of whiteness.

By the time he got to the US, he had got a little more secure with his directorial instincts through his professional acting experiences, although he had done little or nothing in terms of actual directing until after Yale School of Drama. His experiences had been limited to occasional attempts at scenes at the Rose Bruford conducted by Leo Baker, the acting teacher. But the disposition was always there with any show he had watched in London or at Yale, with thoughts about what it took to be a director. As such, he had enjoyed the after-show conversations in pubs or first night parties whenever he was at the Aldwych in London, or Stratford-upon-Avon. It was always an added opportunity if the directors were present.

*****

Every class-year of playwriting at the Yale School of Drama seemed to always generate a favorite playwright. Such a playwright had the advantage of the possibility of being produced, or considered for production either in a workshop set-up at any of the Yale Theater spaces—the studio, the Cabaret—or at the Yale Rep in the Sunday experimental series.

In BBGD's class-year, it was Lainie London, at least in the first year. She was another white encounter with whom he became close, but only as classmates. However, she too almost distracted his studies. She would whisper in class tete-a-tete outrageous advices to go against the system, or gossip about

Yale and their classmates at cafes or at her self-contained apartment at York Towers. One of her plays received a performance in the Sunday series at the Rep., much to the envy of all the other playwrights. But that seemed to have been all for her—she didn't seem to have plied beyond that fame; attention thereafter shifted to another playwright in their second and third year.

He had remained friends with Lainie after Yale, in spite of her having a boyfriend, later to be husband. They were still friends certainly during his two-year stint at the Ethel Walker School, where he was engaged as a mime instructor with an added opportunity to direct plays. Up till that point in the life of the school, they had engaged only a lighting technician, who happened to be a community actor, simply to light school occasions such as graduation, concerts, guest lectures, etc. When the headmaster realized BBGD was a professional actor in England and a recipient of a Yale MFA, he had no doubts of his directorial capabilities, and looked forward to him directing the girls of Ethel Walker, a university preparatory school for young women. There he wasn't given much of a salary, but that excluded free meals at the school and a rent-free accommodation, a chalet overlooking eight hundred acres of the school property. Those essentials went a long way for him to ignore the small salary.

He was very popular with the students. They had always come to him for favors, such as taking them to the cinema in the school's van. He was also friends with Michael Leonard, the house master, and his wife Molly and often went to dinner in their apartment in one of the dorms. Convinced that nobody else in that school knew about theater more than him, especially the way all the teachers looked up to him, he was able to fan his expansive ego around as an authority in theater, and as such suppress any feeling of insecurity. This allowed his creative and inventive capabilities to guide him, that is, in spite of the feelings of animosity the white technician had towards him. Once or twice the technician had tried to sabotage his directing, to no avail.

Lainie leant about his opportunity by phone and immediately jumped the gun:

"Why don't you plan to direct that play of mine? I think you'll do a good job."

"Which play?"

"*The Beast*. The one workshopped at Yale Rep in our first year. I think it will be fun for the girls."

He remembered the play well. As far as his knowledge took him, she didn't really produce any other stuff after that play, and probably the reason why attention shifted to another playwright, Bill Hauptmann in their second year. He wasn't sure what she submitted for her thesis, probably a revision of that play, and all the reason why she would like a full production of it. But it's also possible she suggested it because the play was a right fit for two girls like the students at Ethel Walker.

"What do you think?" she prodded BBGD for immediate response.

"Yes, why not. Send me the script and I'll work on it."

"Wonderful! I'll send you the script immediately."

The more he thought about it, the more he felt a production of the play would be right for the Ethel Walker community; he sincerely warmed up to doing it. He was also delighted about its small cast, which was probably sufficient to test his directing skills. It was easy to sell the idea to the enthusiastic headmaster, Mr. Pierce (pronounced for some reasons "purse"). All the faculty were also excited about seeing at first hand the work of this Yale graduate with superior knowledge through his British professional experiences, some of which had been tested in their classroom. For instance, Michael, also a Yale graduate in English, invited him to come and join his discussion of *Oedipus Rex*. While the instructor, a PhD at that, had undisputable knowledge of the play, he wanted his guest to suggest ideas of staging through his theatrical vision. It was a play BBGD knew very well but rather than go into any analysis of it, at which Michael was probably better, he suggested ideas about the chorus, demonstrating its importance to the text in relation to Oedipus. He also highlighted the messenger's speech in relation to Oedipus' character, and gave a demonstration of the graph of the speech. He used images of an airplane, at start-point, then its movement on the tarmac, at first indirectly, to take-off point; there it gathers momentum, courses down the runway, then takes off; cruising in flight for some time, it begins to descend and then touches down at its destination. The idea was by no means original to him; he got it from a book written by his favorite French actor and mime, Jean-Louis Barrault. But the teacher and student's acclamation of his rendering boosted his ego to substantial heights, which he tried to control with a counterbalancing modesty.

There was no audition for the production of *The Beast*; he knew whom he wanted—two of his favorite students, Darby and Betsy in his mime class. He felt he had a gift for choosing actors for roles by mere instincts, a notion he was to test and be more confident about. Although in most cases he still had to go through the auditions, he was most of the time dead-on with his original sight-picking.

He very much wanted to work with Lainie and as such he invited her to Simsbury early in the rehearsal period to get her take as the author. After the Saturday afternoon rehearsal, they had dinner at the dining hall with the students; at their table was the headmaster and the actors, Darby and Betsy. He also introduced her to some of the other faculty who had set their gloating eyes on her as soon as they entered the dining hall.

"I'm really delighted we're doing your play here," Mr. Pierce pitched his nasal enthusiastic twang at Lainie. "How's the rehearsal?"

"Going very well," came Lainie's quick response with almost equal nasality. "Femi is a wonderful director. Yes, I mean that, my friend," she countered BBGD's modest grin.

"Looking forward very much to seeing it." The headmaster's addendum related more to his admiration of the lucky hire he had made for the school, which Lainie's fanned acknowledgement only confirmed.

"And you girls are doing a great job," she went on to quickly throw an encouragement at the actors. They simply beamed a trickling chortle and immediately bowed their heads to their Cornish hen dinner with rookie teenage shyness.

Lainie had to leave the dinner early so she could get back on the road to New Haven. She got up to say her goodbye to the headmaster and all around the table.

"Hope we'll see you at the opening," Mr. Pierce piped. "We can all have dinner at my house and then go and see the play." He pointed in the direction of the house, which Lainie could only imagine in the hall. Outside as he escorted her to the parking lot, BBGD connected the image for her by indicating the lone house on the hill on the other side of the road, sitting on acres of the school's property. He had come to associate the house with the soirees the headmaster gave his faculty from time to time. First time BBGD went, his eyes boggled at the spread, especially the sumptuous steak cuts being barbequed; he ended up helping himself to two of these, with baked potatoes, cooked vegetables, tossed salad and cocktail shrimps.

"Oh. I'd love to come to one of those. I love soirees," Lainie delightfully put an RSVP stamp on her friend's depiction. Before she entered her car, she gave him one of her cold and puritanical, emotionless shift-to-the-left, sideways hugs, with "Keep it up, my friend. See you soon." Then she paused and linked up with the conversation they had during the rehearsal:

"You mean you couldn't get me even an author's fee for this production?"

"Well, I can try; but as I told you, I don't know whether I could negotiate such a fee in this non-professional set-up."

"Okay, okay. Doing the production is more important to me."

Not that BBGD wanted a more intimate or some emotion-laden hug. For that could suggest an unrequested assumption, or lay itself open to interpretation of intimacy, for which he had no intentions. But there was nothing in the gesture even to support a sincerity of friendship; rather it exposed a dichotomy between words and action. This wasn't something he had felt mainly with her, but what he had observed sometimes ever since he had been in the country and mingled among Americans, especially whites. That it happened with somebody who professed to be his friend was all the more perplexing. It sometimes felt like she didn't reciprocate similar trust and faith he offered her, which made him, at times, not to put complete trust on any compliments she made. Case in point was the commendation she gave at the dinner table about his directing capabilities, which he took with modest calm. Although the comment boosted his ego, it was only because it was made in front of the Ethel Walker community.

He had an inclination to being sincere and taking people at their word, an effort he found was always flouted by unreciprocated gestures of insincerity. Is this a question of hypothetical two plus two not always amounting to the habitual four? That question obviously summoned up his childhood difficulties of coming to terms with that rather conclusive mathematical factor of four.

"BBGD, you can sometimes be so naïve," his mentor had told him many times, when he seemed to have taken situations too much at face value. But his constitution couldn't be bothered to get consumed with doubt. He would rather trust until he was let down, which of course could be too late, he realized. "But you'll learn, I promise you," Br'er Wole had affirmed.

That process of learning gradually began by the time he got to the US to face it nakedly. He started to learn first by being conscious of the lie and, before coming to any conclusions, put his belief or disbelief on hold—an attitude he found somewhat difficult at first. However, connecting his thoughts with his acting exercises at Bruford, the consciousness of different representations had served him well, the reading between the lines and deciphering in dialogue sincere and insincere thoughts and gestures of the characters.

The production of *The Beast* was his first formal adventure into directing a full production, albeit, and just as well, a two-character one-act. A play about impact of Americanism on teenage life, it was successful through gaining the confidence of the writer and the rather rave responses of faculty and students of the school. This placed him in a position to begin to seriously include directing in his artistic career. At Yale, he had read and come to understand the gradual evolution of the director as the artist of modern and contemporary theater, taking the place of the playwright of the Classical and the Renaissance periods. Although a playwright himself, a still grappling one at that, he liked the idea of the modern status of the director and wanted to aspire towards this like his mentor had done. Not having a formal training in the area, like some of his friends in the directing program at Yale, he picked up and browsed one or two books to formally acquaint himself with some of the responsibilities of a director. However, through watching so many plays in England and having the opportunity of interacting with directors at the Royal Court as well as talking to some of the directors of the Royal Shakespeare company on his many visits to Stratford-upon-Avon, mingling with them in the pub after productions, he had come to realize a lot depended on the senses, on the creative and experimental self through trial and error.

The Ethel Walker School had no formal theater areas such as costume, music, scene-shop, etc. The absence had awakened his sense of improvisation, which had been with him since his acting training at Rose Bruford. He had employed the experience to some success directing *The Beast*, taking advantage of the available departments and teachers at the school that could help him. With that understanding, he had approached the sewing mistress, the music teacher, the chapel organist, and of course the lighting technician, who also helped with sound.

He discussed on phone with Lainie the progress of the rehearsal and the ideas he had relating to sound. His idea of utilizing the organ sound for the opening of the play was welcomed by her with excitement. He had a fascination for the pipe organ since growing up in Nigeria, subconsciously taking in the renditions of the organists at his childhood church—the Olowogbowo Methodist Church, now Wesley Cathedral, Olowogbowo. Principally, he had been fascinated by the harmonic manipulations of the English organist, Dr. Thalden Ball, through radio transmissions, which had formed an important part of his Sunday evening preoccupations. The chapel at the Ethel Walker School had a good organ, and it was easy to approach the school organist.

"Is that all you want, not the whole song?" Mr. Sykes asked with his soft voice after trying out the last phrases of "God Bless America" before it was recorded. BBGD had always found it fascinating and ironical that such a short man with a petite figure could command at the organ such power and authority with his hands and feet.

"Yes, yes, that's all I want," BBGD affirmed. He wished he could have more, but that was all he felt the script needed. He had nowhere else within the play he could also fit those phrases or some other phrases of the song. Thinking back, as got more experienced, he discovered he should have had more undertones of the organ for the rather satiric tone he wanted to strike with the play. But at the time, that was all his creative instincts would allow him.

"Of course I don't know the play; I'll just have to rely on you," the organist affirmed casting his face back at the director from his seat at the console.

"Yes, yes, I just wanted it to suggest the satiric temperature of the play. It's about these young girls, products of questionable American values."

"Oh, I see, I see." The idea dawned on Mr. Sykes.

"So, I want it loud and big."

"Okay."

After repeating the phrases quite a few times, sometimes to the dissatisfaction of the director, and at times that of the organist, they both arrived at a workable and recordable rendering.

"Thanks, thanks. That was wonderful," BBGD was delighted.

"Well, I can't wait to see the production," Sykes complimented.

The success of the production, much to the admiration of faculty and students confirming their confidence in him, gave him the self-assurance to direct another show in his second and final year at the school. In order to accommodate the number of interested students, he gambled on a more ambitious play with a larger cast—the "Ants" part of *The Insect Play* of the Brothers Capek.

*****

"Lucky boy!" "Famous boy!" That was the interchangeable appellation that his first cousin Akin Coker's mother always used to accost him. It often intrigued him how the accolade came out of the blue for no apparent reason he knew of, nor which she knew of, in his judgment. As such, he assumed it just came out by some instincts, probably through internalized tonal bites such as Femi... Feme...fame..., ultimately to famous. Yet, the acknowledgement sometimes crossed his mind whenever he felt fulfilled with his objectives by some luck. Perhaps she was a witch or some clairvoyant who knew? Anyway, the supposition appeared to be the case regarding the repetitive luck that seemed to come his way at the beginning of his professional career after Rose Bruford; whether in acting or directing, he had found himself in productions that effortlessly lay on his path for him to accept.

Coming upon Athol Fugard, he had his first professional engagement performing Chume, in *The Trials of Brother Jero*. Then, sighting his performance in that production, Bill Gaskill, the artistic director of the Royal Court, got him to play Second Witch in *Macbeth*, and from there he went on to play Lakunle in *The Lion and the Jewel*. All within two years, he had been thrown into the challenges of leading and principal roles.

Normally, an actor coming out of drama school really needed to develop his professional craft preferably in the regional repertory theaters. But such a procedure was not available to black actors, who had no promising black roles available to them at the Rep, or even if they were to cast color-blind, which was unthinkable at the time. In fact, his only venture with a repertory company was to play Persil-le-Noir in *Irma La Douce*. As such, most of them stayed in London to take on occasional roles, or as it happened employed as "servants and sword carriers" in Shakespeare's plays. Also they might come by small roles on television and films, most of the time, non-speaking.

Of course, having the luck of principal roles had its setbacks. During the period of his engagement he couldn't do anything else other than be consumed by such roles, which however did not come often enough. But he was able to survive the arid periods of non-engagement, partly by acting in radio plays at the BBC African Service, and partly by doing clerical work at the Eagle Star Insurance—a flexible job that often paid his bills. However, he did not stay long enough in London to test his talents in acting, pulled away, by luck again, to the US to pursue his nagging ambition in other areas of theater.

Lord Luck confronted him no less in directing. He must have been introduced to Lennox Brown by one of the artistic directors at the Harford Stage Company, Jessica Desmond. BBGD had met her through a friend, Judy Trenchman, at a social gathering; he had met Judy, a divorcee looking for a friend, also at a social event. Sighting his picture in an edition of Encyclopedia Britannica, in a picture captioned with a Wole Soyinka entry, Judy had introduced him to Jessica as "this famous actor from London, graduated from Yale School of Drama, now a professional-in-residence at the Ethel Walker School." As usual, as far as his modesty would have it, he recoiled a little to being a "famous actor;" but as he would gradually learn "That's the way we do things here—you have to sell yourself." Judy had whispered in his ear.

He got a phone call from Lennox, who hardly knew him, about his intentions to do a play of his at the University of Hartford, where he was playwright-in-residence. Lennox indicated that the production would include professional actors from New York. Called *The Winti Train*, he wanted BBGD to participate in the play. When Lennox sent him the script to read, he felt it had promise and was excited to play one of the roles, especially with the fact that the production would include actors from New York.

Then just before rehearsals began, he got another call from Lennox: "Just learnt the guy I wanted from New York to direct the production can't make it—he has other engagements. So, I was wondering whether you'd be interested in directing it."

"Me?" BBGD sounded a little alarmed. Not even allowing modesty to hedge him, he genuinely thought he wasn't up to it, not so much the fact that the great responsibility was thrown at him at a moment's notice. But perhaps the greatest threat posed was the fact of his directing professionals from New York. His hesitation therefore lacked any pretensions. "Are there no other people from the New York crowd who could direct it?"

"No, I really would like you to direct it." On what grounds, BBGD almost let out. For surely the man had not seen anything of his in directing; not that there was much to flaunt in that capacity.

"I may not be able to do a good job," BBGD continued to find a way out.

"I'm sure you would. You're the only one I see who could direct it," Lennox insisted. Was it because of some special cultural affiliations, BBGD wondered, between Caribbean and African?

"Listen, I'll be at some rehearsals. I will be able to help you, if you need me." Lennox was firm in his faith in him.

He did not consider the gesture as necessarily welcoming or conciliatory, since the presence of the writer might create other limitations of his creativity. On the other hand, he felt it might be a blessing of sorts, especially by the very fact that the production would be somewhat professional. To be able to handle professional actors, though intimidating, was enticing, as it would boost his ego and directorial abilities. The more he thought about it, within those few decision-making minutes, the more he convinced himself he could do it.

"Okay, I guess," he agreed with quiet confidence.

"Great! I'm really excited. You will be a wonderful director," Lennox fanned his ego with compelling finality. The writer's faith went a long way to dispel any uncertainty and inadequacy.

The cast was a mixture of amateur students at Hartford University and professional actors. The students were eager to learn from the professionals and the professionals were willing to flaunt their New York experience no end at the naivety of the students. This was all very well, but it did not speak to the problem of making the relationship work for the director.

BBGD really had no professional experience to go by, except his acting tenure on the London stage. While that experience was legitimate and might mean something more to the New Yorkers, it said nothing about his directorial know-how, for which he was tested every bit of the way. In addition to this, it was obvious that unless the students knew something about London as the world's entertainment center equal to New York if not better, they were more likely to respect the New Yorkers than him. Added to this was the matter of his "foreign accent," which Americans in general were fond of registering and commenting on for one reason or the other. He didn't believe he had a thick African accent; if anything, it was a mixture of British, Nigerian, and American, each of which could come into play depending on whom he was entertaining conversation with. But any Americans he met, be it Caucasian or African American, brooked no such distinctions and could care less making any. All they knew was he came from an alien predominantly black country, or from some "jungle" in Africa—the emphasis was by implication.

Two different levels of actors demanded at least two different approaches. He had to learn that quickly early in the rehearsals. The students needed to be guided and coaxed into developing their characters; sometimes some demonstrative illustration may be needed and should be appropriate to jolt their creative versatility into action. The professionals, on the other hand, needed more flexibility and should be left alone most of the time to develop their character within the concept chosen by the director, which the director should constantly but judiciously bring to their attention. However, they too were not above being given demonstrative illustrations, although as a last resort.

The playwright was present most of the time, but remained in the background. BBGD got comfortable with this after some time, through the discussions they had after rehearsals regarding its progress with the actors. As such, his presence was ultimately helpful to the novice director in gaining confidence and meeting the challenges presented by the actors, especially the professionals, who tested his abilities whenever they could. Through his own acting experience, he knew actors had the habit of talking about the director behind the scene, sometimes blaming him for their own deficiencies or uncertainties. Especially so when rehearsals were coming to an end and they were still insecure with their characters.

Even at these early stages of his directorial experience, BBGD was aware of his fault, an oversight as he would like to call it. He was lax, or stingy, at offering commendations that actors always needed to feel secure. Probably something he absorbed working with WS. He preferred to deliberate on what still needed to be done with their character choices. Regarding this, he was challenged once or twice by some of the professionals.

"Ah," came the exasperated but humorous Caribbean voice of Tony, "you seem to see all my faults. How about me hearing some of my good deeds?"

"My blemish, Tony. I always take for granted those good deeds and more conscious about further development. Sorry about that."

"We would like to know sometimes you know," he insisted with a quiet smile.

"Yes, yes. I understand." BBGD decided to keep the matter lighthearted. "I usually do soon enough, although I'm quite aware this sometimes comes a bit too late in the game."

Apart from such incidental comments, nothing major came from the New Yorkers. He learnt to let them be and work things out whenever he sensed any stubborn opposition to his direction. He realized he must always make actors understand from the beginning that he did not give praises easily, that he tended to be more preoccupied with how to make their delineations even better and in harmonious relationship with the other characters. But he would try and keep in mind as essential what he thought amounted to Pavlov's theory, even though he questioned the theory's full practical applicability with humans.

*****

"I just have to tell you, that I loved your production of *Madame Tinubu*. It's very professional and the best thing I've seen since I came to here." The remark was from an African American Professor in the Department of English at the University of Ife. "I tell you; it could be any of the productions on Broadway in New York. I think this is your forte."

The professor's additional comment about Broadway was rather unexpected, and it seemed genuine enough to make BBGD consider it. It almost finally legitimized what he had felt all along, that he had a natural propensity for directing, an area in which he never formally received training, a talent even better than what he could discern as creative in his playwriting, let alone acting. However, he realized his coming into the area by way of acting and playwriting was very instructive and beneficial. By the time he took up his appointment at the University of Ife, he had already come to a solid understanding of the process and had developed enormous confidence, especially through directing the professionals from New York in *The Winti Train*. Like in that production, the actors' experiential levels were mixed, comprising of theater students and some professionals, who received their training and rigorous grooming in Ola Rotimi's Ori-Olokun company, a professional arm of the Unife Theater. There was a lull when Rotimi was Head of Drama. Under him, it was very difficult for BBGD to do any directing, since every production was all about the playwright. He had to wait until his former mentor took over.

Madame Tinubu was BBGD's first production at Ife and its challenges were a first for him in many respects. For some reasons, the writer, Akin Ishola, had been directed to him as a possible director for his play. He looked at the rather untidy typewriter-typewritten play and was at first thrown off by its very large cast of over 30. Its dialogue was also very formal in places with a kind of Yorubanglish fluency—a term coined by Dapo Adelugba to reflect the Yoruba culture and its rather adept but sometimes clumsy appropriation and transposition of the English language. During rehearsals, once, obviously exasperated by questions of interpretation raised by the script, he let his feelings out, oblivious of the presence of the playwright:

"I don't know, the language of this play baffles me, at times too formal, stilted and contrived." Suddenly noticing that the playwright was sitting close by, he relented with immediate embarrassment, although still stood his ground as a knowing director: "Oh, Akin, you're here. Is it all right if we make that sentence more colloquial?" He would have done that anyway if the playwright were not there, as he had already done in places, although he meant to indicate the editing eventually to the playwright.

"Yes, yes of course." The playwright was very deferential, although BBGD was curious about how he took his off-the-record reaction and comment.

"Your play is very interesting, of course," he went on to engage, "but challenging in places regarding the formality of the dialogue."

"Yes, you can edit it where necessary." That was all BBGD wanted to hear, the trust that the playwright should have in him. Far be it from him to alter the meaning or the atmosphere the playwright intended, as the ego of another director might be tempted to do. As a playwright himself, BBGD was quite adamant about that. But since the productions of *The Beast* and *Winti Train*, he believed he had the knack for eliciting such meaning and atmosphere, and making a new unproduced play be conceived more clearly on stage. It was because of the muddle new plays usually presented that it was essential and productive they went through a series of workshops. *Madame Tinubu* needed such workshops, but he believed he could override these with his penchant for impeccable and disciplined manicure.

One of the major additions he added to the script, which he defended and which pleased the playwright and his critical colleagues, happened in the opening scenes. *Madame Tinubu* honors a figure in Nigerian history, a traditional Yoruba trader who championed Lagos economy through legitimate and illegitimate processes and always in conflict with her Western influenced competitors and the elite power structure.

To be able to celebrate her death with a traditional ritual imperative deserving her status, BBGD decided to introduce some aspects of the Adamu Orisha Play, a festival of Eyo masks, unique to Lagos, usually performed to celebrate the passing of important kings and chiefs. It was an enactment that BBGD was very familiar with as a Lagosian, and even researched it a little when he was assisting WS, before he left for further studies abroad. He remembered, through his childhood eyes, the celebrative parades, along major streets of Lagos, to honor kings such as Esugbayi and Kosoko. He especially recalled moments the key figure of the ritual festival passed by, the Adimu, a ritual sacrifice-carrier supposed to cleanse the community of accumulated evil. Wearing an ass's mask with mucus running down its nostrils like an indulged village idiot, the carrier moaned curses as he slowly moved along. To countervail the evil-efficacies of the ritual utterance, spectators on either side of the street symbolically clicked fingers over their heads to boomerang the highly potent curses back to the carrier. Apparently, this led to the carrier's anticipated sacrificial death at the end of the day's celebration.

With this in mind, BBGD prologued the production with "traditional women" on a balcony chanting a familiar Adamu-orisha-play ritual song, as they swayed their bodies and flailed their hands in the air. Simultaneous with the song, several Eyo-masquerades emerged on stage, manipulating their ceremonial staffs, the *opambata*, as they danced, crisscross, across the stage. To maintain a theatrical balance, he continued the motif in the middle scenes and at the end of the play. In the middle, a representation of the Adimu crossed the stage diagonally in a slow, silent movement. At the end, as an epilogue, a formation of the Eyo-masquerades, amid soft chanting of the traditional women, symbolically absorbed Madame Tinubu, as she moved one step at a time backwards, into the realm of the ancestors.

Also, at the beginning of the play, after the prologue, in order to strike a chord with the might of Madame Tinubu, the director organized a huge traffic of servants/slaves to cross the front of stage with loads of merchandises and supplies, deserving to the status of the famous trader.

Furthermore, with regard to the atmosphere of the play, he reflected through sound the two conflicting parties in the play, the traditional personages and the Western influenced émigré-elite. There was a clashing of traditional drumming and classical music at the beginning, and each of these sounds was then used as incidental music at relevant places in the production. He also simulated the sound of the Big Ben, to signify the sound of the former tower-clock imposed by the colonial government at the commemorative Tinubu Square.

As he progressed in his directing engagements, he was to perfect the use of sound to suggest the overall conflicting factions, introduced from the beginning of production. But it was the responses he got from the production of *Madame Tinubu*, endorsed by the remark about the show's potential as a Broadway or West End piece, that began to establish him as a possible artist of the theater.

*****

He had very much wanted work more closely with his colleague, Chuck Mike, a professional in residence at Unife Theater. The possibility offered itself with the production of his full-length play *The Gulf*. He very much wanted to mount the play through some workshop so he could make necessary rewrites, especially the African American aspects of it in terms of dialogue. Apart from the fact that he hated the idea of directing his own play, at least its first production, he was pursuing at the time a PhD degree in the department of English. It was a follow-up of his Master's in Afro-American Studies at Yale, and his initial agenda to have a doctorate. The Yale fellowship, secured through his friend, Henry Louis Gates, Jr., had taken him away from his academic responsibilities at Ife for two years, but it was during that period that he had conceived *The Gulf*. Back at his job in 1982, not content with coming back with only an M.A., even though a terminal, he had made strides to continue his research and pursue a PhD while still maintaining his teaching duties.

His return from the US had enormously helped him to rethink the script of the play, and he wanted Chuck as an African American to help resolve some of the awkwardness that still persisted in the dialogue of the African American character, Gold. However, for reasons of his own, probably through the intimidation of the Yoruba nuances and characters, Chuck declined taking up the whole directing aspect, but promised to assist BBGD, which he did, helping first with the auditions, and then at rehearsals working with the actors and their choices.

The play was the first consciousness of his aptitude for satire, even though the inclination had been there in some of his scripts all along. Even in the radio plays, which were heavily influenced by satiric postures such as in the Commedia dell'Arte and present in the hilarious characters of Moliere, Ben Jonson and Shakespeare. His African American studies at Yale however had brought the consciousness alive, when he struck upon the Yoruba trickster deity of fate, Esu Elegbara, and made the god the topic of his research and thesis. His first summer at Yale, he had gone back to Nigeria to interview relevant traditionalists, such as Babalawo-priests, Esu devotees and a king in Badagry, where he had heard Esu's worship was prominent. He couldn't have done that research as thoroughly as he did without the help of the wife of his colleague, Professor Akomolafe, then the business manager of Unife Theater. His wife physically took him to the research interviews and spoke in the language that the priests understood. The research and writing of his thesis had made him continue to pursue the god for his PhD dissertation that was supervised by Professor Ogunba, the then chair of English at Ife. This had led to his total revision of *The Gulf* and its satiric emphasis on the accidents that pervaded Nigerian roads, and the characters that had to do with such an epidemic.

BBGD's research resolved the fact that everybody has his or her own fate or Esu, no less the gods. In other words, Esu's devotees, who represent all mankind, as well as gods have their own fate or Esu. This affirmation would be explored more deliberately, from *The Gulf* on, in all his works, creative or scholarly. One of the myths of Ogun recreated in the play recounts the time the god got carried away and tested by his fate through the alcoholic deception of palm wine (apparently the drunken flaw of many gods); the intoxication caused him to massacre all the soldiers (his or foe's) on the battleground. BBGD updated the myth to accommodate practical notions of Esu (fate) and the transatlantic slavery:

BABALORISA (Ifa Priest and Traditionalist)
 Two hundred men had already been rounded up and taken to the Fort—
 Chained, dragged, beaten… It was a lucky day for the slavers.
 And the people of the village of Ire knew that was not the end of it;
 They knew that the baboon, if not checked in time, would come back
 To fodder some more. And on whose head might his chain of insults
 fall this time?
 They would not wait for this. Ogun, therefore, was approached for
 help, and he rose…
 The mighty lion of the battleground rose and summoned up all his
 forces!
 And, along with the able men of Ire-village making up the rear,
 He moved toward the Fort. This would be a battle long to be
 remembered,
 A battle the whole wide world should celebrate! Ogun, let me be with
 you today!
 Let me fight sided by side, blood with blood by your will,
 So that I may relate, or be related by, to future men…
 Ogun meant to penetrate the bushes, to crush with his mighty feet
 Any offending offal of a man gaming for Man,
 He meant to strike a deadly victory on all slavers, masters and
 caboceers alike!
 This must be a battle that should end all battles!
 Ogun, let me be with you today!

 Some distance from the coast, on the hills of the gulf, he surveyed
 The horrible scene of torture… Metals splintered and churned his
 stomach sour,
 Welled up in retches! Pukes and pukes of gunpowder and cannon balls,
 Enough to fight the whole wide world twice over,
 Were the immediate accoutrements retched up by his anger.
 He surveyed the battleground, consoled himself,
 And decided to camp in the bushes till nightfall. And,

To pass the time and refill his emptied stomach, he
Ordered palm wine to be served, the freshest and the
Sweetest he had ever drunk before…

Why then does it feel so strange tonight, this thirst
That could not be quenched, this wine that swells up in him
Certain strength which he never felt before?
Is it the first time he would transform his energies
Into metallic devices and warheads, powerful enough to
Match the ballistic apologies of modern man? This war, to end all wars,
Will long be remembered! Yet, what is this Mettle,
This demon of the palms? Is this a celebration prior to the fall…?
The wine-tapper stood in the midst of the mellow that was fogging his
eyes,
And tendered Ogun more wine—he stood,
A solitary figure, a glowworm in the mist…!
What then are you, demon of the palms?
Such portents of the crossroads Ogun failed to see!
A worm which teases the strength of the lion is no common worm!
Such vagaries of the two-faced one, Ogun failed to see…
Till his lusty spirits overpowered his better judgement,
Roaring with insurmountable vengeance!

Sound of guns and cannons rise and fall in the background

"Ogun have mercy, it's your people you mistake for the enemy!"
Deaf he was, like thunder and lightning, blind like a vampire-bat, wild like
forest fire!

Sound of guns and cannons rise and fall in the background

"Ogun have mercy, it's your people you slaughter!"
On and on the bulldozer raged and roared, tearing apart,
Macheting, uprooting, toppling and crushing every living thing in sight,
Man or beast, enemy or foe, slaver and slaves alike…!
Or so it seemed at dawn as he beheld his night's handiwork, the
Last strands of wine-dew lifting from his eyes.
There he stood, dumbfounded, confounded, an emotion-empty tank,
Cold stare goggling out of his metallic forehead!

Why, Elegbara, why? Will and fate, why? And when
Did the slave-boat creep away unnoticed? Did it sink?
Or, was this part of his drunken vision and imaginings of the night?
Did not a boat stand here, a center of his target?
And did he not mean to release its slaves, and turn the white slavers
their slaves?
Where then is the night-boat, on this fateful morning of night?
Sober-cold, numb and speechless, Ogun sank into the earth thereafter,
No more to see or be seen in whole in the light of day!
Those who seek his goodwill must labor the earth
With sacrifices and the offending wine,
Perchance it yields the creative transformations
Of his being... Perchance it fates a new ordering of the will
For the captives in the new world of fated survival, perchance...
Ogun is a demanding god!‡‡‡‡

True to the attributes of Esu, it was a satiric experience that made Ogun master and capitalize on his fateful/fatal potential in palm wine drinking. Made aware of that potential, he subsequently demanded his devotees to revel in it as a challenge to and control of their equilibrium and conscious state of being.

In the play, symbolic of the Ogun/Esu relationship is the wreckage/representation of a passenger truck/bus that is part of the set. As BBGD did in his direction of the play, the wreck could be utilized in various fateful/fatal flashbacks, as well as serve, principally, in the Prologue as the passenger-bus of Yangi, the driver responsible for the accident that the play dramatizes. An apt name for the driver, Yangi evokes Esu's red-laterite shrine/habitat and therefore one of his praise-names. In alignment with this fact is his father, Babalorisha, whose trickster, dissembling qualities and actions seem to replicate Esu's.

Through directing his own play, an important fact that came to his realization, widening the scope of his scholarship, is the research potential of playwriting and directing. To be sure, and to a certain extent, acting also involves certain investigation, but that inquiry feeds upon the research (consciously or otherwise) that made the play possible for the playwright, and the directorial research that provides for the director his concept of the play. With *The Gulf*, BBGD, as actor, playwright and now director, saw himself as

---

‡‡‡‡ *The Gulf*, pp. 37-39. The recitative in poetic prose, as read by the author at an award's reception, has been restructured here in its rightful poetic form, taking into consideration its rhythmic and sensory flow.

a consolidated epitome of all three aspects of the scholarship, as the true artist of the theater.

But in vain he had looked for the support of his mentor and colleague in his creative abilities in directing or even playwriting. The non-acknowledgment had suddenly dawned on him in the production of *The Gulf*, and, looking back, he had recalled it in some other instances of their relationship. Not that his expectations were dire. For, through affirmations that came from other quarters, he had come to believe in himself as a creative artist, one whose talents were inherent within his ambitions, an innate factor that was simply waiting to be kindled to action. And WS assisted in kindling it. He just wanted a little nod from him to boost his confidence, even a feedback of some sort. Throughout the rehearsals and performances of *The Gulf*, WS was in and out of the country. When he came back, a day or two after the production closed, it was too late for him to see the show. BBGD understood that, even though he felt the departmental head could have coordinated his schedule to accommodate the production of his former mentee. Was it a case of an oversight, or of being taken for granted? However, BBGD's disappointment was not based just on that one show. It was not the first and wouldn't be the last time he felt abandoned or even betrayed.

Earlier on, during his radio-play phase at the BBC African Theater, WS was the judge of a contest for which Shirley Cordeaux, the BBC drama producer, submitted one of his plays as a prospective winner of one of the three prizes. To his alarm and dismay, the play *Tortoise*, a play initiated by his mentor's imprisonment, did not even receive an honorable mention. As the most prolific writer of radio plays at the time, he felt he deserved to win, especially when he placed his play against the winners. Shirley and her co-producer, John Gordon were also baffled. Nobody knew what happened, but he had to contain the possible slight.

So was the much-acclaimed production of *Madame Tinubu*. It came and went without the former mentor's formal presence or comment. He missed the first performances at Ife and the touring performance at the National Theater in Lagos. Actually he appeared during the technical rehearsal in the afternoon of the day of performance at the National. He didn't stay for long but commented on the loudness of the sound being tested. He promised to come back later to see the whole show but didn't appear to have, because BBGD never heard any more about the production from him, until the New York visitors inquired about the possibilities of featuring the production in New York instead of *The Biko Inquest*. His comments then indicated he might have seen the production, but perhaps only fleetingly.

Later, after that production, another slighting occurred, also at Ife, when he directed two of his one-acts—*A Riddle of the Palms* and *Crocodiles*. He went out of his way to remind Kongi the last day of the performance and he promised to be there. He showed up with his friend, the chancellor of the university, but about half-hour after the end of the performance:

"Oh, has the performance ended?" There seemed a registration of some guilt in his tenor voice, his face soused with his favorite drink, wine—like his god, Ogun.

"Yep," disappointed, BBGD's response was abrupt.

"I thought it started at 8.30 or something?"

"7.30. As I said, they were two short plays. Both lasted about an hour and a half."

"It was your fault, Bola," he said, turning to the chancellor and then to BBGD. "He wouldn't let me leave."

"Yes, yes BB, put it all on me," chipped in the chancellor. "We were eating and drinking and before we know what, the time had flitted by. Is there going to be another performance?"

"This is the last one."

"And you can't do it just for us?"

"Bola," WS quickly butted in before BBGD could summon the appropriate response. "Too many things are involved, and I'm almost sure the set is being knocked down right now, in time for tomorrow's lecture."

"Oh."

"BB. So sorry. I'll make it up to you I promise." Although how he meant to make it up, other than by the usual frequent invitations to dinner, BBGD failed to see. What frustrated him, more than anything, was the probability that some woman, or women, were the cause of the tardiness. In Kongi's circle, in which BBGD believed he was, that was supposed to be understood, overlooked and forgiven.

Other similar occurrences had followed, some in directing situations, others in playwriting, all of which he had struggled to contain. It was impossible to conclude the attitude as nonchalant, because in many other respects, there were reasons to believe his mentor-colleague was very fond of him. He couldn't count the number of times they had met out of town or country (incidental or planned) and had ended up in some restaurants or at a friend's for wine over dinner. Neither could he think of it as some sort of creative envy, since there was no cause. He couldn't be a Wole Soyinka even if he wanted to; there was nothing of him to compare with his mentor's creative genius, of which he was proud and had only tried to emulate. If anything, it was him who should be envious; but he was not.

He could only think that the attitude of being taken for granted arose from the fact that his relationship with the eminent playwright started in his rookie days, when he was naïve about so many things regarding life, some knowledge of which he gained from the mentor. His other Ife University colleagues, sycophants really, that surrounded his personage and appeared to fawn him came long after BBGD. All came back home with their PhDs, and dominated their activity and scholarship with Wole Soyinka's intellectuality, creativity, and political activism. BBGD was of course envious of their degrees and wished he could wax in their scholarly fluency, so he could pontificate in that circle. He coveted their academic flaunt only because, ironically, these were the people Kongi seemed to favor and support at every turn. But, thinking further about it, as he began to see through their superficiality, he didn't really want to be in that circle. He could boast of an intellectualism that probably surpassed theirs, only his was introspective, true to his name in his rookie days as "the silent one." Even though Kongi saw through them also, dubbing some of them as pseudo Marxists, he still favored them, or so it appeared.

The thought had struck him often. Both he and WS seemed to share similar cultural interests which surpassed any of the others—WS was a devotee of Ogun, so to speak, while he was that of Esu, so to speak. Actually, as he was an artist, he could also claim an affinity to Ogun as patron of the arts, but he must always consider the god from the point of Esu Elegbara, that is, Ogun's Esu or fate essence. However that may be, he had wondered whether both their interests possibly had to do with that eternal struggle, being human, with Esu or fate. In this case it would seem to be the subconscious tussle that exists within the Ogun-Esu complex, a complex that describes their individuality as respective devotees. However much the thought seemed farfetched, it was still to him a creative idea that seemed plausible and therefore fascinating to entertain.

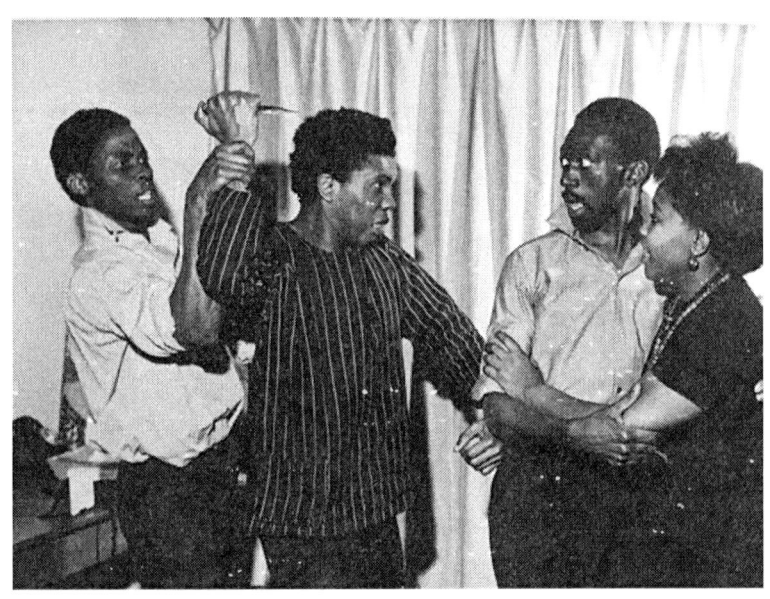

As jealous husband in a BBC African Theatre radio play

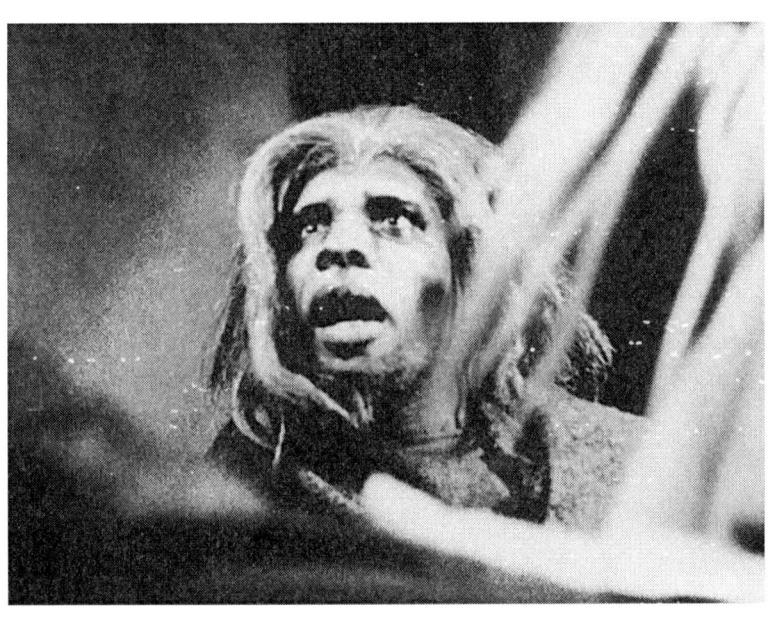

As 2nd Witch in *Macbeth*

As 3rd Murderer in *Macbeth*

As Colonel Moses in *Opera Wonyosi*

Scenes Nine

Re-Experiencing Soyinka: Oyedipo at Kolhuni (2002)

BBGD liked to appear on any scene silently and unannounced. Actually, WS seemed to be like that also—like when he came back home from his studies and experiences abroad. His home coming, to assume a research fellowship at the University of Ibadan, had been well arranged abroad, unknown to any of his friends or family. Few days before he arrived, he had told a friend of his to meet him at the airport, and he was already in Ibadan long before his parents knew. They of course did not find their WS's behavior amusing, but of course they were well aware of the difficult son they bore. BBGD got to know about all this much later when he got into the picture. He had gleaned it from his many eavesdropping on conversation among the playwright and his friends.

However, BBGD refused to make claims to what otherwise looked like an imitation of his mentor's behavior, because it was not. His own attitude, as far as he could remember, dated back before his experiences with WS, back in fact to his high school days. He would creep into the house after school long before anybody knew, thinking he had not got back from school and imagining the punishment he would receive from his father. Then, almost at dinner time, he would appear from where he was hiding, usually in the garret, much to the surprise of everybody. Actually, his behavior happened to be a strategy. By so doing, he kept away from and avoided many evening chores that might get dumped on him. But then, the conduct sometimes landed him in trouble, especially when they discovered his trick and constant hideout.

In England, his surprise disappearances and appearances had also baffled his friends and flat mates. Then his room was always his hideout, which he locked up if he didn't want to be bothered. He only appeared when he wanted to cook and eat, or to go to the bathroom. But sometimes he would disappear for days, when most likely he would have left for Stratford upon Avon. He would mumble something casual to his apartment mates as he left, something that they would remember when they were looking for him. At Stratford, he would similarly surprise his South African Bru-College friend, Alton Kumalo, just before a Friday performance. He could count on Alton getting him a ticket to see a show, if not for that Friday show, for the Saturday and or Sunday matinee.

He found nothing obnoxious about this behavior; it was his way of doing things as long as it didn't bother anybody; it had to do with his introspective nature. Looking several years back, he had always been like that since he was born, as far as he could remember. As a matter of fact, reflecting back on WS's incident, he recollected similar incident when he came back home from abroad for the first time in nine or ten years. He wrote his parents (since he knew he couldn't avoid telling them) only about two weeks before, allowing time for the mail to reach them. However, he was specific about his preference. He told them not to tell anybody else, knowing the need of parents in general, especially Nigerian parents, to make elaborate preparations such as attending church services for thanksgiving, visiting relatives, and undergoing the traditional rituals the homecoming would automatically foster. For all that warning, he didn't quite succeed, precisely because he told them anything at all, what WS had completely avoided.

And so it was in Las Vegas, when he showed up for the rehearsals of *Oyedipo at Kolhuni*. His decisions to appear unannounced was very deliberate; there was some confusion regarding his participation. He had responded and expressed his interests to WS in taking up the role of the Chieftain, which he found extremely funny—for some reasons he had at first associated the character with Peter Ustinov, recalling some of the humorous characters the distinguished actor had played. Contract for his participation requiring his signature was to be sent from the producers through University of Nevada at Las Vegas Conservatory. The contract did come after a few weeks, but he had some questions about the terms regarding artist's per diem, which was much lower than he had expected. He immediately contested it by e-mailing WS to find out whether he could intercede with the producers on his behalf so they could increase the fees. Before he got an answer, Peter Badejo, the designated choreographer for the show called him from London:

"*Egbon*," addressing him by proper traditional code of age seniority, "Long time now."

"Who's this?"

"Peter. Peter Badejo."

"Ah, Peter. Gee, quite a long time. What a surprise!"

They hadn't seen each other for some ten years. After a few minutes of catching up with some news, Peter finally alighted on reasons for his surprise call.

"Are you doing Prof's play?"

BBGD immediately sensed the direction he was going. "I'm supposed to."

"But have you received the contract?"

"Yes. In fact, I got it only yesterday."

"Well, I don't know about you, but what kind of chicken fee is that?" He said this, short of asking BBGD directly what was in his contract, perchance the choreographer was shortchanged.

"I know. Actually, I was thinking of complaining to Prof about this."

"I was also. In fact, that's why I called. I wanted to talk to you first before I did." Convinced that they were being offered the same amount, BBGD felt a kind of satisfaction from Peter. Then they both went on to vent airs about the possibility of declining to participate, although they both knew it might not be that simple—to vent superior airs about their professional rights and call the producers' bluff by rejecting their offer.

"Yes, let's first explore with Kongi the possibilities of getting better terms," BBGD came to the rather judicious conclusion then signed off: "See you soon."

"Yes, Egbon, looking forward to seeing you again."

BBGD was very apprehensive about WS's intervention, judging by experiences of the past. As such, he was surprised by the playwright's e-mail response to his complaint, although disappointed. The playwright had checked with the production agency; apparently the final budget given was less than expected. As to that, BBGD could go along with it as a reasonable man, although up to a point. However, that wasn't the disappointment; it was what followed:

"Look, you could turn it down you know. Let me know what you decided."

That felt like a stab launched at his chest, which he managed to deflect before it caused unnecessary harm. For that kind of the response typically brought back old wounds. Those memories erupted, but he decided for the meantime to suppress and rebury them. Rather, he chose to apply his most annoying weapon, silence. For what could one say? That he wasn't going to participate in a production of his former mentor for reasons of economics? For something he was really looking forward to? That the production agency along with the playwright/director could go to hell? That, at the last minute?

He did in fact e-mail the agency to find out whether they could do better, but again it all came down to the reason of low budget. He therefore resolved, in silence, not to sign the contract until he got to La Vegas, augmented by what counted in his favor as an obvious mismanagement—they had made the mistake of sending him a flight ticket. He vaguely knew, from previous correspondence, where the artists were supposed to lodge, and that somebody was supposed to meet him. Having both information in hand, he felt he could find his way. So, he arrived in Las Vegas, unannounced. As he got off the plane and checked his messages, he realized his wife had called from Baton Rouge.

"There have been two or three frantic phone calls since you left," Addie informed him when he returned her call.

"Oh yeah? Calls from whom?"

"One from Wole Soyinka, one from a guy who said you didn't respond to his last e-mail, regarding travel details. The third was from a woman, who was supposed to meet you. They were all worried whether you were going to come. I said you were on your way. I gave the woman your cell phone number. Did you arrive there safely?"

"Yah. A few minutes ago… Oh, just a minute, somebody's trying to call me. Okay, I'll call you back when I get to the lodging."

The phone call was from the woman, who introduced herself and said she had been to the airport looking for him, with a placard of his name.

"I didn't see anything of the sort."

"My fault, my fault," she apologized. "The letters were probably not legible enough. Anyway, welcome to Las Vegas." Then she went on to describe herself, what she looked like, and promised to be there shortly to pick him up.

Two weeks into rehearsals, another development regarding artists' contract came to a head. There had been undercurrent rumblings since the beginning, but the immediate incitement concerned the health insurance of one of the actors, which raised concern for those of the others. For who indeed would be responsible for their health should something happen? Nothing was specified in the contract, and if there wasn't, why not? The matter didn't at first relate directly to those based in the US, like BBGD, since they supposedly had a group insurance from where they worked. But ultimately the anticipated end product of the rehearsals and the performance in Greece came into the picture. Who would be responsible for their health in Delphi and wherever their journey took them in Greece? Nobody knew. After some tossing of their complaints here and there within the administration without any conclusive answer, the actors decided to confront WS's ears with the grievances. Thus, the decision to do this brought in the other prevailing concerns.

BBGD had arrived some days before Peter Badejo. At first, he thought the choreographer had declined the offer and wasn't coming. When he finally arrived, he explained there had been some visa problems with the three artists that came from Britain, through some incompetence of the administrative agency. That problem initiated the old concern about artist fees that they had spoken about over the phone.

"I thought about it, though—declining and not coming. But I had to think in terms of Kongi. I could not let him down."

"Same here. It was all because of him," BBGD concurred.

"These people are incompetent, you know," the dancer proceeded to blame the administrative agency. "It wasn't all the fault of Immigration, although visa is not as easy as it used to be. Now you had to be called for an interview. But these people did not send the necessary information till late."

Then they talked about the living conditions. They were all put in some dormitory, with beds that recalled hospital rooms, minus conveniences such as TVs. Just four bare concrete walls, with no pictures or something of the sort to capture the mind and tease out the strains and isolation of wandering eyes. They were obviously rooms vacated by the students for the summer, but thankfully, because they were designed for graduate students, they were at least self-contained with shower and toilet. Actually, BBGD made sure of his living condition before he left Baton Rouge. He simply could not share bedroom, bathroom, and toilet with anybody. Without those amenities confirmed, he wouldn't have budged from Louisiana. Not even WS could persuade him without his demands. It was an understanding that he knew the playwright understood. With an affirmation of these, nothing else really mattered because he knew how to make himself comfortable.

Thus, as soon as he surveyed the empty small studio apartment assigned to him, he had figured out the adjustments he needed to make—rent a TV and a small refrigerator, buy a cheap electric pot for tea and coffee, a mug and art work at a Thrift store, then find the necessary snacks at some supermarket. And of course buy some good wine. He could pride himself with the fact that most of these survival comforts derive from his mentor, keeping a good wine in store, for sure, and then look for special crackers and hard salami in a store that sold them. These were delicacies always found anywhere WS happened to inhabit. Even the need to be self-contained also indirectly had to do with the playwright, but he had gradually found it appropriate for his introverted person.

Then, as he had come to realize for such extensive stay, he had the need for a rented car to be able to move around the city, especially to be able to visit his favorite pastime, the casino. Coming to the world of casinos he had heard about so much, he knew he couldn't resist the temptation. His yearning had been accelerated by the slot machines that littered the airport, much to his surprise. The temptation to divert as he made his way to baggage claim was never so great, but he had to resist because he first had to find himself settled in his anticipated lodging.

With regard to the list of complaints that originated from him and Peter, the issues soon spread to the other actors, not only the ones that came from abroad but also those in the University conservatory. They all had something in common that was rife for discussion with the playwright. BBGD and Peter approached him and a day and time was set.

Nobody thought the concern over the per diem could be met and resolved in their favor. All the playwright-director could do was to inquire and then relate the response back to the artists. He seemed powerless to do otherwise, such as making supportive demands on the administrative agency. If the budget as they said was small, then so be it; it was an unarguable fact and nothing could be done. But, as far as BBGD's experience had been with the man, WS's attitude to this kind of thing was much more complicated than that, as BBGD recalled a list of similar incidents, which he shared with Peter's. And, it was not always on monetary terms. In fact, the usual ones he always recalled were not monetary. For instance, with a little effort on the playwright's part, BBGD could have participated in productions such as, *The Road*, in Joan Littlewood's theater at Stratford East in London (1965); *Mad Men and Specialists* at the Eugene O'Neill's Playwright's Conference in New London, Connecticut (1970); and *Death and the King's Horseman* at the Lincoln Centre in New York (1987). Peter's list was more in terms of money. On two occasions prior to *Oyedipo*, WS failed to negotiate a better deal for him. On the two occasions he did the collaboration out of respect for the man, just as was the present case with the production of *Oyedipo*.

WS's failing seemed to be a state of powerlessness he had not been willing to challenge and overcome on account of somebody else, that is, other than himself. As he had intimated to BBGD often, he left such negotiations to his agent, whom he trusted to get him the best deal, even if they were in communication as regards the development of the negotiation. As such, by implication, he expected his artists to do the same. But then, some of those artists did not have agents like his working for them, that is, if they had any at all. With regards to respectful mentees and admirers such as BBGD and Peter, things could become a little more complicated. Invariably, they were often caught between their fondness and their losing out on a project by their favorite and most distinguished theater practitioner, especially a project in which the man himself really wanted them to participate.

The meeting with the playwright-director was short. BBGD, perhaps the oldest member in relationship that dated back to the 1960 Masks, initiated the concerns and everyone else supported. Regarding the matter of money, as expected, there was nothing WS could do. He reminded them that his original plans, to bring more artists from Nigeria, from the old 1960 Masks/Orisun

Theater days, had gone awry as a result of budget. Expected grants that was supposed to affect his collaboration with the distinguished Chinese theater personage, Suzuki, had also failed. As such, he had to cut corners and follow the manageable projections of plan B or C.

The health insurance issue was more feasible, for that was supposed to have been addressed in the contract. At the second meeting in which the playwright summoned the administrative agent, he confronted the agent, called him into question regarding the funds that was supposed to have taken care of the health matter, and demanded change effective for the life of the contract. Issues of accommodation were also brought up. BBGD found out that he was the only one living somewhat self-contained; the others had to share their accommodation, two in a room. He was glad he had put his foot down before he ascended from Baton Rouge and descended in Las Vegas. Since the few other professionals had lived for two weeks with their situation, they felt they could endure it for the remaining period in Las Vegas. However, they wanted accommodation in Greece to be addressed and changed if need be, from shared to self-contained rooms in their own professional rights, that is, as opposed to the students that comprised the bulk of the cast. The administrator promised to consolidate the change with the organizing agents in Greece.

BBGD found the morning rehearsals too early and rather unnerving. This slight discomfort shouldn't have occurred under normal circumstances, even though starting at 9 am was a little demanding. But in this circumstance, it meant waking up early to go for breakfast in the dining hall (thankfully two stories below his apartment), hurrying the food down, so as not to be late for rehearsals, which was some 15-minute walk away. As far as waking up, that was not difficult; it was an attempt to coordinate this with breakfast that seemed to be the problem—there were certain perfunctory duties that needed to be attended to before and after breakfast, the major one being waiting to void his bowels of the previous day's clutter. Sometimes the move came at the right time, but at other times it had to be waited on, even with the assistance of inducing aids. He would rather not build on the accumulation with new supplies from breakfast if he could help it. Of course, he was convinced that there was nothing peculiar about his particularity, that is, if people would face up to nature and openly speak their mind. Somebody that had addressed this successfully was no other than WS, judging by his central character in *The Interpreters*.

Complicating that preferred morning duty was the sudden attack of hemorrhoids. It started early in the rehearsal period. He hadn't had it that badly for some twenty years at the University of Ife. It was so bad then that he contemplated surgery, which he refused to do recalling what his father felt about surgery. Against that judgment, the doctor believed it was only a question of days that he would come hopping back to the clinic for the surgery. And that prophecy would have occurred, regardless of his parents warning, and the threat of the constant power failure that beset Nigerian communities and hospitals. He would have succumbed, but for what he could call nothing but a miracle of the traditional medicine he sought through a friend at the last minute.

This time around, he didn't know exactly what had caused his ailment; possibly diet or stress from pressure. Twenty years before, he was more inclined to think it was diet, the many protein and sugar-rich stuff his mouth was given to, such as fried plantains, his constant lunch or dinner dessert. In terms of pressure, given his knowledge of WS's rehearsal practices, there should have been no need to fret. But there he was doing just that, fretting and giving in to pressure more than ever before. This he attributed to the time lapse between the present and the last time he had worked with WS in a play written and directed by him—some eighteen years hiatus. But then, in reality, what difference did that make? There was that constant mistrust between him and the playwright, he taking his time to grasp the character, and the director running out of patience to accommodate his fond actor. Compounded with this was the fear entertained by most actors in his situation—trying to do justice to the many levels of the character in the effort to align their interpretation with the director's concept.

In spite of his ailment, he had struggled to get to the rehearsals on time, and did the best he could to keep his agony under cover. Until the day he was called by the stage manager to have a conference with the director—BBGD was among the actors he needed to see.

"How dare he call upon me among these people?" BBGD mused as he waited for his turn to be called. He knew exactly what was coming.

"H'm, Bem-Bem!" he was accosted as he entered the room. BBGD did his best to ignore the appellation. The calming it was supposed to effect merely elicited a curl of mistrusting smile on his cheek. "How are the rehearsals going for you?" WS added, as BBGD was settling to his seat.

"All right, I suppose."

"I just wanted to talk to you about your character. How do you see him?"

"Well, as I told you before, there's something Ustinov about him, especially in the comedic oddity of his costume. That's what I'm trying to find."

"I see your point about Ustinov. But nothing is coming through yet. Right now, it seems you don't quite understand the character. You seem to be still reading it."

"Well, as you may know, I can't interpret the lines correctly until I find the character."

"Find it quickly then. We have no time."

"Come on, we're just a week and a half into rehearsals."

"I know, I know. But you are a professional—I should count on you to set an example for the others. Look at Ofeigbo. He came in late into rehearsals only a few days ago. But look at him, he fell right into the part."

Quite frankly, BBGD did not appreciate being compared. He tried to control himself, but couldn't help what came out: "Well, we all have our different approaches to character. Mine takes longer, that's all."

"Okay, that's all I have to say. Do try and get on with it."

That was when BBGD felt he had to bring up what he had tried to keep to himself. In fact he didn't know what brought it out exactly, except that it came out as he rose to go. "This has nothing to do with anything—it's not an excuse. But, if you must know, I've been battling through rehearsals with acute hemorrhoids."

"How come?" WS appeared sympathetic.

"Don't know." The reluctant actor shrugged.

"Do you want to see a doctor?"

"Well, I've already called my doctor in Baton Rouge. He gave me a prescription that seems to be keeping the pain in control."

"Okay, let me know if you need further assistance."

He walked out of the room determined not to allow the director's apprehensions to waylay him. If he didn't know any better as a professional, the conference was enough to depress and frustrate further efforts. He knew, given time, he would do better. He had been there before.

But a thought suddenly began to fester—his love-hate for acting, and probably the reason why he hadn't submitted himself to it formerly as a profession. Since his London days, in the US and at Ife, he had been more on the other side of the theater process, as teacher and director. Through those years he hadn't felt any urgent inclinations towards acting. Gradually, the reasons began to take form before him, the struggle the actor had faced, and now the various challenges he must overcome in the rehearsal process and at performance of *Oyedipo*. Thinking back on it, he realized how acting had always drained and exhausted his energies, emotionally—that is, the character and lines he must constantly accommodate before rehearsals, through rehearsals, and realizing them in performances. During those processes, everything else—reading, writing, partying—was always on hold, incapacitated by his struggle not only to clinch the character, but also to improve on it from moment to moment. On that strain, impelled by creativity it demanded from day to day, not one performance of his was like the other, for each was always created anew. And, perhaps, if directors understood this actor's turmoil (and some did), they could be more sympathetic to the actor and therefore know how to relate better with him or her.

There was a knock on his dormitory studio room. He had just got back from rehearsals. As he was wont, he had walked from the rehearsal building to his room in slow steps and deep thought for about an hour, trying to resolve the issues that arose from the day's work, especially relating to the progression of his character. He had come back in those streams of thought and had decided to lay down on the bed for a little while before dinner.

"Announce yourself!" He was expecting nobody, although probably Peter or Folabo had decided to drop by. As such, his response was more of humor than of deterrence. In fact, he himself had received several of such responses knocking on the door of WS's house back in the Ife years.

"Stranger." The deep tenor on the other side, followed by a familiarity-chuckle, made no serious attempt to conceal its owner.

"H'm!" With an easy knowledge of whose voice it was, he slowly got out the bed, wondering what else could have brought his visitor to his room. He hoped in wasn't a continuation of the talk they had before rehearsals.

"BBGD!" the usually fond appellation accosted him frontally as he opened the door, as if nothing had happened a few hours before. But he was quite familiar with the attitude and nature of the man.

"Oh!" The feigned surprise was immediate, but completed with, "For what do I owe this honor?" He stepped back from the door to let his visitor in, but WS chose not to follow the yield. "I was looking for you after the rehearsal but you were gone. Listen, I was wondering if you could come over to my apartment this evening."

"Dinner?" A quiet smile lit BBGD's face. Being a Saturday, he was hoping to go to the Strip after clearing his thoughts; but of course, that could pass.

"Yah. Folake is in town. So I thought you and Folabo could come, you know, family." He stressed that to indicate none of the other actors were invited.

"Sure."

Folake was wife number two. That is, discounting the probable English marriage, of which he was uncertain. Laide, the first wife he knew, but only as girlfriend through his go-between responsibilities during the days of his apprenticeship. By the time they were married, he was already in England, and when he got back formally to the Nigerian scene, some 13 years later, they were already divorced although with four children. Folake happened much later on first as a customary relationship, when she was a student at Ife. Then, to everybody surprise, marriage struck, apparently with some reluctance on the part of WS. But, again, BBGD had missed that event because he was back in the US when it happened. He got the news straight from the horse's mouth in one of their encounters in the US.

"I'll pick you and Folabo up, about 6?"

"Sure. Thanks."

He was hardly expecting the million-dollar apartment on a street fittingly called Howard Hughes Drive, which contained only two similarly structured, somewhat octagonal high-rise buildings. The concealed drive into the secured parking garage further escalated his confoundment as he noticed the kind of cars that parked there—two or three Rolls Royce, an uncommon Mercedes Benz, one or two Porches and a Lamborghini. What else could he expect of lavish in the largest world of Casinos?

"Exactly what I needed," explained WS. "Nobody can get to me unannounced by the Security guy in the lobby." BBGD remembered the poet/playwright/director was still literally in exile, and still being hunted by the Nigerian terrorist current Head of State. The elevator, key control, led directly into the huge two bed-roomed apartment, with its own balcony and garden. The atmosphere was like that of a single family house.

"How much are you paying for all this," mystified BBGD was curious as WS gave them a tour.

"Not a farthing." The playwright went on to explain further that the apartment, temporarily donated to the School of Modern Letters, was part of the deal for bringing him to UNLV to develop that department's area of study. "But you're right, it's a million-dollar apartment. Makes me feel like it too, but alas..." He allowed the temporality to drift and dissolve into a humorous oblivion.

He called Folake, and she presently appeared with her two kids, who immediately, without any hinting, fell prostrate on the floor to greet BBGD. He was very impressed by the traditional gesture of greeting their parents had instilled in them, even though both were born outside Nigeria, and probably hadn't physically seen home. Immediate memories flashed to the last time he too had to undergo this formality to an elder. That was the day he escorted his brother to Ede, a historical, traditional Yoruba city, where Akin was conducting some interview with the then traditional ruler, the Timi of Ede. BBGD was well into adulthood and had been away from home (in the UK and the US) for some 12 years or so. As soon as the king appeared to sit on his throne, he followed his brother's example by prostrating. But the knowledgeable king would not have it so: "Come on now, get up. Get up!" he insisted, "You educated people shouldn't have to do this." Nevertheless, BBGD thought, it was the right thing to do.

The sumptuous dinner was expected, especially with the presence of the wife, although not because he had ever tasted anything of her cooking. In fact, the first time he met them as husband and wife was at the Soyinka Symposium in Canada, when he took him, Folabo and Yvonne Brewster to dinner at a Chinese Restaurant, famous for its Dim Sum specialties, a first for BBGD. The fact was that, typically, from the University of Ife days, eating with WS was always an epicurean lavish, whether at a restaurant or his residence. But, apart from looking forward to seeing Folake once again, he knew the capabilities of Yoruba wives. And a wife of Epicurus Soyinka to boot.

It was during that dinner (of pounded yam, fried rice, fried plantain, spinach with crushed melon (egusi) stew, pepper-fried fish steaks, and constant flow of wine) that it dawned on him, like a ticklish thought, the epicurean implications of his acronymic name. The thought probably had germinated long time before then. For it was always assumed that, more than just the name of a rotund soldier of a tired platoon walking up a hill, Bem-Bem-Gu-Du was associated with the many delights he had devoured as a child. Stories abound of his crouching at the top of the stairs, trying to access a craned vision of the outside kitchen at the further end of the small courtyard, craning and shouting to one of his favorite aunties "S'Aike (a conflation of Sisi Agbeke), wawa, shushu (an alliterated sound for beans and yams)." That was all his child imagination needed to convey to let everybody know he was hungry for his favorite delight. The conclusive supposition that titillated him to the quick was its present connection with WS, who always took pleasure of sounding that acronym without even knowing half the story behind it. As he surveyed the spread, he felt the accosting was probably compelled by a fascinated attraction of one epicurean identity to another.

The rehearsals were grueling. Nothing could be done about the bottom-line professional per diem they were receiving. But the achievement of the health insurance issue assumed the comfort of working under better conditions. As far as his character went, its presence in the play did not materialize as he had thought in the beginning. He had desired and thought he had got a small but interesting role. But what it turned out to be, illuminated by the rehearsals, was different. Once the Chieftain entered the stage, which was really not far from the beginning of the play, he was on stage for the more than two hours length of it. This came as a surprise to him, how he missed that glaring fact when he was reading the play. However, as he realized, smallness in terms of dialogue did not necessarily determine the actual physical presence of a character on stage. At any rate, he felt it was quite possible to miss this presence in his preliminary readings, especially not knowing the playwright's or director's intentions. And then, not far into the rehearsal the director had to divert some of the Priest's lines on to his.

BBGD's difficulties with his continuous presence was, of course, not oblivious to the director. Apparently, as probably the oldest in age and relationship among the actors, and because of his additional hemorrhoid ailment, he commanded WS's sympathetic attention.

"Watching you standing there for a long time," the director later reflected with a tongue-in-the-cheek lightheartedness, "I wanted to ask somebody to get you a seat. But ultimately, I said, 'Nah. Let him suffer—it's good for him.'" BBGD took it as it was meant—a joke. Even though he would have preferred a seat, he didn't think it was practical in a space that did not call for such a prop.

"The visitation is ill-timed. As if the famine is not enough to worry about, there comes a new affliction of a different kind." He had problems delivering that first line, which was not unusual in his acting experience—difficult lines were only to be expected. But regarding the Chieftain's lines, he couldn't for a long time make the necessary visual connections. On the one hand was the connection between the "visitation" of the exiled king, whose ship ran aground, and the "famine" being referred to; on the other was the connection between the ill-timed afflictions of the famine and the impending volcano-eruption of volcanic Mount Ngaliur. The Chieftain's outward gesture went on to implicate the anticipated calamity of "wretched cone" that had been "dead for over a thousand years" but now has chosen "this time to add to our woes." The actor needed to see the visual images very clearly and connect them before he could project them clearly to the audience.

Compounding this problem was the timing of his entrance, for which the Priest on stage gave a somewhat inflated introduction. Furthermore, exactly where he was coming from to this space was difficult to image. Ordinarily, he was good at imagining what was not visible, as was demanded by Ms. Bruford herself when he was a student. But the problem here seemed to hinge on the landscape of overlaid cultures (Greek, Australian, and, to a certain extent, Afghan—not to talk about the Yoruba of the Chorus) that confronted him.

The timing of that entrance during rehearsals was one thing; that of the actual performance on the physical stage at Delphi was another. Even if he had struggled with it and gone the length of rehearsal period to finally master it on the rehearsal space, another timing had to be worked out for the performance on the physical open stage. This could also have been worked out, except for the overriding problem—nobody saw the set within the performance space until the day before the one and only performance. Until then, it was very difficult to rely on just the model. Scheduling the various productions of the conference only allowed for one rehearsal on the set, which was also the tech night. As such, all the actors were seeing the whole set for the first time that day. The director had warned everybody about this, and the possibility of having a long rehearsal into the night. As it happened it was well into the morning of the performance day.

Prominent was the protruding front hull of the wrecked cargo boat and its towering mast, as demanded by the script. BBGD admired the set, surveyed it around to determine his character's entrance task. The distance from behind the stage to the front, with stairs leading to the raised stage, was long, much of which was in view of the audience. He realized he would have to time his long walk against his introduction by the Priest, which fortunately was long enough. No rehearsal prior to the one on the actual space could have projected it, certainly not in the rehearsal space allocated to the company at Delphi—a kind of school auditorium. His wandering mind for some reasons took him all the way back to a timing he had to effect in some play at Rose Bruford. All he remembered was he had to open a door into a conversation concerning "shank's pony." Apparently, that timing, for again only one production, was so right that it received an immediate applause. But this one on the Greek stage obviously demanded a different skill. He believed it was an actor's challenge and therefore his problem. As such, he would rather work it out and realize it on his own and then surprise the director. He decided to practice it with the Priest several times before the performance.

6 o'clock in the morning! What kind of tech is this? He knew they had no choice, for there were many challenges that had to be set right. But he couldn't remember any rehearsal in his professional experience that took that long. The sun was already rising when they left the space. Much earlier on, the director had gathered the actors together to relate to the production they saw the day before, the Greek National Theater postmodern and Brechtian rendering of *Oedipus Rex*, which, apparently, was lauded with an extraordinary applause.

"Don't be disheartened," WS had tried to raise their spirits. "Actually, I didn't see any surprises in that production. Very academic, which probably suited an audience of many scholars. Ours is very different, and much more challenging."

BBGD understood what he meant and was resolved to do his best to make it a successful production. But getting to the hotel at a time when he should be waking up distressed him immensely. He knew he couldn't have much sleep, certainly not the kind that would make his mind, body and voice function very well. He doubted whether his usual sleeping pill would do any good, what with his mind racing riot in preparation for his performance that night. However, he decided to give it a try.

As he was getting ready to turn himself in, there was a knock on the door.

He couldn't think of anybody so bold. He opened the door with some reluctance and gingerly pull the door slightly ajar to peep.

"What a night." It was Margie, a UNLV student and one of the Chorus women.

"Yep. What a morning," BBGD responded with caution.

"You're not going to sleep, are you? I know I won't be able to."

"Oh, I have to get some." He felt the pressure her body was applying on the door to gain access into the room, but resisted.

"What's your room like? Are you the only one?" She stubbornly craned his neck through the door to look.

"Yep. Pretty much."

Getting the message of his resistance, she finally complied. "Maybe I should try and get some sleep also. See you later then."

He breathed a sigh a relief. He determined that the moment wasn't right. Any other time, but, alas, not this. Since the beginning of rehearsals in Las Vegas, a kind of flirtation had developed between him and the woman. There was even a moment, during the director's notes after rehearsal, when she brazenly came and hoisted herself on his lap. Kongi's eyes had made a double-take that landed briefly on him, eliciting a knowing smile, and then ignored the rather seductive act. In that brief moment BBGD read some envy in the director's eyes.

In spite of such signals, nothing tangible had developed between him and Maggie, even though everybody, including her jealous UNLV peers, felt it was a done deal. Her problem was how to separate herself from those women friends; all his efforts to make her do so were fruitless. In fact, one of them had confronted him during a temporary break at a rehearsal to say: "You're a tease, aren't you?" A remark potent with jealousy, if he ever knew one, he thought. Thus, he had abandoned the idea until a probable time she would choose to present herself more insistently, perhaps far from the familiar gaze at Las Vegas. That she had to choose that morning at the hotel to do this was simply unfair.

He knew it was probably his one and only chance; but his performance body, mind and voice, obviously, had to come first. He would rather think it was trickster fate-god, Esu, that had confronted him with the seductive problematic, a test of his artist willpower? It would be rather dangerous to fall for it, like Ogun or even Obatala submitted to the intoxicating spell of the god, knowing the devastating result that might follow. It was necessary to place these mythic experiences against his experience in order to acknowledge Esu's test as only a directive to the awareness of his artistic potential, which must not be compromised in the situation.

"*Olukoso... Olukoso... Olukoso...*"

By what now became obvious to him as an irony of fate, the play was not a celebration of an Ogunian spirit, or what seemed to be a triumphant dramatization of an extraordinary, combative will over a human remorseless power, as was customary in many Soyinka plays. Rather it was a celebration of Sango, and for the first time, a god that the author had, for so long, brushed aside as too erratic and mischievous for his Ogunian temperament. It would seem now this neglect was perhaps unjust. BBGD came to that conclusion as the Chieftain in the production of *Oyedipo*.

As stated, he found himself on stage for most of the time, but not just as that character, Chieftain. More important, he was a kind of assessor and intercessor, interjecting here and there in the developing situations for most of the time. In this capacity, he was able to follow Oyedipo's fate from moment to moment. Like Sango's or Oedipus', it is a fate process that has dogged the character from years before, through ravaging internecine wars, through repercussive blindness (mentally or physically), to being a wandering exile. Thus, through an acknowledgement of Oyedipo's process of fate, BBGD had come to fully understand his own role as Chieftain in terms of his god of interest, Esu Elegbara.

The more he thought about it, the more it made sense to him. As a botanist, the Chieftain traps butterflies, by extension, erring human beings; his assorted costume and cultural affinities all suggest the richness of Esu's vestment and accoutrement, as often displayed by his dance wand symbol carried by his devotees. Furthermore, the Chieftain's wisdom, humor and laughter also smack of the trickster-god's satiric beguilement. But, as BBGD confessed to himself, he, as the actor, got distracted from his character-focus halfway through the production, by a certain unexpected incident that happened on stage. Rationalizing this in hindsight through the function of his god, he concluded that he must have allowed himself to be distracted by the panic he had read on other actors' faces, for he had subsequently weathered the fear through sheer professional instincts and skills.

It all started as early as the formal choral invocation of Sango, aligning the Yoruba god with the Afghan's Diorakos through the praise-name of Oyedipo:

CHORUS: "*Olukoso... Olukoso.. Olukoso... Sango o, a l'aka le ile...*"

ATONA: The gods must be tested to reveal their being.

As if in response to Atona's daring, rain clouds began to form, seemingly out of nowhere. BBGD in character saw it coming over the mountain overlooking the makeshift stage. Soon, there was a rumble of thunder, complemented by sudden gusts of wind. There was no forewarning; it had been a lovely day, and till then the outdoor production was faring well on the Grecian summer evening. As such, BBGD thought of it as a passing affair, expected to settle within a few minutes. But it had continued and the interference began to be somewhat intolerable on stage. Cyclonic wind dusts began to rise. Stage set (mast of the grounded boat that had up till then been admired as a well-crafted piece of structure) began a spasmodic rocking movement and sound that was menacing. Props, temporarily laid on the stage by the warrior-actors, shifted, and were in danger of being blown away.

"*Esu Odara, Laroye,*" muffled BBGD, inciting the god with praise-names "What kind of shit are you pulling?" For a second, he was tickled as he considered the ludicrousness of his query. For if, as he had conveniently positioned himself, if he, the Chieftain, was acting on behalf of the god, was he not accosting himself, and calling for an assuaging of his own unpredictable temperament? He immediately reconsidered and became convinced that the deed must have been fashioned by Sango's Esu, since even the gods were not immune from fate, and therefore were accountable for their own fateful/fatal action. It was this challenging, comparable power of Sango he felt BBGD the actor rightly confronted and demanded answers.

"But then, why must Sango show his dangerous might when, apparently, he was being honored?" For answers, he recalled the intoxicating power of praise-chants, which makes heads swell to certain delirium. It is the euphoria of the ululation that makes Sango be beside himself to dazzle the invoking devotees with magical bolts of his might.

"Ahhh." That understanding satisfied his nervous curiosity, concluding, with certain conviction, that he must remain calm. He looked around the stage as if to assuage the obvious panic he saw among the other actors.

No good. One of the warrior-shields had already escaped the hand that tried to contain it and was dancing a slow waltz to and fro, back and forth from the actor's reaches. A total betrayal, he read on the actor's face—very comical, BBGD thought. A shield that was supposed to be metallic and made to look as such, was dancing before their very eyes, like a feather? A laughable betrayal of realism, if ever there was one. The owner of the shield, at a propitious moment, gave his kneeling position a slight lift, enough to reach out a hand,

and with dexterity manipulate the offending prop to his control. He could almost hear a snigger from the "orchestra."

But then the threat and dismay had continued into the audience, which began to dwindle. "All is well," BBGD consoled himself, convinced that, in spite of physical evidence, there would be no rainstorm. He wished he could extend his prediction to the European audience. Given the fact that they knew nothing about the attitudes of Yoruba gods, they seemed also to know nothing of those of the Greek gods being celebrated indirectly. For, as the playwright claimed parallels with his Oedipus/Diorakos/Sango construct, all under the dramatic canopy of Oyedipo, the complex demonstrated obvious affinities with their Yoruba countenance. If there was any curiosity at all, it was hardly strong enough to sustain the untrusting rather faithless spectators. One by one they dismantled themselves from the illusion being presented on stage and rushed down the terraced aisles to make for their ungraceful exit.

It was unfortunate, BBGD thought, and wished they could hearken to his prediction. As the Chieftain's speeches for much of the play came intermittently, he used them, whenever he could, to offer professional assurance and security to the actors. He seemed to succeed, for they all seemed to be resolute to a collective will and determination to continue the performance till the end, rain or no rain, audience or no audience. It would probably have taken the playwright/director, wherever he was in the orchestra, to stop the performance. That decision, however, knowing the playwright as he did, would never happen unless the threat posed a serious danger to all and sundry. Perhaps both BBGD and the playwright were on similar plane of thought that nothing like that would happen.

Thus, just as the threat came, it ended. There was no rain, and the wind all of a sudden ceased, although not till the final stages of the show. It happened to be a statement and to that extent it was symbolic. For it ceased around the time all the conflicts were resolved, and the deportation orders of passengers of the grounded boat by the insensitive authorities failed. The Chieftain summed it all up—on both realistic and elemental levels—like the Esu-incarnate he was:

"The impossible does happen sometimes. The name for it is—miracle." He then followed up with the conviction, "Only the gods are supreme." Just in time for the immortalization of Oedipus/Sango/Diorakos complex to begin.

BBGD felt that, like the author's celebration of Ogun in *Idanre*, the play demonstrated poetry at its best. Both works resonate affirmation of the creative power that only a few could achieve. Both are vehicles of immorality, such as is chanted by Oyedipo's Chorus, amid the symbolic eruption of Mount Ngaliur:

You will not falter; you will not miss your step.
The mountain goat steps nimbly on the sharp-toothed crag
It neither slips nor stumbles. The spiked caterpillar
Freezes on a twig of thorns and the chrysalis is born
Its dark sheath heaves, the butterfly emerges
Its moist wings flap but are never impaled,
Not though its molting took life on a twig of thorns.
...
Voyager whose pouch is bare of earth's provisions
The gods await you with immortal fare.

BBGD was convinced that such immortal welcoming awaited heroes of the disorienting yet soothingly poetic chthonic realm of the creative process, the mettle or prowess that "moults" and "moulds" (disintegrates yet reintegrates) the creative fabric of exceptional artists such as WS.

Scenes Ten

The Artist-Scholar: Coming Full Circle with Death and the King's Horseman

More than anything else ever since he heard about and set his eye on his mentor, he had seen himself in his guise as a theater practitioner and scholar. It was on such terms that he was sent to England, to complete the necessary qualifications that would get him into a university and like his mentor, get an academic terminal degree. In the old days, getting a PhD was not required to teach at a university. This he knew when he was assisting WS in his research into African indigenous drama. Some of the professors he met at the University of Ibadan through his mentor had only Masters. But, as requirements became more streamlined, he knew he would have to do better than that and aspire to acquire that ultimate degree, a PhD. His mentor, he realized, could get by with an MA to do anything he wanted, for he was one of a kind. As such, he wouldn't limit himself to just that.

However, as BBGD copiously stated in this endeavor, things didn't go quite the way he had planned at first. He was to do a preliminary study at the Northwestern Polytechnic in London for two years, and then apply to do a B.A. at a university such as Leads (his mentor's alma mater) or Bristol, the best institution for Theater at the time and where he was really focused. But, to relieve his parents, especially his mother, of the rather costly expenses of living in London and for the university study, he had to divert from his plans after one year at the Poly. Receiving a fortuitous Nigerian scholarship, he went to study acting at the Rose Bruford College of Speech and Drama. With Bru's diploma, he was almost guaranteed at least a teaching position at the University of Ibadan where his mentor was. A testament to that was Ebun Clark (then Odutola), his former girlfriend at Bru. With her Bruford diploma, she was appointed to teach, first at Ibadan, then later at the University of Lagos.

"You seem to have an intellectual and academic mindset," Rose Bruford had alerted him at the graduating conference he had with her. "Somebody like you should be at a university."

He got that encouragement when they were trying to get him to accept a special certificate for foreign students like him, instead of the authentic diploma, on account of some deficiency in his application of Queen's English. While he rejected the certificate proposition, which made him do extra summer tutorials in other to obtain the real diploma, the principal's idea of a university study resonated with his convictions and ideal. As such, even as he made his professional career in acting on the London stage, he had the academic idea at the back of his mind as a possibility in future.

Between the time he entered Rose Bruford and the time he was following an acting career, new universities had sprung up in England, some of them with theater departments comparable to that at Bristol. Thus, securing a letter from his mentor and another from Rose Bruford, he had applied to one of the universities, Essex University, near London. He was hoping his diploma at Bru, his background experience on the London stage, and the acquired references would be enough to get him an admission. Actually Essex would seem sympathetic and willing to give him an interview. Alas, in the end, all was to no avail, but he was not willing to land all the blame on the University. Lack of demonstrable evidence of his intellectual and academic standing might have gone some way to blow up prospects of his admission.

"I see you've done some acting on the professional stage."

"Yes." Not knowing where the interviewing professor was heading, BBGD was very excited about the acknowledgment Professor Hunt caught from his application papers.

"Well, we are willing to consider mature students like you. Okay, if we were to give you admission here, what were you anticipating getting from us?"

Was that a trick question, he wondered, seeing a kind of English smirk on Hunt's face. At any rate, he thought some of those details were outlined in his application. "Weeelll," he strained to remember what he actually wrote in the application. Not quite remembering, he proffered what he thought might emphasize his penchant for an academic discipline: "Since you have a directing focus in your discipline, your department should help me develop my directing potential, especially for Shakespeare's plays." Good enough answer he thought, and he was still basking in the sound bites of his response when his interviewer probably spotting this, launched his test question.

"Good, good. Tell me, which of the Shakespeare plays would you consider your favorite?"

That was easy enough. His mind immediately went to the literature professor during his polytechnic days, Mr. Hart. Even though he didn't quite like the guy, he was nevertheless fascinated by the way the professor read *King Lear*, especially the storm scene. He remembered the way Hart would read the speeches, such as the one ending with "I am a man more sinned against than sinning," delivered with such mournful self-pity that he felt replicated Lear's.

"*King Lear*," BBGD proudly identified.

"That's a great play isn't it?" The smirk had not left his interviewer's face, but his supportive acknowledgement somewhat eased BBGD's mind. But before he could relish his somewhat braggadocious claim, his interviewer tossed him the final piece of the trial taste: "Just for curiosity's sakes, how would you direct the play? I mean, what is a key factor for you to consider as a concept?"

BBGD felt the question was a bit cumbersome and probably unfair. But rather than boldly front his interviewer with anything oppositional, he decided to supply what he thought should demonstrate his intellectual capacity. Actually the idea wasn't entirely his; he had gathered much of it from some interview on television and had acquired it as experimentally sound. "Well, I've always thought of the Fool as King Lear's alter ego."

"Possible, possible…but can you give me an example? How might you suggest that?"

That was when BBGD came a humpty-dumpty tumbling down. He errrred…mumbled and fumbled, with unintelligible guesses, exposing his ignorance to the quick, and landing all his supposed intellectual integrity to a helpless crash in the dumps.

"Okay. That's fine. Fine," was all he could hear from his interviewer's conclusion, ending with: "We'll certainly consider your application and let you know."

At that juncture, he knew all his previous intelligent guesses were to no avail and that nothing good could come of the interview. For the interviewer's smirk had lingered to the end, and now it seemed to betray a triumphant glee.

As he began to query his mind about the incident, he felt the admissions professor probably had no intentions of giving him a favorable trial beyond that interview. As a non-traditional candidate, and perhaps black, with no qualifying requirements, he was expected to demonstrate his abilities twice or thrice as visible. However, he resisted qualifying the failure as a significant race thing, since he had good references, especially one from his mentor, who knew the man. Regarding that, he could not help feeling he had somewhat failed his mentor. Much later on, however, he had reconsidered that deliberation and modified his suppositions to admit what he had sometimes considered his penchant for chronic self-deprecation. He had remembered, from his readings, one dramatist that was always given to that condition— Anton Chekhov. Not that his understanding and acceptance of this characteristic in Chekhov was a rest-cure for his situation, but only to confirm for himself that the habit was real and a fault.

At any rate, he felt his eagerness to sound intellectual and academic, driven by his anxieties to succeed, had failed him. He shouldn't have encouraged it, but he was simply naïve. He doubted whether the professor took the trouble to see that naivety, and why should he. He pounced at whatever he saw and just took undue advantage of it. As BBGD got to know more about directing, he realized Hunt's test question was too broad and wickedly unfair. It wasn't anything any candidate could have answered successfully without a serious consultation of the script. A director could legitimately conceive an idea, however wild it might be, but that idea would have to be put to test on close reading of the script. Whatever curiosity drove Hunt to ask it, it was a reckless question that he knew would land his victim in trouble.

It would not be the first and last time BBGD played into the lion's den with such naivety, regarding his attempts to initiate himself into directing. Another occasion was when he interviewed for apprenticeship at the National Theater. Now that was simply British racism rearing its ugly head at that moment in time. They had no intentions of given him, an African, any such chances. Being a professional black actor in London was hard enough, let alone being a director. But he had had no regrets; the time and timing were simply not right.

*****

His first encounter with *Death and the King's Horseman* as an artist was at the University of Ife, when he played Olunde. Before then, he had been a professional actor in London a few years back. Between that and the time he came back home to take up a position at the university, he had been in the US to study playwriting at Yale. After that, for the next few years, he found himself unable to put anything down on paper to justify his training as a playwright. It was quite a contrast to his BBC Radio playwriting period, about a decade before. Then he could knock out a half-hour radio play within in a few days, at the most a week.

Through his usual self-analysis, he felt there were at least two significant factors responsible for his mental blockage. The first, he thought, was because of his exposure to an academic environment though artistic discipline, which opened up his critical faculties but to a fault. The second, an extension of the first, was brought about by the rather destructive criticism perpetuated with impunity among his playwriting peers during workshops. It was during these reflections that he started to feel his studies at Yale was academically incomplete and he wanted more.

*****

222

"My boy, you're a child of circumstance," concluded his high school chemistry master. He had gone to him to contest his grade and to beg for leniency. Instead, he was met with, "My boy, you're a child of circumstance."

He had no idea of what that meant; it obviously had done nothing to change the grade. He knew the solution to the equation in question, but unfortunately for him time was up before he could complete it. That argument failed to hold water with Mr. Effiong; he refused to reconsider. That was just too bad, the tutor insinuated through the thick glasses hanging on his nose and his rather square Ibibio face. Too bad that he didn't finish resolving the equation? But did that make him a child of circumstance?

Somehow, Effiong's remark began to gain traction, when he had a better assessment of himself through certain fateful experiences. He began to associate "circumstance" with luck and ill-luck. Ill-luck, regarding the situation with Effiong, but luck in certain other cases. For sometimes, probably more often than not, certain favorable circumstances just happened, handed to him, as it were, on a silver platter, situating himself in the right place at the right time so to speak. Such was his fateful encounter with the academic milieu he had sought for so long, going to Yale. But this happened through a series of luck and ill-luck circumstances, sometimes one in connection with the other.

The possibility of pursuing and securing a more academic degree had stirred his heart, intermittently, throughout his acting career on the London professional stage. After the University of Essex fiasco, he was almost at a dead end. Then all of a sudden, he got a letter from a Professor at UCLA in Los Angeles, a friend of his brother and WS. Dr. Povey wrote to ask whether he could contribute to the African Arts Journal, of which he was editor. He was seeking features about the African Theater scene in London. With his background experiences, acting in Soyinka's *The Trials of Brother Jero* and *The Lion and Jewel*, BBGD felt the mail was godsend. He could write about experiences in those productions of the Ijinle Theater Company, the group that was created under the direction of Athol Fugard. However, having no real academic experience that could bolster him as a frequent contributor to the journal was a handicap. What came out, as his one and only contribution, was more a polemical complaint, about what went wrong with the only African Theater he knew, than a critical insight into various African or Black Theater happenings in London. Povey probably wanted to explore in London what was already happening in the US with the black theater.

As to that, what else could he have said? There was really no physical African Theater to talk about, apart from the radio plays of the BBC African Service. To him, those didn't offer much to write about, although on reflection he could have done something to expose those new plays. But by the time of

Povey's interest, the Ijinle Theater Company that could have developed as a legitimate African Theater was defunct. That happened after Athol Fugard went back to South Africa. Funds suddenly became scarce or nonexistent to continue to maintain the group.

He had broached his feelings about an academic pursuit with his brother, who suggested he contacted a friend of his in Michigan. Through that friend he had applied to the University of Michigan, which appeared to have a good theater program that combined the artistic with the academic. The response to his application was quite promising at first, receiving a letter of interest from the Acting Dean, who had taken into consideration his artistic background at Bruford as an equivalent of a BA, and his experiences on the London stage. What probably was more in his favor for a possible admission was the promise of a fellowship from the University of Ife in Nigeria, where his brother worked as chair of Music. Things had appeared to have gone smoothly with the Acting Dean and it would seem his academic dreams would be realized. Then the rather unexpected setback happened.

He had been awoken by a vividly recalled dream. Having had such a dream before, he got up quietly and unamused. All he heard himself saying was "All right, let's go and get this over and done with." He calmly removed his pajamas, put on decent clothes, got out of his Earls Court small studio apartment, descended the stairs two levels towards the ground floor, walked over to his mail box in the lobby, opened it and there was the letter, exactly as he had dreamt it. Knowing what might be in the letter, he didn't feel anxious to open it until he got back upstairs. And there it was again, almost word for word, or image for image, as was in the dream, the content of the letter from the Acting Dean. The AD was very sorry he couldn't convince the Dean when he returned to office from leave of absence. The Dean overrode the former enthusiasm of the AD to grant admission to the African candidate, which the AD went on to imply as a political power play.

However, as luck would overturn it, there was a surprise addendum. What BBGD had gathered foggily from the dream now became clearer to him: "Why don't you try the Yale School of Drama? They sometimes accepted late application for admission of people of your maturity and experience. In your case, you also have the funds."

It was in June, when all admissions would have been finalized. He felt a bit disappointed about Michigan, but thought it worthwhile to take up the acting dean's suggestion. He knew practically nothing about Yale, although he had heard of the name. He directed his application to the address supplied in the letter and in the meantime decided to get himself acquainted with details about School of Drama. He found out that, more than just being another school of drama in the nature of Bruford, it was an establishment of Yale University and, more important, a graduate program offering an MFA. Not exactly a PhD program he had anticipated but he felt being in a university environment might not be a bad thing. At any rate it might lead to other opportunities. Given the fact that he had written a few noteworthy radio plays, he felt his best bet was to apply for an MFA in Playwriting and Dramatic Literature. That combination with literature pleased him immensely.

He was surprised to receive a response within two weeks. As conjectured, his application was rather late, but the Associate Dean of the school, who signed the letter, was willing to give him what amounted to a temporary one year admission. This could be regularized afterwards to a full admission depending on how he fared after a semester. He was a bit cautionary about that but thought his accumulated background experiences should serve him well.

But before he could make his final decision on the Yale offer, he had to settle with what had come to tease his mind as a viable alternative. This was with regard to his acting career and ties to London, even though this didn't seem at first to be a competitive match against his academic pursuit. As he would later identify upon reflection, the situation of things he was faced with was a symptom of his frequent dilemma, the vacillating toss between two equally positive possibilities at the crossroads. The question was always which was more fatefully positive and viable.

Normally the opportunity to explore new ventures in the US would have been easy to snatch. However, at that time there was a romantic circumstance that further complicated the decision making. In hindsight a naïve notion, but he felt his relationship with Robin, daughter of a member of royalty, was moving in a positive direction. That circumstance was an added important factor to his main consideration, the prospects of joining the National Theater Company, which at the time was looking to incorporate young black actors, like him, into the company. Both factors, in unison, were in direct conflicting struggle with the "American dream."

"What do you think?" he posed the question to Mae Bleazard, his agent.

"Well, it's up to you. Don't expect any substantial roles at the National, or anything beyond servant roles," she responded, putting a damper on his enthusiasm.

"But consider this. What they are offering me for fees is small. Can't we push up the amount a little more, say, 25 pounds a week for rehearsals and 30 for performance?"

"Their offer is standard, but we could try, although I doubt whether they'd go up. And if they disagree, that's the end of it, you realize that."

"Well, let's try anyway. So be it if they don't agree." He was seriously hoping they would increase it, since some of the directors had seen him on stage. But he was also using whatever decision they came to as a positive sign of fate to his own resolve.

As his agent surmised, they rejected his counter offer. He felt a little disappointed about it, not because of the rejection itself, but about the fact that in reality his counter-offer was really not that much. But it demonstrated to him that they were not really serious in engaging a good black actor; rather, a token.

"Don't worry about it though," his agent tried to console him. "You've taken up bigger roles, leading roles. Playing servants and sword carriers is not worth your time. A talented actor like you must be patient to be truly recognized."

The romantic part of his dilemma took a little longer to resolve. He waited a little to tell Robin about Yale. When he did, he caught a little disappointment on her face, which at first played on his bias and sentiments. When she saw her again the second day, somehow she seemed to have resolved the matter and feeling very positive about it.

"Yale is a good school. I'll miss you, darling, but I'm sure we can work it out. Besides, I can come and see you in America."

The encouragement lifted his spirits up with a feeling that the rejection he got from the National was a signal as to what he should do. Yale was the more positive step, and he believed all would be well with Robin. Of course, counterbalancing his hope, and still on his mind, was the attitude of her parents when she took him home, a small castle in Perth. To her mother, he was a "blackamoor."

"You've come to see how rich people live," was the welcome she fronted him with at the medieval entrance to the castle. Her whole demeanor was rather uninviting, and he realized the lecture awaiting Robin about the African she'd brought "home to dinner."

Her father was a little conciliatory, but told Robin point blank that the time was not right for a relationship they were both thinking of. Probably relating to that and certainly because of her mother's attitude, he wasn't allowed to stay for more than one night, and alone in the attic.

He had been warned about the opinions of the royalty concerning blacks, lumping them all up as savages, with blood that would taint the blue of royalty. They seemed to have a ready example in Shakespeare's *Othello, the Moor*, not in the least an honorable yet a savage man. In spite of this knowledge, BBGD still entertained some attendant faith in Robin, and his resolve was based on the fact that his going away would be a kind of test of love for both of them, especially for her.

Within a short time, the irony of course became very obvious. In spite of all presents, self-picture, and one romantic poem to boot, which Robin tendered to relieve any pain of their separation and boosted their hopes for a promising future, the relationship was dead as soon as he entered the plane. When he tried to call her from New Haven a week later after he had settled in somewhat, her excuses, hesitations and subterfuges underlying her "Why did you have to go away, darling," spoke catatonic volumes.

His recovery to normal state of affairs took some time, but preoccupation with his studies finally helped cast the memory into oblivion. Yet, he maintained himself with a kind of hubristic pride and tongue-in-the-cheek royalty, that is, thinking of the way Yale came to be presented to him, as it were, on a silver platter. An irony of fate?

*****

The University of Ife, at the time of *Death and the King's Horseman*, was rich and rife with nascent scholarship—Nigerian, African, international, rejection of colonial European ideals and their consequent neocolonial African parallels. In addition, Marxism began to receive an African ideological aspect among a few professors on campus. WS came to reveal them as pseudo-Marxists, especially the way they used their ideology to challenge his possible objectives in *Death and the King's Horseman*. For BBGD, the dialogue generated a lively and enviable debate.

It was also a time that WS's concepts and ideas in his almost impenetrable book, *Myth, Literature and the African World*, were spawning a healthy, scholarly discussion. The idea that seemed to have singlehandedly got tossed about the most, and dissected for illumination in scholastic circles, vis-à-vis conversation and article, was the "chthonic realm."

BBGD felt rather limited in these circles. He had been to and graduated at one of the best Universities in the world, as he came to realize, although had made no bones about it; yet, he had found his knowledge to be mostly backed by the artistic rather than the academic. Thinking back, he probably should have taken fuller advantage of Yale. There, he could have made a possible change of studies from an MFA to a DFA, but then the focus of the doctoral would have been towards becoming a literary critic, which didn't really interest him.

Rather than participate in the debate of *Death*, he kept his disagreement with the Marxist view of the play silent. The critics contrasted the author's non-committal political position in the play with the political dimension he had claimed and demonstrated in the real world, a dimension on the other hand that distinguished his earlier plays, such as *Madmen and Specialists*, or even *Kongi's Harvest*, and definitely in the early satirical skits he launched, *Before the Blackout* and *After the Blackout*. They had wondered whether the man had mellowed and compromised his political stance and activism. A play that came out around that time and which the Marxists constantly cited and analyzed against *Death* to support their argument was Ngugi wa Thiong'o's *The Trials of Dedan Kimathi*. BBGD had hastily gone on to read that play; his reading didn't support the Marxists' criticism of *Death*, unless he was missing something, which he doubted. However, he did not have enough critical background, let alone knowledge of Marxist concepts, to launch a strong defense. Whatever he had in mind to say he decided to simply hold in his thoughts.

As a creative artist and a great admirer of WS's creativity, he thought the Marxists were missing a significant point. A creative artist is not beholden to any particular stance, especially one that might limit his creativity, which is primal. He felt there was no reason why both political and traditional couldn't exist side by side, or interwoven in a creative venture. It was a view he upheld with WS. It formed the basis of the distinguished playwright's creativity even in his more political plays, such as *Madmen* and *Kongi's Harvest*. He thought this should only be expected of any true creative artist. He didn't believe one should be totally political. Such an agitprop stance was probably not possible in any creative venture of merit.

One must constantly draw from one's own culture, in this case the Yoruba, which is potent with traditional precepts and rituals that could help mystify the political aspects and lift the play to larger than life magnitude. A ready example is most of Shakespeare's plays, perhaps with the exception of, to a certain extent, the historical plays that constitute the War of the Roses. Even then those plays are littered with images of Elizabethan culture. He had wondered whether it was the war mongering politics of those plays that had often drawn him away from them.

At any rate, the conditions of a particular moment in time might be very influential to the playwright's process in determining the level of the political versus the social-traditional, a seesaw, so to speak, that could swing either way to result in a product that favors one more than the other. Who knows...who knows the various intricacies of the creative mind?!

The Marxists were probably expecting the socio-traditional aspects should not be dramatized at all, or be used to vividly support a political agenda. As a matter of fact, that kind of support is evident in Soyinka's use of the traditional,

228

to a greater or lesser degree, in *Death*, depending on the political factor that motivated the play. As expected, Kongi responded to the "pseudo Marxists" argument in an essay he titled, "Who's Afraid of Elesin-Oba?" Reading the article, BBGD felt his thoughts were justified.

He was more interested and in intellectual tune with the "chthonic realm" idea, even though he did not have the scholarly clout to participate in the debate. He could hardly penetrate the essay which featured the concept, "The Fourth Stage," an appendix to *Myth, Literature and the African World*. He gathered it had to do with Ogun's fate, as was recalled in the myth when the god, along with the other gods, descended from their ancestral world to reconnect with their human counterparts. It was the god's creative, metallurgical inventiveness that forged the machete which he used to brave the elements, cutting through the dense forest and marsh encountered (the chthonic amorphous abyss) to carve a path that led to the human world. In the process he almost got annihilated. But through his combative will he fought through to the other side where he reintegrated and reassembled self. Soyinka sees him as the first artist, who championed the amorphous space that many creative artists face when creating, a process that describes the artist creative/destructive/re-creative potential. As a creative artist, BBGD was at one with this reality, and the fate of Ogun was to later formulate his own concept of fate and satire, modelled on Esu-Elegbara, the Yoruba trickster-god of fate.

It was in an effort to pursue Soyinka's concept of Ogun that he was delighted to participate in the first production of *Death and the King's Horseman*, although not at first as an actor. But the more he thought about his taking on the role, rather than just assisting the director, the more he felt it was to his advantage regarding his pursuit. As it happened his rationale was correct. Playing Olunde, Elesin's son, gave him the opportunity to graph Elesin's fate, from the beginning demonstration of his willpower, through his erring, to his apologetic demise. It also allowed him to place Olunde's willpower against his father's, so he could engage the role and be able to accomplish the character's rather unfortunate but necessary resolve. It would seem to him that in terms of Elesin's fateful/fatal graph, there is an erring from an already defined direction of fate, an erring through a kind of temptation that tests his potential and the façade of strength and will he projects to the market women. He woefully fails the testing, but turns around to overcome his failure only too late. BBGD contrasted it with another myth of Ogun he had read, which he then interpreted more realistically. Overconfident Ogun, a battle leader, was given to the pleasures of alcohol during a lull on the battlefield, a miscalculation for which he failed with catastrophic results.

Both Ogun and Elesin went on to right their apparent respective error, perhaps tragically a bit too late. But there seemed a remarkable difference in their effort to apply a corrective measure. Surveying the massacre-consequence of his alcoholic error that killed enemy and ally alike on the battlefield, Ogun's response was immediate. Elesin, on the other hand prevaricated from one rationale to another, blaming everybody and everything else but himself. Brought into confrontation of his error by Olunde, who exposed his disservice to the community, he did not at first want to be judged harshly, obviously because of the reasons he was churning in his mind and was to later verbalize. He delayed any positive action as he tried to convince himself of his need to continue to live longer. It was not until he was confronted with his son's death, an example of demonstration of will in service to the community, not until that tragedy of his prevarication and delay that he sprang to a definitive action.

Thus, BBGD as Olunde saw his character's fate in contrast to Elesin's. Arguably, his own potential also underwent some testing. He had come home to complete the burial ceremonies for his father, confident that all would be well. His confidence, based on what he knew of his father's willpower and the ritual precepts of his community, made him match his traditional ritual belief against a British ritual belief in his debate with Mrs. Pilkings and the colonial excrescences and indulgences going on in the background. That confidence came under crossfire when he realized his father had veered from traditional beliefs. BBGD/Olunde saw his community in danger of growth, continuity and survival against his own growth and survival in terms of his established fate as a medical doctor. Traditional affirmations of the community and modern speculative realities as defined by Western ideologies were in conflict. His choice, to participate in the traditional for its survival and consequently against his fate as a medical doctor, was probably coaxed by the elders of his community and therefore unfortunate. But, ultimately, that difficult decision would seem to hang heavily on him the next of kin and as duty to the community, which made it all the more tragic. It spurred an overbearing impact on Elesin to complete his belated and delayed fateful direction, by which he fatally ended his own life.

BBGD felt he needed to express Olunde's conflicting conflicts of the process in his mind; hence his experimental angst in the delivery of his lines: "Eater of left overs," which the director-playwright rejected outright, without any consideration of any other choices. At first, he was reluctant to admit the playwright's interpretation of the line at that rehearsal of the first production of the play. Eventually he was able to accept it and made it be consistent with his own rendering. His thinking was, by the time Olunde made that statement, those conflicts were not really present, not until community pressure was put on him and his personal and medical priorities. Years later, he would confront that interpretation again as a director of *Death and the King's Horseman.* But by that time, a span of about forty years, his development as an academic and theater practitioner had been buttressed by many experiences.

*****

"Come on, go ahead and write it," pleaded Skip, assessing BBGD's continued reluctance with his customary mischievous gaze. "It will be good to have it in the contribution." He had deliberately brought the matter up again in front of WS, who was at his typewriter in an armchair at the dining room table of Skip's Yale University college-apartment.

"What are you asking him to write about?" the poet-playwright halted on the electronic typewriter, curious about the conversation.

Skip immediately took advantage of WS's curiosity, which was the attention he wanted in the first place. "I've been asking this guy to write me an article on that first production of *Death and the King's Horseman*, which you directed, right?"

"And he won't write it?" The question, preceded by a chuckle, anticipated the director's knowledge of the situation.

"No, he won't. Been asking him for over a year now." Then turning to BB sitting across from him in the living room he went on to rub it in for WS, "Just think about it. The one and only production, and you alone could write about it. It'd be super in the collection I'm editing for Wole's 50th birthday. You among all the important scholars and writers I've asked to contribute."

"I know why he doesn't want to," WS's subtle interjection under his breath was loaded. Casting a deliberate buried look at BB, the playwright threw the coin to land on his target's face: "Am I right or wrong?" He then proceeded to tantalize his victim, humorously humming the tones of his nickname: "Bem-bem-gudu!"

"Why? You guys know something I don't?" Skip's curiosity was arrested, flashing eager-roguish glances from one to the other at almost equidistant angles. He seemed fascinated by the tonal sound offered by WS but for the moment his ears popped up to be enlightened about facts of BB's hesitation.

"He'd like to bury that hatchet, I'm afraid, the experience of his performance. I don't blame him really."

"But what happened?"

"Ask him there, sitting with you." WS was at his most conniving, tweaking a smile on his face.

BBGD, glowing with a blush for being put on the spot, remained silent.

"Hey, what happened…" Skip tried to imitate WS's tonal appellation, as if that would incite an answer. At any rate his imitation failed woefully.

"Bem-Bem, do you want me to tell him about that debacle?" the playwright challenged.

"Yes, yes," Skip jumped to the cue.

"But what do you want me to say?" BBGD querulously defended.

"Tell him what happened, that performance night." Without waiting for BBGD to respond to the challenge, the playwright decided to initiate it: "It was embarrassing. Nobody could hear him; even I couldn't."

"It wasn't that simple," BBGD decided to contest WS's submission. "The A/C was in full blast. My voice couldn't pierce through."

"How come it was only you?"

"I'm sure it wasn't only me."

"You lost your voice, plain and simple, my friend." WS then turned to Skip to make his point. "I warned him about this the day before. 'I can't hear you; you're losing your voice.' He said he could handle it."

Try as BBGD could to rack his head, he couldn't remember hearing that warning. But he decided to continue with his own side of the story: "And there was that terrible woman who played Mrs. Pilkings. Acting is supposed to be give and take. I couldn't take anything from her. She was simply dead."

"True that," WS acknowledged. "We had a terrible Mrs. Pilkings. She was born in England, I think, before her parents came home. She had this phony British accent, and she couldn't act. In fact, it was one of the reasons I decided to squash further performances."

"Well, what are you waiting for?" Skip cut into the banter, "It would be a fantastic article if you could write about that experience. Come on, my man. The one and only performance of the first production!"

"All right, all right, I'll think about it." BBGD felt he'd had enough of that conversation.

"I've heard that before. I want it in two weeks." Skip decided to pin him down to a deadline.

"Ahhh, two weeks?"

"Yes, okay, write it during the Xmas break. It shouldn't be that difficult to churn out."

Thinking of all he must do before the break, he felt he could probably manage it. He had come back to Yale to obtain a graduate degree in African American studies, on leave of absence from his position as a lecturer in the Dramatic Arts department at the University of Ife. WS as department chair had helped BBGD to secure the leave. The poet-playwright colleague had been invited to Yale by Skip, as a Visiting Professor for one semester in Afro-Am Studies. In fact, BBGD had chosen to TA for WS's undergrad survey in African and African American drama. He had subsequently been dumped almost all the papers to grade at the end of semester. Apart from that, he had his own seminar papers to write. He had begun these and should finish by the end of the semester when the papers were due.

He really couldn't refuse Skip anything, even though he had lingered for so long to commit himself to the essay he wanted. Coming back to do this study was due to Skip's efforts and negotiation. A year before that, when he was on his usual summer vacation in the US. Skip had suggested the idea. The professor was then living in the same block of apartments that BBGD was staying with his friend, Don Amechi Ifejika. The fellow Nigerian had graduated in Architecture at Yale at the same time BBGD got his MFA at the School of Drama. But Don had stayed on for a while in New Haven, involved in some business, which his enterprising qualities had merited.

BBGD had snatched the opportunity to come back to study, partly because he wanted to have a more solid background in African American cultures, which he lacked when he was at the School of Drama. But more important for him was the opportunity to further his development as an academic, so he could be at one with his fellow more scholarly colleagues at Ife.

"Okay, what's that sound again?" Once Skip had gotten BBGD's commitment to the article on *Death*'s first performance, he flipped back to entertain his curiosity. He tried again to make the tonal sound, this time more woefully. "What does that sound mean? Didn't you promise to tell me about it?" He directed his statement to WS, thinking he would more likely get the answer from him.

"I promised you nothing of the sort." The playwright was curt and abrupt as he resumed his typing.

"Okay, tell me anyway."

"I will certainly not break the oath of secrecy to you or anyone."

"You mean an oath was involved?" Skip tested the waves.

"It was a secret between me and him."

Skip wasn't satisfied with the rather nonchalant response, but decided to leave his apparent embarrassing defeat at that for the meantime. He probably hoped to bring it up again at a more advantageous time, perhaps during dinner with gushes of wine at some expensive restaurant. All he could hold on to, to counter his inadequacy was: "Hey, write that essay!" as he got up from his armchair and clumped his club-foot shoe into the bedroom hallway.

*****

233

He got a call from the theater administration of the Lincoln Centre, through Wole Soyinka, regarding the forthcoming production of *Death and the King's Horseman*. At first, he thought they wanted him to come for an audition in order to participate in the production—what he would have liked very much. But it was for something else. Soyinka would be arriving a day or two late for the start of rehearsals, and he would appreciate it if BBGD could fill in for those days, to prepare the actors with the Yoruba cultural background, nuances and word pronunciations in the play.

At the time in 1986, he was a visiting professor at the College of William and Mary, filling in for a professor who was on a year's leave; but there was a hope of regularizing the Theater and Speech position if the department could get a budget slot from the university. He was on his way out of the University of Ife, but was still retaining his position there until he could get a more permanent engagement in the US. He had been nervous about the growing unstable political situation in Nigeria, which was slowly rendering the intellectual integrity and autonomy of academic institutions ineffectual or nonexistent. In addition, WS had retired from the university two years before, their last collaboration being the production of the film *Blues for a Prodigal* in which he took a principal role.

He and the director-playwright had talked about possible future collaborations, which might be difficult if he were away from Nigeria. An event happening in the US might be possible, that is, if he could negotiate a leave to be able to participate. Such would have been the case for the production of *Death and the King's Horseman*, but he knew nothing about it until the Lincoln Center call. Not knowing about it was the kind of thing that always infuriated him about his mentor-colleague. Prior knowledge might have made it possible for him to audition. His membership in the British Actors' Equity was still in force; he could use it to act in the US, as he had done once before. An initial thought about his former mentee by the playwright, when arrangements about the production were being made, might have helped and gone a long way.

He knew the man had just been honored with the Nobel Laureate. He had learnt about it from the public radio the very morning the award was made. He had immediately sent an e-mail of congratulations—which probably didn't get read in the euphoria of the award. That didn't bother him since he knew his mail was among thousands. Apparently, the acclaimed Laureate was on his way to Nigeria from Paris when he was called by the Nobel committee; he had turned right back to Paris to celebrate the occasion among friends and well-wishers. BBGD had mourned the fact he could not be there to celebrate it with him.

234

Waving off his disappointment, he accepted the small request and offer being made by the Lincoln Center, obviously an afterthought of the playwright-director in desperation. He felt he could use the small participation to his advantage, by doing a closer reading of the play, and actually having a group of chosen professional African American actors under his direction. Albeit for a short preliminary time.

"BB, great that they contacted you." He heard from the director about two days after the Lincoln Center call. "I wasn't sure you were around. I was hoping you or Niyi Coker could help; I told them to check with you, first. Glad they found you."

"So am I," he intoned with subdued calm, knowing that the offer could easily have gone elsewhere. But he remained composed with the knowledge that he was first option in his mentor-colleague's mind.

"Go over the script with the actors a couple of times and get them acquainted with the nuances and difficult pronunciation of the Yoruba words."

"Certainly." As usual, even at this stage in his career, he was at a loss for words. He had so much he wanted to talk to him about, but he blanked out.

"See you in a bit."

"Y-yes, see you soon."

His pre-rehearsal sessions with the actors went very well. He spent a whole day with them, working at the play twice, and answering any questions they asked, except for the few that demanded the judgment of the director. He felt acknowledgment and honor from them, giving him all the respect due to a person they thought was highly knowledgeable of the play, and a professor at William and Mary at that. He was in fact acquainted with one or two of the actors before—when he was at the Ethel Walker School and directed *The Winti Train* at the University of Harford. He lamented the fact that they brought him for only two days, in reality one; he was gone the third morning, not even able to see WS.

"Thought I'd be able to see you and have dinner," the director indicated on the phone.

"That'd have been nice. But they booked me for only two nights," BBGD explained.

"Not to worry. I'll make it up to you. You're coming for the opening, I hope."

"Yes, I'd love to come. They didn't mention the possibility." He knew full well the administration didn't put that in their budget.

"No, no. Consider it done. I'll arrange it."

"Great. Please don't forget."

"I'll put it in my notes, right away."

He had wondered while working with the actors how they would all turn out at performance. Particularly the person playing Elesin. WS was not always good at casting. He was sometimes deceived by the voice, timbre and delivery of some actors when he conducted auditions. As such, he had made some bad choices that were discovered early or late into rehearsals. If early enough he could replace them, but when one was dealing with contracted actors, even that could be difficult.

It turned out that BBGD was right about the person playing Elesin, a well-known actor, with rich Shakespearean voice. His lines were delivered well, but that simply was not enough for Elesin. His stalwart stature must be matched by his various attributes: his *joie de vivre*, his sexual vigor and attraction, his crafty seductive movement among women, indulgent effervescent humor, and his twist of the tongue in riddles and proverbs, as encouraged by his culture. Needless to say, his movement of course involved spontaneous and deliberate dancing. The Elesin at the Lincoln Centre was no match for all these qualities. This was more noticeable at two key moments of the production.

As it became obvious to BBGD, the "Not-Bird" sequence that Soyinka created is probably one of the most difficult speeches ever written. Poetic and laden with cultural images. Its storytelling and narrative sequences must be projected and made compelling not only to Elesin's audience of market women surrounding him, but also to the theater audience. As demanded by the rhythm and the images being created, an actor playing the "thoroughbred" must display and match fluidity of body and movement with voice, poetic eloquence and spontaneous reaction to his audience of market women. And there's the rub. As if threatened by these demands of the narration, the Lincoln Center Elesin was uncomfortably rooted to a spot most of the time, his face lacking any definable emotion. He was supposed to be full of life and master of his stage, that is, the whole theater space. As such, that scene was not as spectacular as it should be, although the director found other ways to make it so, by using the women around him to surrogate his movement and vivacity. More important, the thread and images of the narrative, as difficult and foreign as they could be to an unfamiliar audience, were hardly conveyed to the straining ears and mind of the theater audience.

The other moment, perhaps the most important for Elesin, also had to do with movement and more significantly, dance. It was at the end of scene three, when Elesin was accompanied by drummers and the praise-singer, Olohuniyo. The euphoria of the drumming was supposed to induce dancing and his willing himself gradually to the world of the ancestors, to meet and accompany his waiting friend, the dead Alafin, through the gates into ancestral world. Following his movements behind should-be the praise-singer as quester, seeking to get a glimpse of his passage across and what constituted it, from moment to moment.

Again, here, at the Lincoln Center production, Elesin's actor found himself transfixed and rigid to a spot during his progressive dialogue with questing Olohuniyo, who assumed the voice of the Alafin as visualized at heaven's gate. But worse, that state of stasis continued even when the Olohuniyo took over the dialogue with his sweeping narrative of amazement at Elesin's forgone concluded journey. As such, the actor's rather counterproductive inertia failed to image for the audience the progression of crossing in the numinous passage (Soyinka's chthonic realm) linking the physical to the metaphysical. It is the passage, as WS informs, that links the three existences constituting the Yoruba worldview—the living, the ancestral and the unborn. It is an amorphous passage through which supernal knowledge could be gained of the metaphysical order, an information that the questing Olohuniyo, on the other hand, is trying to glean from Elesin.

"The man was pathetic, I'm telling you," WS was explaining to BBGD at dinner after the first night's performance. "In fact, I tried to let him go. I called in the producer to come and see for himself. He himself suggested a number of ways we could get the man through his difficulties, but failed. And no luck at letting him go, without facing complicated problems with Equity. As you saw, I had to ultimately build a movement around him with Olohuniyo."

"Well, that was very effective," BBGD admitted.

"Well, yah, up to a point."

Part of that effectiveness was due to the presence of Tunji Oyelana, the only Nigerian the director was able to get invited from London to participate. Remaining in the background, and in consonant with Elesin-Olohuniyo's movement, he softly incantated a recitative in Yoruba. The surreal and theatrical effect evoked the image of the Alafin in the numinous passage, summoning and guiding Elesin through the passage with hypnotic incantation-power. It was as if the Alafin was prompting the conscience of his friend regarding the pact they had long since made, as companions to death.

*****

It was the second time he would come to Washington State to workshop *Death and the King's Horseman*. The first time was a few years back, when he was invited by the National Museum in Seattle to do a lecture and workshop on the play for an invited audience as part of a festival. He got the invitation out of the blue, initiated by a former University of Ife student of his and her boyfriend, a white American that came to Ife to study how to play Yoruba

237

dundun drums. As far as he got it, he was to do a reading of the play with some actors, then select a scene for a workshop presentation. And even though he was paid handsomely, he wasn't wholly satisfied with the project. While he could cope with the actors he was given to work with, a mixture of amateur and professionals, the whole project was cumbersome, disorganized, and uneventful.

The scene he chose was the very same and difficult end of scene three, when Elesin was dancing himself from the physical to the metaphysical world. The difficulties posed were manifold. The allotted open space for the presentation was conceivable, since the scene identifies an open market location. But he wasn't made aware of this until the moment of the presentation. What he understood was that everything would be indoors, probably in the room that the whole play was earlier read. As such, with no time to access the performance space beforehand, the BBGD found himself at the last minute racking his head as to how to set the scene and group the actors.

But that in itself would not have been difficult. He was used to last minute changes and, consequently, to making quick decisions, insights and inventiveness demanded by the change. All of these were within his creative abilities. But he found himself doing this when the audience was already in place, and with actors, mostly amateurs, who were hardly flexible to being drilled into quick directions. The play was tough enough with regard to its cultural nuances and dramatic demands, which they were all still struggling to access.

His former student, Toyin Ajayi, and her white American boyfriend did much to help. As previously arranged, she had brought with her a dancing group she was managing at the time, which consisted of two or three Nigerians who were familiar with the Yoruba dance mode. She was also a fantastic dancer; BBGD knew of her dancing abilities way back at Ife. She also brought some drummers that her boyfriend had trained.

As he expected, the semi-professional African American actor chosen for him to play Elesin could not dance. Consequently, Toyin, instructed by the director, had to hastily create a dance around him. But by doing so, the biggest handicap was balancing the sound of the drumming with the important dialogue and narrative, and projecting this to a rather fidgety audience, who needed to be engaged with the unfamiliar nuances and poetry of the piece. In this regard, as BBGD later confessed to himself, the scene was probably a bad choice. But then, what other choices could he have made to demonstrate the play and playwright's genius without involving the crowd, an important feature of the play? He had hoped that the audience could probably be mesmerized by the totality of the spectacle (the drumming, the dancing and the grouping), that is, at the complete expense of the spoken lines.

The museum-producer of the project, an African American, seemed to think the presentation was successful, but he personally wasn't satisfied. For him it was a disaster that should have been avoided, which meant turning down the project in the first place. But then, how was he to know and anticipate what it turned out to be? His preliminary communication between him and Toyin promised nothing but a worthy and exciting enlightenment for the Seattle community. Furthermore, he very much wanted to help her fledgling dance company, which he knew she was trying to promote.

The workshop at Pullman was a totally different experience. The department of Theater and Dance at the University of Washington wanted to do a production of the play; he was asked to come and do a series of workshops for a week to prepare the student actors. It was in celebration of WS who would be invited to the show. He was excited about this fact.

When he first learnt about the production, through a letter from the chair of the department, he had attempted to make them commit the directing of the show to him, for which he would be available. But he couldn't get them to do so, since they had a director of their own in mind, one of the faculty members, a director in his own right. His attempt to get them to engage a good choreographer also ran aground. He was thinking of somebody that would be familiar with the play, such as his friend at the University of Kansas, Folabo Ajayi-Soyinka. It was made known to him that there was a capable choreographer in the dance program who was excited about doing the show. BBGD realized they had to think in terms of the budget and would rather have a person on site, to minimize the expenses; to argue against that notion was fruitless, but he tried.

They ultimately settled with the agreement that he would come twice— initially for the first week of rehearsals do a workshop, and then the last week of rehearsals to help with the final notes before the opening. He immediately e-mailed WS to tell him what his plans were, and to verify whether he was truly invited and was coming to the event—he knew the playwright's position about attending productions of his plays. He got an immediate response from WS with confirmation of his attending. The playwright was delighted about BBGD's involvement and both were looking forward to meeting again. The former mentee and colleague treasured such moments since they now seemed to be rare.

At once, he could see the problems that could afflict the production. The direction by a white director could prove to elicit a good production, as it had been with certain productions in the past, especially in Europe, based on what transpired to him from the media. But, as he did not know anything about the work of this director, he had to put his speculations on hold. However, he thought the dance might be in jeopardy. For, if anything at all, and most likely than not, the dance forms would not be the Yoruba demanded by the play. Rather, it would be something in the nature of the Senegalese form, familiar to most African American choreographers and dancers. But he was willing to be proven wrong.

The opportunity to do a workshop made him consider the script again, and in greater detail. This time, he confronted the various songs in it, incidental and specific, remembering the productions he had seen, especially the one at the Lincoln Center. He called his friend, Folabo Ajayi-Soyinka, the playwright's sister, to confirm what he knew, what he had forgotten and the ones he intended to include. He then scored all the tones, since giving Yoruba tones the correct accent was a difficulty posed by the language.

Actually he felt enormous enthusiasm among the students as they all sat in the round to learn the songs. The doh-re-mi-fa-so… of the scoring helped enormously; all the actors could write it down and practice on their own. He also made a solo recording of the songs and Yoruba words, to sharpen their reception as they struggled on their own with the unfamiliar tones. On the whole they got it almost right and beyond his expectations, an attribution of the repetition he insisted on and encouraged at every session of the workshop. They also went over the script with him and the director a couple of times, stopping severally to explain the cultural background and nuances; then tried out the songs with the scenes in which they occurred. He felt satisfied by the time he left at the end of one week, and hoped they would constantly return to the recording he made if they were in difficulty.

"Don't mind them," WS explained the offer made to him. "They suggested this ridiculous amount. I was going to turn it down." They met in Pullman the day the play opened. BBGD had arrived a day prior, to catch and help with the last-minute details of the rehearsals as was previously planned. They were sitting over snacks and wine in the playwright's hotel room at the same place BBGD was staying. "They said they didn't have much in the budget," the playwright continued to explain, probably to sound BBGD's feelings about it.

"That's what they told me too," he confirmed, although he managed to get what he wanted.

"I accepted only because you were going to be here—haven't seen you for quite some time. Accepted the offer as family price." Both chuckled at the understanding. He knew under certain terms, the Nobel Laureate overrode his agent to accept fees that were far below the suggested, or the standard equitable to his stature. "Anyway, how are the rehearsals coming?"

"Oh, I arrived back only yesterday—my second time. I first came, about five weeks ago, to do workshops. Then I was supposed to come back the last week of rehearsals. For some reasons I was sent a plane ticket for yesterday. Anyway, I saw the dress rehearsal yesterday. Well, they've come a long way, but let me warn you, there are some things that would irritate you."

"Oh God," the playwright gave his familiar deep sigh of 'What did get myself into!' "You mean, I'm going to have to sit through…"

"No, no, no, I think you'll enjoy much of it. I'm just warning you. For instance, I told the director he could cut part of the Not-I sequence. Apparently, he didn't."

"But is the Elesin any good?"

"Well, not bad. He's a professional—the only professional really."

"But we know how that goes, sometimes," the playwright sniggered, recalling his own experiences, about which BBGD knew so well.

He wouldn't go further than the example he gave, but he knew of other incidents that the playwright would frown at, concerns that came to his notice but was too late to correct at the dress rehearsal he saw. He would rather not increase any level of frustration. On the whole, he thought the student-actors had come a long way in five or six weeks. The workshops he did on cultural nuances and songs had been put to advantageous use, although there were some lapses, which he tried to correct. He couldn't do much with the directorial choices made, but subtly made his feelings felt. For instance, he wanted to know why "Rule Britannia" tune had recurred again and again in the long scene change between scenes two and three. It was obvious its intentions were to allow some changes of costume, but the replay went on for far too long that it became ridiculous and annoying. When he pointed it out to the director, he did not receive any definitive answer.

"Yes, why is that?" WS queried after the performance.

"He gave some reasons, which I couldn't follow."

The Laureate's frustration was greater than BBGD had thought. Where they were sitting during the performance, at the top level of the orchestra, he could feel the frowns of annoyance exuding from the playwright. Both of them found many of the directorial choices unnerving. On such choices in productions of his plays, the playwright had always maintained: "That's the director's prerogative, as long as I don't have to sit through watching it." With that in mind, he very rarely saw a production of his own plays. He felt he had that right to decline. But once he accepted the invitation and physically entered the theater, he felt he had committed himself to live with whatever images confronted him and the self-inflicted pain they might impose.

"Are you coming to see the actors and meet the director?"

"No." BBGD was afraid that would be WS's response. "Help me say hello to them and him." However, the director was sitting almost in the same row and BBGD could see him at the end of the row, waiting to meet the man of the hour.

"Too late, there he is."

"Oh God!" The breathy sigh almost met the anxious, boisterous yet nervous "Hello!" of the director.

BBGD introduced them, but the playwright had not much to tell him except to mumble: "Good performance, all told."

"We were very nervous, hoping it would meet your approval."

"Well, err..." the garbled response faded into a quiet grin. Then hastily added, "You must excuse me, but I have to go to the restroom. I'll talk to you later."

"I'll see you later Ron," BBGD nodded something positive, as he made to follow the playwright. He needed to ask him where to reconnect.

He felt he had to go and say hello, at least, to the actors backstage, so he established a place to meet the playwright afterwards so they could drive back to the hotel in his rented car. He just couldn't avoid complimenting the actors who he felt had worked so hard in spite of what his feelings about the whole production might be.

"What did he think? I have a feeling he didn't like it," the director confronted him as he got backstage.

"Oh no, he liked it," he quickly responded. "As I told you, you should have cut some of the passages of the "Not-I Bird" sequence. He also felt the same, but I think he liked your choices in general,"

"Oh good." Whether the director's response was also condescending, he couldn't tell; he moved away to congratulate the actors.

*****

"Would you be interested in directing *Death and the King's Horseman*," WS posed him the question.

"Where?"

"Here."

They were sitting at the residence of the President of Kalamazoo College, enjoying a Nigerian treat reception in honor of the playwright—he had given his lecture in the main college hall. The weekend event was almost like a reunion of the Ife University group, since both the president and her husband had been colleagues there a few years before. Folabo Ajayi-Soyinka, the celebrity's sister and BBGD's friend, was also there.

"Yes, of course, I'd very much like that. When are they thinking of doing this?" BBGD was curious, not because he foresaw possible conflicts, although it would be better if he could coordinate this with the responsibilities of his job at Louisiana State University.

"I don't quite know this, but let's ask Sope about it." The president's husband happened to be passing by at that time. WS beckoned at him and he came by. "Sope, the theater director told me he was interested in doing *Death and the King's Horseman* here and was looking for somebody to direct it."

"Oh y-yes, y-yes sir. H-He told me about it," Sope responded with his stutter-ridden excitement. He had always displayed the customary elder-respect for the playwright, although they were within the same age-range.

"He said he was thinking of Chuck Mike," the playwright explained further. "But I think BB might be a better choice."

"Oh...O-hh yes. Yes," casting what BBGD thought was a condescending although agreeable look at him.

"Can you please, please suggest me to the director?" BBGD tried to give him an extra push. The guy had not always been on good terms with him. There seem to have been some understood professional dislike between them since Ife; in fact, BBGD had often found the apparent animosity unjustified and trifling, knowing the possible source of it.

"I-I will. In fact, I will introduce you; he was here a few minutes ago but might have left."

"Okay, that's settled." WS put his final stamp on it and went on to enjoy his plate of pounded yam with rich condiment-laden vegetable stew, pepper-fried snails and some fried plantains. BBGD piled similar stuff on his plate, including jollof rice. He realized he had a much-bigger appetite, since the playwright generally didn't eat much, which was an irony, considering the sumptuous spread that often lavished his dining table at Ife.

He didn't fully believe Sope's promise and he meant to prod him if he did not hear anything from him soon. However, praise be, he affirmed to himself. For it was really one of those rare occasions that his mentor had suggested him for a project; in fact the only time of its kind. That is, not counting the failed attempt of a few years back, when he was at William and Mary. The project really never got started. The playwright surprisingly threw his name at a group in New York who were thinking of producing *The Bacchae*. He met the group at a location, only to find out that it was rather disorganized, and they were still thinking of how to raise the production money, or what to do to begin doing just that. That was the only time he met with them.

He finally got a positive response to the possibility of directing *Death*, although not without a few promptings of Sope. These sometimes felt like harassment on Sope's part and almost resulted in a non-compliant attitude of an exercise of power, which didn't surprise him. Sometimes he wondered whether the quiet antagonist attitude was also a result of some professional jealousy. That would surprise him, for which he felt there was no need. But he wouldn't put it past the president's consort.

He got to meet the Kalamazoo College theater director at that year's biennial National Black Theater Festival at Winston-Salem. Professor Sope Oyelaran, by virtue of his residency in that city, had for years been the coordinator of the International Colloquium segment of the festival. BBGD had always looked forward, every other year, to participating ever since the beginning of the colloquium, even before Sope's dexterous takeover. The Kalamazoo director, himself a developing playwright, brought a work-in-progress to the festival, after which he sat with BBGD to talk about prospects of the production. He brought along with him one of his workshop actors, an African American professor at Western Michigan State; he was introduced as the person intended to play the role of Elesin Oba.

BBGD did not appreciate the definitiveness of an already chosen person to play the role. He would have loved to select the person through a normal audition process, or at least have two or three choices to pick from. He happened to talk with Chuck Mike on the phone sometime later, at which conversation the Kalamazoo production came up.

"Seems they already have somebody in mind to play Elesin," Chuck confirmed their initial attempt to engage him as director. "I told them I'd rather make the selection myself, but I never heard any more from them."

"Well, they approached me to direct it." BBGD felt there was no need to hedge the fact from Chuck since he would sooner or later hear about it anyway.

"Oh, you're going to do it?"

"Yes, although I too don't like the stipulation of an already cast Elesin," BBGD intimated. "However, I met the man at the Black Theater Festival in August, and felt it was possible to cast him. I still have my reservations though."

"Well, at least one of us is doing it."

BBGD registered a feeling of disappointment from Chuck, but decided to leave the matter at that.

2008. *Death and the King's Horseman* had been with him for more than four decades, since 1976 when he was Olunde, the character that launched his questing. He felt it was quite logical and an honor to have the opportunity to direct the play, which logically was his ultimate desire. The time was right, but found he had to jump through some initial hurdles—coming to terms with his guest director fees, and making sure his accommodation was consistent with his convenience. He also had to think about his mobility around and outside campus for a period of six weeks.

Regarding his fees, he came to an agreement that the only way to make it acceptable on both sides was to teach a course within the duration, conveniently to fit their quarter-term system. The free accommodation that the contract included he insisted must be self-contained, as he was not in the habit of sharing even a bathroom, let alone a toilet. He was glad he dealt with this stipulation before he sealed the deal, for the initial plan was to accommodate him in a regular guest house for artists, which had a common bathroom and toilet on each floor. As he wasn't sure who else they were planning to accommodate during that time, he declined, in spite of efforts to persuade him through Sope and the President. Ultimately, they found a hotel accommodation for him outside campus—the chalet guest house of a small castle, catered by a friend of the theater director. It was exactly what he wanted and felt very pleased with the last-minute find. The location reminded him, some years back, of the chalet he had at Ethel Walker School overlooking 800 acres of the school's property. Here the overlooking castle was recently renovated as a hotel complex, so to speak. Having a free breakfast there every morning was also an added blessing. With that and a rented car he could drive to and fro rehearsals and outside campus whenever he felt like it, everything else was secondary—even his guest-director fees.

He knew what he was getting into from the start—that it was an educational theater set-up with student actors, and the only professional would be the African American professor to play Elesin. But he didn't realize that black students would be scare. He had thought he would be able to cast the principal roles (the Yoruba characters) at least with black students, an effort to maintain a kind of authenticity. The auditions did not produce sufficient number to choose from, certainly not for a strong character like Iyaloja. As such, he had to insist on auditioning possible people from outside. He had also got the director to understand that a good choreographer was essential, and fortunately, through his aforethought prompting of the person he had in mind, he was able to get hired his friend, Folabo Ajayi-Soyinka, then a professor of Dance and Theater at the University of Kansas.

He was quite surprised to see a known face among the three that auditioned for Iyaloja, in fact a professional that he had met years before when he was at Ethel Walker School and took part in Derek Walcott's *Dream on Monkey*

Mountain. She had gone on in age, but if ever there was a person that looked like Iyaloja, she would be it. Folabo agreed with her, and because the woman read well and seemed to understand the part, even though she struggled with some words, which was understandable, he was willing to gamble with her.

However, some three weeks into the rehearsal period, he was constrained to change his mind. She was very hard to direct in terms of getting her to understand what she was saying and the choices she had to make with it. For a professional she said she was, versatility was lacking; instead, she always chose to blame other people for her rigidity and obvious ineptitude. So, consulting with the Theater chair about the ramifications of equity contract, he came to the difficult decision of letting her go. That decision, fortunately, was encouraged by the audition he gave the possible substitute the chair invited. In spite of her many conflicts, which he was willing to work around, she proved a hundred percent a worthier choice.

Early arrival of Folabo was also a blessing. He insisted that she should be present at the auditions. She would need to have an idea of the flexibility of the bodies to be cast as market women, whose essential presence on stage involved dancing. The choreographer also helped him to finalize his choice of actors.

The directorial challenge for the director was to coordinate the diverse variety of the actors on stage, two professionals, a few theater students, and other students from various departments within the university and with no significant background in acting. All of them with diverse cultural upbringing—Indian, Caribbean, African, etc. As such, he expected enormous flexibility on his part and the need to exercise patience.

Some of the conflicts were not within his control, based on past experiences in American Colleges and Universities. One was the enormous power and pressures that fraternities and sororities imposed on students. These strictly limited their efforts to satisfy other responsibilities such as theater rehearsals. He had not clearly understood this pressure that made it impossible for the young human mind to be flexible and to compromise themselves to other equally important and perhaps more enlightening concerns. In the past, he had tried to work with it; at Kalamazoo, given the massive challenges the play posed, it almost seemed impossible to overcome.

One of major tasks of the play for the director had to do with coordinating the Yoruba dancing of the market women. That was why he had insisted on Folabo as choreographer, who he knew could perform wonders on uninitiated bodies. Added to that challenge was his inability to find all black students to constitute the Yoruba community; in fact, the opposite was the case, the available students were mostly white. To get these culturally foreign bodies to respond to the Yoruba nuances and subtle dancing movements was the task ahead for the choreographer. However, the enthusiasm and the eagerness to learn among the students went a long way to win half the battle from the outset. The attitude made him somewhat optimistic to leave them in the secure, capable hands and direction of his friend.

His disappointment with the professional actor playing Elesin had gradually grown over the length of the rehearsals. He understood the man's sensitivity, as a professional, to being criticized in front of the other actors; as such, the director exercised enormous control when giving notes. He went out of his way to have several tête-à-tête conferences with him during intervals at rehearsals; even then, the actor did not display any visible improvement regarding what transpire during those sessions. He had discerned early enough the kind of actor he had in his hands, one that had taken for granted the challenges of the play, thinking he could overcome them with no difficulty. What the actor had read and probably fell in love with through sheer artistic fancy was different from the reality of the demands that confronted him. This was very much the situation in this production, in terms of the rich poetry and cultural nuances woven into the rhythm of the play. The actor not only lacked the capacity and the resources to confront these encounters, as time went on, he seemed given to constant blanking out, and to rely on being prompted.

The various cuts that the director found necessary to make, given the actor's difficulties, were very judicious, careful not to destroy the rhythmic flow and the meaning of what the playwright intended. From experience, he knew that the "Not-I Bird" sequence was too long to hold the attention of the audience, to bring the moment off with success. It would need a very versatile and creative actor and, more important, one who also knew the culture and the nuances embedded in the images of the text. As a matter of fact, he hadn't seen any actor on this side of the continent that had successfully brought it off completely, even the ones directed by the playwright himself. Added to this problematic, and this was unfortunate, BBGD also had to look into some of Elesin's long speeches to see how he could trim off some of the lines for the benefit of the present professional. To his dismay and frustration, all of this did not stop the actor from blanking even during performances, almost always at the same places. This left the director no alternative other than wonder whether the actor did any work or soul-searching self-criticism outside the theater space of rehearsals.

"Oh no, he didn't!" came the exasperated sigh of the director, covering his eyes with his hand in embarrassment, as the actor did it again on opening night, and in front of invited guests and the critics. "What is this man doing?" There

247

in front of that audience the actor just stood still, blanked out, with no remorse, waiting to recall the lines. That was why his acting lacked the magical power and stature that Elesin deserved. It was as if he wasn't acting at all, but was for most of the time trying to remember his lines.

BBGD was glad the critics saw through the problem and noted the actor's serious lack in their reviews. Although there was no indication they held the director responsible, he nevertheless felt personally humiliated to the very core, considering the disarray this must have created among the other actors on stage or backstage. Fortunately, he had told them what to do should such a thing occur during performance, but he knew only too well that advice of caution was easier absorbed than realized by spontaneity on stage, especially so with inexperience. Even professionals were sometimes caught unawares that they had to scramble for improvised solutions. He sniggered at the irony the student-actors might have entertained—the fact that it was one of the two professionals that messed up and let the side down. And if they did consider the ironic fact, who else could they turn to as a worthy role model to give them the moral support they needed? Not even the apology rendered at the end of the show sufficed, as far as the director was concerned. It became redundant and ridiculous since the mess up and apology continued almost every night thereafter.

"Yet again?!" This time BBGD ducked his head down into the flex of his horror-compelled hands, casing his occiput in shame. That happened on the night the playwright came. Yes, he felt shame for the actor and for himself, that is, for his inability and helplessness to have the guy fired long time ago. But shame for the actor?—he reflected to confirm this. Yes, an unsympathetic shame, for shaming the profession which included him as director. He was sitting with WS and he could feel the playwright's disgust at that moment.

"I don't want to see him," the playwright stated as a matter of fact after the performance. "You can say hello to the other actors for me, but that guy…?" He couldn't find the right expletives to express his emotions. Wole Soyinka, short of immediate expression to vent his feelings? That was a first for BBGD.

"I did my best," the director explained. "That was the guy they gave me, unsolicited and unconditionally." His clarification was probably redundant, since he had warned the playwright; but he felt he needed to restate it.

"Yes. I feel your pain." WS's response probably summoned up the experiences he'd had with failed actors, such as the Elesin at the Lincoln Centre production. But he went on to relieve his anger by diverting to the moments he liked and those he didn't like in the production, although he realized some of these were directorial choices the director was entitled.

He was hoping the playwright would at least say hello to the woman who played Iyaloja. He had grown to be fond of her and enjoyed working with her as a fortunate well-cast person for the role. Knowing the wandering mind of his mentor, he felt the playwright might have wished to explore his curiosity over some dinner, at least to discover her professional probabilities. Perhaps he would have, were it not for the actor that played Elesin.

John, the Elesin actor, was present at a kind of postmortem session with the playwright, the following morning. WS spoke frankly about what he liked and didn't like, but made the present actors feel comfortable by assuring them that he enjoyed their performances on the whole. BBGD, from where he was sitting, away from the playwright, noticed Sope Oyelaran down in the first row near the playwright's podium. The man was nodding his head at the mention of any critical moment the playwright felt could do with some improvement, as if to say, "Yes, I felt that too." In fact, as if to make sure BBGD saw and registered his gesture of agreement with the playwright, the president's consort turned around to locate BBGD, as if to make his reaction prod the director's conscience. Their eyes met, but BBGD immediately deflected and ignored the onslaught. He wasn't surprised about the indiscretion, knowing the kind of person the man was—somebody who took delight, wittingly or otherwise, at probable mistakes or errors of his declared enemy. Whatever the man's nodding might have translated for him in his thoughts, BBGD professionally brushed it aside. For Sope Oyelaran knew nothing about theater and the processes it took to mount a production. The choices of any director could always do with some improvements. BBGD knew that, a perfectionist that he was.

Any production, he confirmed for himself, is always in process and could always be done differently by the same or another director. In fact, in this regard, there is a lot to take into consideration. Given all the collaboration staging a play demands, the director may not fulfil all of his objectives, let alone satisfy every member of the audience. And there is the question of the actor as an essential part of that collaboration. The director could do all he can to work with a very limited actor without achieving the satisfactory results he wanted. What did Sope know about all this? Reflecting on it, BBGD couldn't help but snigger at the man's glaringly obvious ignorance and inadequacy, as far as theater was concerned.

When the session came to Q and A, Elesin's actor got up. Firstly, he apologized for his failed memory that made nonsense of two moments in the performance. But rather than leave it at that, he went on to make a justification for the failing. Something about the inability of Americans or people like him to measure up to the poetic language of the play. He compared the lack with the competence of British actors, or those who trained at a British conservatory, who were quite familiar with such language because of their knowledge of classical acting styles, a requirement available to them but not to many American actors.

He shouldn't have said that. For the playwright couldn't resist having his say, short but to the point: "I understand and appreciate that, but that's not the case here. You just couldn't remember the lines, point blank. You put the rest of the actors in disarray."

"Yes, the audacity of the guy," WS agreed with BBGD after the session and on their way to find a restaurant to eat and drink. They both would have loved the choreographer, his sister, to join them, but she had to leave earlier that morning to catch a plane and connect with her flight to Senegal where she had another engagement. They had talked about her achievements in the production, working with the mostly white market women and dancers, and turning them within six weeks of rehearsal into almost Yoruba dancers. BBGD didn't think it would be that possible and he was nervous about its success in the beginning; but thanks to Folabo.

"Yah, she came up to par with her abilities." The playwright rarely praised his sister in front of anybody, even when praises were warranted. Might have to do with being siblings. But then he rarely praised BBGD also, an inclination that could be an extension of the sibling attitude—since he always considered his former mentee one of the family.

"Anyway, I'm glad I did the production," BBGD concluded. "Directing it realized a kind of completion for me in my process of understanding. Of course I would have liked a more professional group and there's always a possibility of that in future. But…" He let his voice, thoughts and senses trail off expectantly into that unknown future.

Epilogue

Some After Thoughts: "A Prophet Unrecognized…"

Tick, Tick, Tick in my flesh! The words of the experimental theorist, Ann Bogart, struck his ears with persistent significance, initiating thoughts that floated backwards through the rocky roads of his career. He was making an effort to assess and establish a justification for a recognition as an artist/scholar par excellence. He was not one for tooting his horn; yet he felt he merited it, as a good example of such a person. Surely, a spade should be called a spade— begging the pardon of the derogatory connotation that the phrase sometimes punned.

Bogart's words, meant as a humor, in fact had a foundation and was reflective of those rocky roads. She was giving a lecture about her theory and practice to theater students and faculty of the Theater Department at Louisiana State University. Introduced with some familiarity of her by the chair of the department, Michael Tick, Bogart complimented with an equal familiarity as she got to the podium: "Thank you, Mike…tick, tick, tick in my flesh!" a pun loaded with images that drew enormous, tearful laughter from the audience.

For BBGD, the word/name of the pun adequately summed up the human form that responded to and imaged the character—short, slender; a compressed and pointed Jewish nose hanging a Scrooge-eyeglasses; and a kind of sly, undulating swagger as Chairman Tick identified and progressed towards his victim. BBGD was a victim and both he and the victimizer had their many fall outs, over various issues regarding his artistic and scholarly development. This growth, BBGD often thought, Tick had deliberately slowed down, or suppressed—for whatever reasons, he couldn't quite figure out, although they were very glaring. If the man had not sometimes shown some flashes of friendship, whose genuineness he sometimes often queried, BBGD would have categorically labelled him a racist. But then again, he could legitimately call him that, as far as he was concerned. For those gestures of alliance often seemed pretentious to him, given the radiating superficiality he felt when confronted with them.

However, he'd rather say no more on the matter; all's well that ends well, he sighed the Shakespeare's title to himself. He'd prefer to let vicious mongrels lie, or, to complete the image he started with, spray off the "ticks" that had attempted to leech on his progressive legs. For, however slow his academic development may have been, all seemed to have turned out well in the end with long overdue recognition of his artistry and scholarship, even if that appreciation was still short of what he would regard as the ultimate. Many times, that *ne plus ultra* had come his way, only to be knocked down with a discriminating political cudgel before it could reach, let alone celebrate him. And...

"And here's my wonder-boy-genius." At moments of self-doubt, the accosting appellation from Addie Russo always invaded his mind to soothe his raging thoughts. Not that he had complete faith in Addie's attribution. But the acknowledgment had come so often at every introduction of him by the colleague professor in French and Comparative Studies, so much so that it felt genuine enough. And perhaps it reflected the unspoken feelings of many others that had commented favorably on his work, especially in directing. That certainly must include the rather premature but foreshadowing observation made at the outset of that area of his career, back at the University of Ife. That is, the African American professor in the English department that glowed over his production of *Madame Tinubu*, compelled by what the professor thought was at the level of a Broadway show. Thereafter, with each subsequent production, he had grown to believe that directing was his forte, that it had something significant to offer its audience, something that, perhaps, could have landed him some awards if he had pursued it more vigorously the American way.

Farfetched as it seemed, that speculation was conceivable, not even counting the awards he received at the KC/ACTF for his production of Athol Fugard et al's *Sizwe Bansi is Dead*, in 1995. On seconds thoughts, those awards should matter, all the more because, given at both state and regional levels of the competition, they were meritoriously awarded, unmarred by the usual political lobbying that accompanied that festival. In fact, as he was told, the production could have ascended to the Kennedy Centre finalists, if it wasn't waylaid at the last minute by the very belaboring political agents. For what did it matter if another production of the same play was a finalist the year before? More kudos to the play and its directorial capacities, it would seem. As such, he had always questioned the convoluted reasoning behind the non-inclusion of the production for that final honor.

Filling himself with momentary pride, he decided not to get into any of the detriments or the so-called unprofessional ticks of saboteurs that sometimes invaded his thoughts, vying for a hearing—for the injustices that had plagued him, often through pure professional envy or because of the color of his skin. As such, he tried to vanquish any self-doubts these intrusions tended to foster; he would rather pursue his critical self-study with a more productive philosophical deliberation. For, as they say, a prophet doesn't often get the merited recognition in his own country. But then, one may well ask in his case, in what or which country?

As a citizen of three continents and at least three cultures (as multiracial and multi-cultured as he could be), he almost always found himself in some abyss in between, and therefore at a losing end. Dangling, as it were, in the chthonic realm of some sorts, to borrow WS's term. For him, it was always a case of struggling for acceptance as oppose to claiming the advantages of being multi-cultured. As if pursued by something, or in pursuit of certain satisfaction of the mind and intellect, he was always on the move, shifting from one world or culture to the other, not sufficiently grounded in one long enough for him to be recognized as a significant and worthy artist and/or scholar. In his teens, he left his culture of origin in Nigeria to go and study in England and then stayed on, to explore his talents and to try and achieve some professional standing, but only for a little while. From there, he went on to the US to study some more, but also left that culture before establishing himself, to go back to Nigeria to take up an academic position. Seemingly secured at that location, his first home, he was always running back and forth, any time he could, to the enticing US to test the waters of his career, not really satisfied with his academic standing. Then, just before he could ascend to full professorship in Nigeria, frustrated by the daily-festering political unrest and the uncertainty of academic freedom, he left for the US in hopes of a permanent stay.

Yet, he had often wondered whether his ultimate choice of home in the US had been the very best for his development, what with the culture's background of racism, capitalist rat race, political mud-slings, corruptive democracy, mafia impulses and superficial objectification of dreams. Given his inclination to acute rationalizing, especially on matters of fate, he had wondered whether any of the other cultures (in the U.K. or in Nigeria) would have produced better results for him. Who knows…as WS might have stated with no remorse. Who knows…?

If he had somehow returned to Nigeria at some point, which would not have been in his best interest, another set of issues probably more destructive might have confronted him. Really, he had had no compulsive reasons for him to go back. It used to be the consideration of his aging parents, but after both passed, he was free to follow any intentions he wanted. Thus, he had followed his dreams to the US. It was his choice to emigrate, like many of his friends; but unlike some who had returned home, he had stayed on no matter what.

"My country, 'tis of thee..." had claimed the diehard returnees. Or better still, "Dis na ma country a no go lie/ Na here a go live and eat and die." He chuckled, recalling the lyrics of the song, or some semblance of it, waxed into an album by WS during one of the terrible corruption-laden times in Nigeria. With such an affirmation it should be possible to face off any problematic encounters more squarely and better, culture for culture. But it was an argument he just could not buy into. For one, there were the glaring, endemic problems of infrastructure and looted economy to wrestle with, let alone the lack of, or the deplorable common conveniences that every human being deserved to make life a little more comfortable. In fact, some of those friends that went back eventually had to give up and return—to the lesser strains of evil in the US, it would seem? That question mark must linger...

"Evil?" What else could one call it? For evil, as in "money is the root of all evil," not only exists but metastasizes, corrupts and kills with impunity. A human condition anywhere one chose to reside?

Whenever he landed on the idea, he could not help entertaining the thought of it as one of the detriments of globalization. Like democracy (demon-crazy, as he often called it). The Western notion of it, he believed, was foisted indiscriminately on the so-called underdeveloped countries, whose socio-political neo-capitalists not only embraced it but exploited it against their people, indiscriminately. Despite its positive values, and perhaps the fact of it as an enabler of miscegenation, its corruptive influences were impossible to escape. Its manipulating wings took flight across the African continent creating autocratic states of despair that bested those of its Western counterparts. To support his claims, he recalled leaders such as Idi Amin of Uganda, Mobutu of Zaire, Abacha of Nigeria, to name a deathly few, leaders that WS had in mind in his consciously political plays—*Kongi's Harvest*, *Play of Giants*, and *King Baabu*. Digressing a little, although nevertheless a related subject, he had always regretted his inability to participate in any of the productions of those plays, through no fault of his to be sure. But all this was to say he did not see Nigeria as any easier or better solution for his artistic or scholarly growth.

If, on the other hand he had stayed in the UK, what then? He probably would have been driven more towards the artistic than the scholarly, given some of the initial setbacks he encountered in trying to pursue his more academic pursuits. He believed he had the talents it took to become an excellent creative artist as actor, writer, or even a filmmaker, but opportunities to flourish at that moment in time was not readily available to a black man, let alone an African. However, given the later successes of a few of his peers and the black British-borns, perhaps he would have made it. His accomplishments would probably have landed him an OBE, like it happened to one or two of his friends, or an MBE, or even a knighthood from the Queen! He cleared his throat, shifted and chortled, British style, at the thought. Sir BBGD! Not inconceivable, he dared say, especially if his fledgling relationship with Robin, a royalty, had blossomed to material substance. Who knows, who knows...? And would that have satisfied him and banished into thin air (like Macbeth's witches) all his more academic interests? Who knows, who knows, in the indeterminate manifestations of Fate?

Thus, he had ultimately concluded, the location in which he had finally settled, given its many crucial conflicts and setbacks, was exactly where his fate had landed him—that is, the fate-head that his body had chosen in the metaphysical world. He was relating to the Yoruba worldview of his culture of origin, which, believe it or not, still informed his critical judgment. Indeed, that concept of fate had motivated most of his works, producing his seminal study of satire in black culture, *Archetypes, Imprecators and Victims of Fate.*

He had evoked the vision as he understood it: there, in the metaphysical world before birth, his molded body had walked into an enormous room full of fate-heads. He had looked around, examined, thoughtfully considered, and chosen his fate as an artist/scholar. Thereafter, Esu, the fate essence, at the chthonic crossroads between realms of existence, sanctioned his choice before he passed through his mother's womb into the living world of fateful-fatal encounters—obstacles he had had to combat and overcome in his pursuits, in order to realize his chosen fate. And there's the rub, the difficult processes of aligning oneself to one's chosen fate; the difficulty of maintaining its balance of good and evil complementarity; the persistent difficulty of every human being.

> *Eeee, t'Esu Odara*
> *(Ah, it is the matter of Esu Odara)*
> *Lo so soro o*
> *(That is difficult)*
> *Bakare o j'adi o*
> *(A Councillor—that he is—does not eat adi* [§§§§]*)*
> *T'Esu Odara lo soro*
> *(It is the matter of Esu Odara that is difficult)*

[§§§§] Adi, palm kernel oil, apparently, is an allergic agent that unleashes Esu's satiric venom to act upon and avenge an offending victim. See Euba's *Archetypes, Imprecators and Victims of Fate*, Ch. 2.

Consequently, in his settled location, he had entertained no regrets. In spite of his aversion for self-promotion, almost a given in the American Dream culture, he had combatted the fateful-fatal obstacles encountered in the slow but incisive way he knew how to. Rather than participate in the rat race, his belief was to always maintain his cool, unruffled, letting the particular opposing obstacle run its course till it exhausted itself. For in due time, as he believed, the assailant's intentions would always become visible, with his/her "evil" rearing its ugly head like a python, only to be toppled or to self-destruct. He realized this, of course, was a risky strategy; it wasn't a given that it always worked that way. But in the event that things didn't work out the way they should and he got bitten instead, as he sometimes had, he may have felt the venom or almost got crushed by it, but only for a little while. Applying the correct, applicable antidote, he had miraculously sprung back to life and had moved on. As such, he felt the strategy was a risk-approach worth taking no matter what. In fact, it would seem the only weapon his constitution could handle.

That modus operandi, a kind of sacrificially demanding but grace-full turning of the other cheek, as opposed to the instinctual and vengeful Judaic eye-for-an-eye, no doubt had developed with his Christian upbringing. Even though he had diverted from that religious direction, or at least had modified its tenets over the years in the mix of reassessment of his traditional precepts, that thinking seemed to have lingered as positive practice. It described a moral fiber that had constituted his rationale of being human in the face of odds. As he well understood, this characteristic inevitably resulted in his persistent tendency to self-deprecate, a by-product trait that WS had observed and often pointed out—as he did during the festschrift celebrating BBGD's accomplishments in 2014. The idiosyncratic peculiarity, he felt, was not without some justification. He had come to link it with the constant self-doubt that society imposed on one, in his own case through those various "ticks" that had infected his career development as artist or scholar. However, perhaps what he had acquired as a probable weapon at his disposal was Satire, that art that does not avenge but makes aware, an art consistent with his fate, his Esu, an art that litters his works. And therefore has fueled his satisfaction?

*****

"You are one success story of the American dream," Tola Pearce's voice, on the phone, fondly whiffed her envy-laden conclusions across the electronic waves into his ears. She had been his academic colleague and friend at the University of Ife, since renamed Obafemi Awolowo University, after the name of that famous politician and nation builder. She too, a comrade Lagosian, had been disgusted with her corrupted country and had left, almost at the same time as BBGD, in pursuit of possible better climes in the land of opportunity. She had subsequently settled in Missouri, just as he had in Louisiana.

"I don't know about that," BBGD objected with his usual modest integrity.

"You are, you are," Tola insisted. "I mean, look at you, you have been able to pursue what you wanted and have gained recognition in all of them—as actor, playwright, director and scholar—more than did any of your peers I know. And have secured property-investments to boot! What else do you want?"

"Well, the property thing was really not my idea, you know. I don't really consider it success. It happened because of the persistence of my African American wife, Addie."

"Yes, a good influence, and companion. You have married well, even though it took you so long. But that's more than what I could say for myself."

"Believe me, we have our ups and downs."

"What married life doesn't? Look at those around you, which had to end in divorce. In spite of those obstacles you imply, very minor compared to others, you've stuck with the marriage. You stuck with it and haven't looked elsewhere, not because you couldn't—I knew your capacities at Ife! You stuck not because you couldn't get out of it. You didn't need to. So what does that tell me, other than the fact that you two are compatible, right?"

"I guess."

"An accomplishment many of us, alas, did not make."

Her argument recalled examples of such disastrous societal entanglements, one of which she experienced. Surveying the past among their friends in Nigeria and abroad, he knew what she was talking about.

"You must be thankful," she concluded.

He must be thankful; he couldn't deny it. For Tola was right in her summation. If he had to do it all over again, he doubted whether there were many other choices he could have taken. And then, luck had to do with it. He wasn't really looking to be a billionaire, the ultimate of the American dream, but something just enough to make himself and his wife comfortable. "For what we have we hold…"

The lines from WS's *Madmen and Specialists* for some reasons came to his aid, although totally out of context with the playwright's meaning. And that with sarcasm. The full speech in that play was indicting colonial and neo-colonial imperialistic imperatives and ambitions, which exploited and looted the economy of the people. He hastily revised it: "What we have, as veritable outcomes of our fate, we hold in appreciation; and should be thankful."

Appendix
Conversations

[Conducted interview at the 2014 Praise at the Crossroads, a festschrift that was done in honor of BBGD and his works]

BJ (Biodun Jeyifo):

Well. It's hard for me to resist being too personal in moderating a discussion in which I've been instructed, and tact also demands that I play as little as possible a role. Mine is just to facilitate the discussion; but I can't but help raise a note of which is very personal and note of a small grouse against WS.

In 1970, when he came back from the long – which the world knows – incarceration and we all danced with joy to have him back. The very first thing he did was to cancel Orisun theater productions on television! And this was a source of pocket money for me!

[LAUGHTER]

I was an undergraduate, and I was earning good money in these weekly television productions at the Orisun Theater. But as soon as he came back, he took a look at the productions, and said, 'This is substandard.'

[LAUGHTER]

So, I raise this to move into the moderation, once I have gotten this out of my system. I can now ask, you know, questions that will connect Femi and WS to say that in my mind, the two roles that kind of stand out as exemplary in their collaboration as playwright and actor is Femi as Lakunle. Try as much as I can, I can't think of any other person playing Lakunle although I have in fact seen other Lakunles, but Femi's seems somehow to be the essential Lakunle. Then on the other hand there's also the role that Femi played as Chief Mujeyo in *Blues for a Prodigal* which is almost a kind of world away from the Lakunle type. So, how did you manage? How did this play out? First of all, you {gestures to WS) and then (gestures to BBGD) I'll turn the mike to Femi.

WS:
Thank you very much. I'm glad to be back in Baton Rouge, and I just wish I could stay longer. But first, I think, having been charged with economic terrorism, I need to defend myself a little bit. See, that's part of the danger of locking people away, away from reality. So, when you come back, you're no longer thinking of human beings. What you see is a certain deterioration. But at the same time, it was a rather ungracious kind of reaction. Because, the television series was very well-intentioned. Dapo Adelugba, who was sort of in charge of the series, wanted to keep Orisun Theater going. And so, he took on a weekly program on television –

BJ:
– weekly pocket money!

[LAUGHTER]

WS:
…You see, how these things linger. [laughter] Alright. And I came and as BJ knows, the kind of standard that we tried to keep up with at the time was really very high. And in relation to the talent, not just human talent but of the

material which existed to turn out weekly, it was beyond their capacity. And I tell you – one look at it and I said, 'I want to go back to prison.'

[LAUGHTER]

Now, you're so right, I also agree with you that Lakunle I believe till today was the peak of Femi Euba's acting. It is pure instinct that made me recognize the fact not just physically but the emanations that came from him, that he would fit (that character) You see, Femi has this self-deprecatory attitude towards himself, and Lakunle was not a tragic figure or anything of the sort; he was also somebody who laughed at himself. We all would tease him endlessly, there's my sister there, his colleague, when they came to the University of Ife, there's no kind of tease that wasn't thrown at him. There's just something about Lakunle which was Femi. Now, Mujeyo was more difficult, the transition, I thought; also, the manifestation of the kind of talent which Femi had. Mujeyo was an accident; he wasn't supposed to be Mujeyo. I had kind of a person (in mind)…anyway, he wasn't, and then I thought, well, let's see, let's see him as Mujeyo. And, we tried it. And he just, you know, segued into it, almost naturally. But Lakunle still comes out to me as the real pinnacle of his acting career.

BBGD:
    Anyway, Lakunle, Mujeyo, they were years apart. And I think, before we can actually talk about collaboration, we have to talk about apprenticeship, and there were years of apprenticeship before the collaboration. I was in London when Lakunle happened, and in all honesty, I mean, although we've collaborated before then (before I when to London) Lakunle happened after Athol Fugard directed me in WS's *The Trials of Brother Jero*—I was Chume in that play. Got great reviews and then Fugard told me they wanted to do *The Lion and the Jewel* at the Royal Court. That's how Lakunle happened. But before I came to London, I was an apprentice. How did that happen? In '59, I was dozing in my favorite arm chair, you know, I had just gotten out of high school, and in the middle of the doze I heard faintly that Wole Soyinka was back in town, and he was going to be doing some research. Then I got wind of it that he was going to be traveling across Nigeria, that's what really got to me. The first time I would ever actually travel across Nigeria. So I told my brother to help contact him, because I would like to do anything at all to avoid doing an office job (laughter). So my brother did, and we met, and he (WS) said, "Look, Femi, there is no money in this." I said, "Well, I don't care, as long as I can travel!" And that's how we began to collaborate, first, as an apprentice, I

was also kind of a research assistant. And this took me everywhere. He was kind of brother to me then, you know, because he was the only person, I found I could emulate, so I copied him in every way, in every aspect before I found myself. And then, after all that apprenticeship and training as an actor in the UK, Lakunle happened, and then of course, afterwards, Mujeyo. He said I wasn't the person he was thinking about – well, I was not aware of this; this is the first time I'm hearing that I wasn't the one! [laughter] But as it happened, I think I really enjoyed the role...we rehearsed in London, I mean, no, we rehearsed and filmed in Nigeria, then went to London for some location filming, then came back to do more, and so it was... But till today I don't know what happened to the movie; somehow, it wasn't released.

WS:
All this money money money money business. There was none to distribute, so all I did was exploit their enthusiasm. That's all I did.

[LAUGHTER]
BJ:
Well, still on the subject of the early period, at the time I became conscious of WS in Nigeria. I was not yet out of high school, and, in fact, I think I may have told him (WS) once, I have another personal story to tell. At the time I was trying to grow a beard, and my father objected very strongly. He liked all of us to be clean shaven. And so one day, in his exasperation, he said, "I will not allow you to become a Soyinka, or an Ojukwu in my house." Because of their very prominent beard. I think I barely knew the name, so I needed information, and I said, "Who is this Wole Soyinka?" who wants to prevent me from becoming (a man)? So, I began to read up on it, and I went to University of Ibadan to watch the productions of his plays...and because of that, to this day, I still have kind of a romantic view of the work that was involved in the 1960 Masks and the early stages of the Orisun Theater, traveling almost every day back and forth from Lagos; it wasn't a fully professional company, people were very, very, you know, inspired enthusiasts, and, you (WS) brought them into shape! And then fast forward to the period of the eighties when you are now head of acting at the School of Drama at Ibadan, and then later, the Head of the Department at Ife, the University of Ife Theater, and things kind of radically changed. And so, while I – of course, at that stage I was part of the theater group, but still very much looking at everything from a kind of romantic view I had had of the 1960s Masks. So, can you share some reflections, both of you, because, you know, I was still very much...barely out of high school.

261

But, let me add one final little personal anecdote. In my first or second year, I played the Court Superintendent in the production (of) *Kongi's Harvest*. And one particular night, I had gone to town and I had gotten very soused. I went, and you know, the Court Superintendent appears only once in the play. I went downstairs to the basement of the Arts Theater and because I was a little drunk, I slept up completely. And someone had to fetch me and wake me up in the basement. Meanwhile, he (WS) had had enough with this quite unprofessional attitude, because he was looking 'Where is he?' I doubt that he remembers (gestures to Wole Soyinka).

WS:
[nods his head] I remember.

BJ:
You do?
[Soyinka nods head]

[LAUGHTER]
BJ:
So at any rate, I got up and read my lines, and probably went back to sleep. But I woke up the next morning, I didn't go to my hall to sleep. So, just to give you a sense of how much fun, how much joy, and how much excitement and opportunities and possibilities that were there. But those two periods are quite different – the days of the 1960s Masks and the days of the University of Ife Theater, livened somewhat by the creation of the Guerilla unit of the Theater.

So could you please, both of you, reflect on this.

WS:
When you said "you still remember," I assure you I don't (forget). It's the bad moment in theater that I remember; I never forget any bad, excruciating moment. Whether as a result of my own ineptness as a director, or the hell, to which I was plunged by people like that, I don't forget the bad moments, at all. People always look askance when they hear the expression "the good old days" or whatever variations there are. But the fact is that it may be a cliché, but very often it is true. There was a kind of excitation about that period. You're talking about the environment – Nigeria at the time – Nigeria was not a hollow space as it is today, nobody can argue about that. Anyway, within certain environments, some forms of art evolve, most naturally. There's a good flexibility, experimentation, more leisure in thinking, improvisation is almost the order of the day, including even recruitment. Very often those who were

pulled into the 1960 Masks or the Orisun Theater I just saw coming to the Theater, watching, obviously interested, and then it's a question of "Look, you keep coming here, you have nothing better to do, okay, come on stage, be the prison guard!" And then they end up drunk downstairs.

[LAUGHTER]

And the political atmosphere required a certain attitude with both a sense of proportion and, at the same time, a measure of anger, but it was manageable anger, and there was even the possibility of interacting with the enemy. Today, it's a lethal thing to try – and for many decades now. And when I returned, my first idea was to create a fully professional company. So I ended up with the 1960 Masks, which was part professional, professional in the sense of capabilities. Some of them I stole from existing amateur companies, and already well-trained. But within that company, I was already grooming a young, aggressive group who would then constitute the first experimentation in Guerilla Theater. They were the ones who did the sketches, because the members of the 1960 Masks, they held jobs. They held civil service jobs, they held company jobs in companies, so they had to be very very careful, and I was very frustrated in certain directions when I had only the 1960 Masks. I mean, they were people whose careers I could not risk. So all these people lounging on armchairs doing nothing, they had nothing to lose. So I began to find them and recruit them on the spot, sometimes students [gestures to BJ] as he was at the time; he wasn't a full member ever of anything, you know, he was so busy with his academic business; but at the same time, he was fascinated by Theater, no question at all about that. So eventually I was able to pull out the young thugs, and turn them into a group in themselves: the Orisun Theater. They were the ones in *Before the Blackout* – we had a series like that – who were constantly attacking the establishment. They were the ones who, with rehearsal, with actual rehearsal, went into self-defense training – unorthodox use of the fire extinguishers, because we were constantly threatened by the politicians on account of the sketches that we did. So then, we had pleas from their parents, "Look, leave this WS alone. This thing you're doing, you're offending our friends, you know, your father's friends, your parents' friends. And, it's not right. Pull aside, go do something else. Go become a first-class clerk, something like that." But they stuck. They stuck with it, and that sense of risk-taking, and risk-taking not only politically, but artistically – ready to try anything, anything at all – that really was what was so beautiful at that time.

When we lost, when we moved from that season, which I would date right around the Civil War, when everybody scattered, that was the period when I was incarcerated. So Dapo Adelugba tried to keep that spirit going on television every week. Once we passed that stage—as we say in Nigeria, "Everytin' skata"—it became a totally different game. We were more careful, more conscious, of things we didn't used to worry about. [Gestures to BBGD] Do you remember, even in Ife, *Requiem of a Futurologist*—which was a spoof on religion, generally—things had got so bad, even at that time, about religious sensibility, that I refused to allow the play to be taken to certain parts of the country, since at that time, once we finished post-production, I could not be with them, and I wasn't going to risk them in that area. There were already killings, for things which you just laughed about, among the same people—a radicalization, I hate using that word for what is really a reactionalization to things which you just argue about; now, it's a question of "I'll cut your throat or move in this area."

So there was that change and we've never really recovered. I've tried to replicate the same thing when I became head of the Department in Ibadan—in Ife, I beg your pardon. It was still (there) when I was in Ibadan—civil war hadn't really begun then; but in Ife, things became really, really tense, the establishment began to be apologetic about its content. But, as I've always believed that the drama department is useless without a laboratory, the laboratory was the company. So, we started again, and we went out, but it was different, the excitation had disappeared. Even though we said we were doing Guerilla Theater, there was something formalistic about it, so different, totally, from the old Orisun Theater.

BBGD:

The only thing I want to say is about the two periods is this. From '59 to '62, I was one of the founding members of the 1960 Masks, which later changed to Orisun Theater. So I was part of the beginning part of that excitation, really, before I left for England to study drama. And then in the middle of that study was the civil war. I stayed in England more than I wanted to at first. I had missed all the excitement of the Orisun Theater by the time I returned. In fact, I didn't return for thirteen years, really, first to the University of Ibadan, and then to the University of Ife in 1976. At Ibadan, I didn't see any sign of Soyinka, so I decided to go back to the U.S. I came back home, formally, in 1976 to be part of the University of Ife, about the time WS returned from exile. But I came back now as a professional, and one of my naïve actor ways of thinking was that a professional shouldn't really work with amateurs. [LAUGHTER] I thought there was something I would lose, you know. But it took WS to actually get that notion out of my head. The first production we did was *Death and the King's Horseman,* and before we began rehearsals, I said I wasn't going to be part of it because…

WS:
He was snooty!

[LAUGHTER]

BBGD:
And then he (WS) came to me and he said, "Well, look, you know, nobody else could play Olunde, so you have to play him." And I said, "Well, okay, yeah." I couldn't resist him. But then I got into the part, you know, and I really enjoyed myself. But for the grace of his direction, and the way he made me feel, that "Yes, you are a professional, but how can we help these others if you're not in it?" – that's how I got to realize I could work well with the company. So, three years of apprenticeship and collaboration with the 1960 Masks 1959-62, and then some thirteen years later when I got to the University of Ife, from 1976 on, we became more collaborative. We did *Death and the King's Horseman* and *Opera Wonyosi*, and then we did *Biko's Inquest*, which we brought to the U.S.

WS:
[points to BBGD]
But you haven't told them what happened during *Death and the King's Horseman.*

BBGD:
[laughs]
Well, I have two different stories about this. Here was I, trying my best to act, you know, acting is a give-and-take, isn't it? So I had this Mrs. Pilkins, who was, for me, really dead as an actress. I just couldn't get through to her, you know? But the bigger thing is that we were doing this play for the first time in a theater that had just been built. There was, err…I mean, the air-conditioning inside the theater was so dense. I thought I was reaching the people above there [gestures with hand as if to balcony of the theater] but in fact something happened between my voice, trying to reach, and the air-conditioning, so that I couldn't get through, you know, to the audience. They told me this afterwards and I said, "Well, I tried my best!"

WS:

Listen, he lost his voice. And I kept warning him, I said, "Femi, you are losing your voice." [mockingly] "No, no, no, he was a professional, he knew what he was doing" "You are losing your voice." [laughter] And that day, you couldn't hear him from the front row. I nearly killed him; I nearly beheaded him. But it's true, he had one terrible girl, who thought she was an aristocrat or whatever. Anyway, she had airs about herself, oh, she was a pain, a real pain. So he had to cope with that, yes. He expected a different kind of, you know—he was used to acting on a professional stage; he had expected the same thing from students who were not even professional students, most doing drama. I said, "You have to help her, you have to help her." And then I think she disappeared, to make matters worse, she disappeared for about two weeks before the production. Came in just once or twice…oh, the horrors of theater! [LAUGHTER]

BJ:

Now, we've mostly spoken about work done in Nigeria, the times, but you also both happened to have collaborated in experimental commission to plays outside. And one that comes to mind is the adaptation of *Oedipus at Colonus*, so do you want to share reflections on that?

WS:

That was not a successful production. It was another one I don't like to remember, especially the part at which one of my favorites on stage froze. And when I say froze, I mean froze. He lost his… He had a black out, there's no other word for it. And, it is one of those terrible things that happen on stage. Also, the style, afterwards, the style which I adopted for that production, was not a successful one; it just didn't work, for a number of reasons. But the horrible moment was when this fellow Anthony, completely froze. And after that, the play never recovered after that one moment. Everybody, on stage, died, it's as simple as that, as elementary as that.

But since he (BBGD) also works in both his writings—creative writing and academically more so—in the province of myth, I think there's something I should narrate about that production, which might interest you. It's not the first time that sort of thing has happened. I adapted it (the play) and used quite a bit of traditional liturgy. I recreated the person of Oedipus with some kind of affinities to a Yoruba anthropological character, particularly Sango (the god of lightning and thunder). During the Delphus, the drama season, it's known as a notoriously dry, bone dry season. It's an open-air theater. The nearest thing to thunder you would hear would be single-engine planes that were flying from somewhere, or else learning-student fliers. Which is why, when I heard the sound of a rumble in the sky, I thought it was just one of these planes. All day, all throughout the rehearsal period, there was not one threat of rain or thunder, nothing. Nothing that day up to the beginning of the play, and for the next, for at least, I think, an hour, no, nothing. When my traditional chanter began the liturgy –

BBGD
– of Sango

WS
– something unbelievable happened. Yes, liturgy of Sango specifically – Sango is the god of lightning, and thunder, etc. etc. As we say in Yoruba, *Bóòlo yà'nmi* – "If you can't move, make way for me." It was one of the most unbelievable thunderstorms. They themselves, the people there, said they'd never seen anything like it. I thought at first it was a plane, then my concern was for the actors on stage, because the riggings, the set, began to sway. I just wanted them safe; I forgot all about, I didn't care about the plane. It was really phenomenal. And, after the chanting stopped, everything just went back to normal. It was a very strange experience, and it was not the first time.

BBGD:
And I must say that we really kept on going. Luckily for us, there was not a single rain, just the wind storm, and lightning, which got us thinking: "What are you going to do if something happened?" The audience members were leaving in droves, you know, wanting to beat the rain.

WS:
Don't worry, they were already bored with the production.

[LAUGHTER]

As I said, it was not a successful production.

BBGD:
But I was glad I was part of it, and actually one of the interesting things that I've come to realize, since that production is the fact that we (that is, himself and WS) have two different approaches to a play. From his point of view, his actors' lines were very important—that's very good, they are very important to me also. But, initially, he would like to get all that out of the

way—by going over those lines many times in sit down rehearsals. During those rehearsals, I didn't make a budge. For me, I have to really see the character first. I have to know the character before the words can come right. So, he called me into his office one day to ask me. "About this character," he asked, "What are you doing with it?" I said, "Well, you know, I'm trying." "Try harder!" he said. I said, "Don't worry, I'll get it, you know," [gestures to indicate WS's protest] "Proof. I want proof." But then, I got it eventually after many rehearsals, and I—[turning to Soyinka] "Did you like what you saw?"

WS:

Yes, well I'll tell you frankly. Yes, I did. In fact, Femi's problem when we started – this is a densely poetic play and I tried to put that poetic spirit into it. What I picked on, the style I picked on for the figure—(to BBGD) he was to be the comic figure you know, and that was what he found difficult to start with. And eventually, by the time—(to BBGD) in fact you became, that episode became the most successful on stage, because now the audience was able to relate to that. They (that is, the commissioners of the production and the audience of mostly classical Greek scholars) wanted a very strict, classical style, of both production and acting, very stylized is what I wanted to say. The kind of stylized of probably…that Japanese director…

BBGD
Suzuki?

WS

Yes, Suzuki. They wanted a mannerist kind of approach to the Greek classics. Whereas I went a different way, tried to merge Yoruba liturgy and style of acting with the Greek classical style. As I said, it didn't really work. But your role, (indicating BBGD) you really got into it properly. As you know, he can be a bit stiffish, and here was I, I wanted this clownish, researcher – botanical researcher – individual to come in there (on stage), breaking into what is supposed to be a kind of Grecian dramatic mold. And I wanted that sort of…wanted some impurity in that particular style. That was what he found difficult, but eventually I just said, "Listen, this is what I want. Imagine that you are a stock character in a soap opera, you know, the figure of fun, in the midst of seriousness. Now, let's go for it." And then, as usual, he netted into it. (To BBGD) Your role was very successful. I didn't tell him.

[LAUGHTER]

BJ:

Well, this is an old question, but it's a question which I think needs for us to revisit now and then. And I'd like to pose it, even in part, around my own experience as an undergraduate at Ibadan when – and I'm thinking Theater History, World Theater History. You had started written plays, you'd written theoretical essays, "The Fourth Stage" was already published. But there was a very decided air of defensiveness in claiming that Africa had—I mean, people like Ruth Finnegan had said that theater did not exist in Africa, period. By a kind of construction of what theater is… I mean, they, first of all, constructed what theater is and was looking everywhere. And once they didn't find their preconceived ideas of theater, it meant that theater did not exist (in Africa). And so, in my undergraduate days in theater, World Theater History, these ideas about the heritage of World Theater had begun to be seriously challenged. But still it was on a kind of defensive basis. Then, fast-forward, by the time—long before the Nobel Prize—by the time that you and others actually began to achieve prominence, locally and globally, things began to change a lot. And so part of the contribution to this was actually the series of essays and plays that you wrote, bringing the diversity and separateness, assumed separateness, between African, ritual, mythic, expressive traditions and Western dialogue drama, and sort of marrying them, fusing them together in quite unprecedented ways. So, instead of asking you straight away the influence of African and specifically Yoruba performance and ritual traditions in your work, because there is really a lot of scholarship on that, instead of that, what's your reflection now on where we stand now in terms of ideas of world theater when you started, and when you actually began to throw out ideas which at that stage were quite new and unprecedented. A kind of roundabout way of –

WS:

Well, first of all, I deny that I was defensive about –

BJ:

Not you! No, no! Not you in particular—I said African theater scholars, Dr. Adedeji and others, who were trying to prove that we did have a theater tradition but were doing so on very very defensive grounds. That's why I said that – that in spite of the fact that you had started writing…

WS:

Well, it's almost like the Amos Tutola when he wrote *The Palm-Wine Drinkard* and people said, "Oh, this is not a novel. This is not a novel; it's just an ungrammatical folk tale," whereas poets like Dylan Thomas coming from an environment not too remote from mythology, fantasy, etcetera etcetera recognized the enormous talent that went into writing that novel. And so, I was just amused that anybody should suggest that there was no theater, so my position was just to ignore it and do my own theater; execute my own vision. I could very easily, in fact, have joined the folk opera tradition. But, Duro Ladipo, Kola Ogunmola, and Herbert Ogunde of course, they were enjoying themselves already in that, that area, so I had no curiosity, no… I had my own vision. The research I'd done, in fact, had produced so much material that I felt the only service I can render is to render it anew, utilize some of these traditional forms of both theater as well as the existing themes there were. And I just was so—amused is the wrong word—I just thought the position you're talking about was so wrong that I could ignore it completely. And that's why I wasn't even interested in theorizing about it at all. This material is there. Good. They don't think that it's drama? That's their business. By the time we started putting things on stage, those who were interested would come. So, it's a strange attitude that people should actually, from within that—the richness of the material—suggest there was no theater.

BBGD:

My comment about that is that there was an incident when I was still in Nigeria with the 1960 Masks. I saw these mushroom theaters—music drama productions—happening, so exciting. I went to him (WS) and said, "Don't you want to do this kind of thing, because it's popular theater, you know?" In fact, one of the members of a company had approached me and said, "What are you doing with Wole Soyinka? You can come to our company! Why don't you come and join our company? You know, we make money!" It was in that state of mind that I went to him (WS), and said, "What are you doing about this drama thing? Why are we not like those theater companies" He said, "Look, Femi, if you really want to go and join them, go ahead, but I'm sure you won't really like what they're doing. We're trying to do something better than that." After that, I asked no more questions regarding the matter. I stayed with him. The question arose in the first place, not because I really enjoyed the type of drama they (those groups) were doing, it's just the liveliness, the moneymaking factor [turns to Soyinka] That money again—that made me think, you know, that they were somewhat in the right direction. Obviously, my rookie naivety. As it turned out, it wasn't my type of drama either, although it has legitimacy.

[APPLAUSE]

[At this point, the questions that follow had been put previously to the both WS and BBGD to respond to. And so here, the interview moves from spontaneous to deliberate.]

BJ

Let me ask both of you, in what sense are the aesthetics and poetics of your theater enriched and energized by expressive resources from Yoruba culture in particular, and African culture in general? How has your theater negotiated its multiple sources of inspiration, especially the Western heritage of theater and traditions of theater and performance in Africa, especially with regard to colonial and neocolonial perspectives? How do your poetics embody the powerful and complex metaphor of "the crossroads" re-centering the world through your own irreducible individual experience(s) as an author continuously moving between worlds and cultures?

WS

I recognize both conscious and unconscious interferences – note, I avoid the word 'influence.' The latter is always a precarious claim. The former means that a writer makes a deliberate choice, you know, admits other minds onto his creative template. Let's take a cursory look at the variety of dramatists into whose works I have delved at some depth – both formally as a student and as a foraging mind: Eugene O'Neil (on whom I wrote my extended essay), Strindberg, Ibsen, Lorca, Chekov, Moliere, Pirandello, Durrenmatt, Brecht…and of course the Ultimate himself—William Shakespeare, and so on and on. Mustn't ignore specific genres either – such as medieval Mystery plays, Greek tragedy, Japanese No Theater, even the cinema – Ingmar Bergman, or opera – Richard Wagner, Verdi etc. Engaging the dramatic works of a playwright means a far deeper immersion in the worlds of those authors, far deeper than prose fiction. When you come to write your own plays therefore, there is great danger of being sucked into theirs because you are bombarded with encounters with those cultures in a dynamic form – beyond stylistics. This is where your own cultural centeredness stands at the crossroads, directing the cultural traffic, neutralizing here, re-directing there. Whiffs of those traffic fumes blow past and in your face. Inevitably you retain some in your lungs.

[LAUGHTER]

BBGD

WS has put it so succinctly, and humorously. In my playwriting book, *Poetics of the Creative Process*, I have had to confront that question, and therefore went on to explore what I think develops as the voice of the playwright—an amalgamation of so many experiences, through reading, observing (plays, novels), analyzing (critical works), hearing or listening (to music) and experiencing various cultures that describe one's adventurous educational development. And as WS implies, one is constantly measuring or contrasting these experiences, subliminally, with those of one's culture of origin—which really never leaves one, and forming the basis of one's voice. A playwright professor of mine, after a class reading of one of my plays said, rather jokingly of course, "I ban you from reading Shakespeare ever again!" He was referring, you know, to what he saw as influences of Shakespeare, especially the dialogue. That was all he saw. What he didn't see was the driving culture underneath, a culture whose characters and, yes, dialogue, have certain similarities with those of Shakespeare, Moliere, Marlowe, etc., that is, in terms of behavioral and vocal characteristics. Until my professor challenged the authenticity of my characters and dialogue, I wasn't conscious of the fact. When I became conscious, I began to explore and experiment with those characteristic nuances more, rather than disclaim them. By the way, it should go with saying that WS also had significant effect on my work.

[APPLAUSE]

BJ

Edward Said frequently quoted Hugues de St. Victor or Hugonis de Sancto Victore, a 12th century Augustinian monk, who wrote: "The man who finds his homeland sweet is still a tender beginner; he to whom every soil is as his native one is already strong; but he is perfect to whom the entire world is as a foreign land." How has mobility across the Atlantic, with special reference to your life in London and the U.S. affected your cultural politics? How are these reflected in your theater?

WS

As subject matter, yes, the entire world – including mine – remains foreign territory. "Amaze me" challenged Diaghilev on meeting the young Nijinsky who was brought to him as the latest thing in Russian ballet. My land never ceases to amaze me; hence I remain its permanent tourist. Remember however that there are different kinds of tourists. Some "do Paris" in one day, then take off for Tokyo the next. Others visit Ethiopia and stay put – cancelling the rest of their itinerary. At the Royal Court Theater, London where I sojourned at the beginning of my creative career, I joined in dramatic experiments with other writers – John Osborne, Harold Pinter, Ann Jellicoe, Arnold Wesker, the West Indian Barry Record among others – but knew instinctively that I was not part of that movement. Technique is a different matter from impulsion. I couldn't wait to return home and commence my own experimentation.

BBGD

Yes, I'd like to consider myself a citizen of the world to the extent that it constantly challenges my creativity. In other words, whatever is happening around the world affects me as a writer and artist to the point of wanting to express it in any way I could. However, my point of departure still remains my country, from where parallels can be made with things happening in other places in the world. Let me extend this further. In the mobility of globalization, it's almost impossible to avoid "miscegenation," but that doesn't mean one should forget one's roots. As I implied earlier, my various backgrounds (Nigeria, Europe, the US) have constantly informed by work either as a playwright, director or scholar, since parallels can be made across, even though ways of going about them may be different from one locality to the next. Curious thing, there was a time I'd like to consider myself apolitical. But I wonder whether there's such a thing as an apolitical writer. At any rate, looking back at things I have written, the statements (dramatic or fictional) have been overall both social and political. Oh, by the way, I also had similar experiences as WS's at the Royal Court. During my London days, in the '60s, Bill Gaskill, the then artistic director of the Royal, tried to revive the workshops for writers and directors in which I participated a few times. Even Gaskill, I think, regarded these as just a way of getting together, to keep the participants' minds somewhat active. I participated when I wasn't working, so I guess they served for something.

[APPLAUSE]

BJ

Okay, how would you define the key concept of the Drama of the Epidemic? Does the notion of drama of the epidemic have any direct or indirect and subliminal bearing on societal issues in Nigeria specifically, in Africa in general, or throughout the African diaspora?

WS

Now that is a question that should be directed more usefully at Femi Euba. Thoughtful playwrights have their unique way of viewing and translating the drama of the life around them, offering the reader or audience their responsive lens or prism – witness Antonin Artaud's Theater of Cruelty or – responding to a dialectical need – Brecht's "epic" or didactic theater for example. None of these quite captures on its own the totality that embraces both arenas of drama – life and art. How would a dramatist, wishing to extract from today's African reality the stylistic vehicle for a coherent expression – Theater of tumult? Chaotic theater?

[LAUGHTER]

BBGD

Yes, I guess I can answer that question more appropriately, since I coined that phrase "Drama of Epidemic." As a matter of fact, I was following Artaud's idea in his essay of "Theater and Plague," which also develops his "Theater of Cruelty" in his book *Theater and Its Double*. For instance, Artaud relates to experience of plague or epidemic as both destructive and therapeutic and therefore instructive, that is, from the point of view of the community. Therefore, applying this, for example, to the "epidemic" of motor vehicle accidents in Nigeria, which was on my mind when I was writing *Archetypes, Imprecators and Victims of Fate*, the epidemic not only was violent and caused lives, it had the potential of a sobering effect or the need to do something about it, even if that therapy is short-lived—lasted only for a short period of time. In fact, this cause and effect situation is the province of satire, whose grotesquery of ridiculousness and seriousness is supposed to make people aware and sober up, again, if only for a short time. This is how the "Drama of Epidemic" is born, which is then applied to those African and African American plays that have this "epidemic" satiric potential.

[APPLAUSE]

BJ

What is your current relationship to Nigeria as one of the world's emerging nations of the 21st century and "crossroads" of the global world? Along with its political turbulence and economic growth, how does the current state of Nigeria affect the cultural climate and role of the playwright, poet, and novelist?

WS

For the foreseeable future, Nigeria will remain the world's unfinished business. Will remain so because it has yet to overcome its deeply flawed beginnings. Even if – ironically – it becomes the economic hub of the continent, it will continue to be undermined from its deeply fissured foundation. Art will survive because art is at home even amidst fragmentation, and because it is not nations that produce Art in any case. My creative relation to that nation has been shaped, and remains shaped by what I perceived early as its inchoate heredity. Each time I find I am about to be proved wrong, something happens to sustain the view that was expressed in my play *A Dance of the Forests,* which many have come to refer to as prophetic.

BBGD

I must confess, at the time we did *A Dance of the Forests*, just out of high school, I had no idea of that message. I was more excited about assisting WS and travelling with him, and being in his company, more excited about these than figuring out what the play actually meant. Of course I read about it, and WS spoke about it, but it simply escaped my naivety. Yes, I eventually got it— when the chaos started and was observing it, unfortunately, from London, where I was at that critical time. Since that time, the chaos has persisted, and I was able to witness much of it when I went back to Nigeria in 1976. I have witnessed it through the time I left, in 1986, to the present time. In terms of art, it's a potent subject for satire, which is the basis of many works by present Nigerian writers, including mine. Will there be change, through this jabbing of satire. That, unfortunately, is not a guaranteed province of satire. However, I continue to hope it will result in a better understanding and awareness that will bring some form of future change.

[APPLAUSE]

BJ:

Well, thank you very much on that note. It's been my pleasure to moderate this discussion, and I'm sure that you'll join me in showing your appreciation of the richness of this discussion.

[APPLAUSE]